Oliver Ellsworth and the
Creation of the Federal Republic

# Oliver Ellsworth and the Creation of the Federal Republic

WILLIAM R. CASTO

*Published by*

Second Circuit Committee on
History and Commemorative Events
New York
1997

LIBRARY OF CONGRESS CATALOGING-IN-PUBLICATION DATA

Casto, William R., 1946–
    Oliver Ellsworth and the creation of the federal republic / William R. Casto.
        p.     cm.
    Includes bibliographical references.
    isbn 0-9618400-2-1
        1. United States—History—Confederation, 1783–1789.   2. United States—
    Politics and government—1783–1789.   3. United States—History—Constitutional
    period, 1789–1809.   4. United States—Politics and government—1789–1809.
    5. Ellsworth, Oliver, 1745–1807.     I. Title.
    E303.C29   1997
    347.73'2634—dc21
    [B]                                                                      97-27882
                                                                                 CIP

DESIGN AND COMPOSITION: Judith Martin Waterman of Martin-Waterman Associates, Ltd.

COVER ILLUSTRATION: Portrait of Oliver Ellsworth by James Sharples, courtesy Independence
National Historical Park.

Printed in the United States of America

*For*
*William Richard Casto III*
*my beloved son*

# Contents

# Illustrations

# Foreword

*T*HIS PUBLICATION, AND THE EXHIBIT which it accompanies, are sponsored by the Second Circuit Committee on History and Commemorative Events, chaired by the Honorable José A. Cabranes, United States Circuit Judge. The exhibit opens at the United States Courthouse in New Haven, Connecticut in November 1997, and at the United States Courthouse in Manhattan in the Spring of 1998.

The Committee gratefully acknowledges the assistance of the Federal Bar Council and the William Nelson Cromwell Foundation, the continuing participation of which in the historical activities of this Circuit remains greatly appreciated. The Committee also wishes to express its thanks to the Texas Tech University School of Law, Lubbock, Texas, for its support of this project.

The Committee has been fortunate in having the participation of Professor William R. Casto of the Texas Tech University School of Law. Professor Casto is recognized as the leading authority on the life and public service of Oliver Ellsworth, a central figure in the formation and early years of the federal judiciary. This publication by Professor Casto represents the first major study in nearly a century of the role of Oliver Ellsworth in the political and judicial history of this country.

THE SECOND CIRCUIT COMMITTEE
ON HISTORY AND COMMEMORATIVE EVENTS

# Preface and Acknowledgments

ᖴOR A NUMBER OF YEARS I have been gathering materials for a full biography of Oliver Ellsworth and was delighted when the Second Circuit Committee on History and Commemorative Events indicated an interest in publishing a short book on Ellsworth. As the title suggests, this monograph concentrates upon Ellsworth's role in the creation of the federal government. In addition to the process of drafting and ratifying the Constitution, I define the creation to include certain vital legislative activities in the First Congress like the Judicial Act of 1789 and the Bill of Rights. In my judgment, the creation concludes with the Senate trade bill that coerced Rhode Island into ratifying the Constitution and completing the Union. I treat other aspects of Ellsworth's life (except his religion) somewhat summarily. I give his religion detailed consideration because it provided him with a sophisticated, powerful, and abiding philosophy of life.

My research would not have been possible without the aid of countless organizations and individuals. My knowledge of Oliver Ellsworth is based primarily upon primary sources gathered with the assistance of grants from the American Philosophical Society and the M.D. Anderson Foundation. In addition, I appreciate the continuing support of Dean Frank Newton and the Texas Tech University Law School Foundation. Like Ellsworth, I labor with pen and ink rather than a keyboard. I would therefore like to give special thanks to Lynda Levels who typed my manuscript.

Although I have visited many archives, collection, and documentary projects, I am particularly appreciative of the assistance that I received from Charlene Bickford, Kenneth Bowling, Helen Veit, and William diGiacomantonio at the Documentary History of the First Federal Congress of the United States of America Project and Maeva Marcus at the Documentary History of the Supreme Court of the United States Project. In addition, John Gordan, Wythe Holt, Mark Valeri and Wesley Horton carefully read drafts of this book and provided many valuable insights and comments. In addition to his valuable editorial comments, I particularly appreciate John Gordan's many administrative contributions to this project. Finally I would like to thank Judith Martin Waterman for her able efforts in the design and composition of this book.

This book is based in significant part on public and private sources from the 1780s and '90s and contains many quotations. I have made a conscious effort to reduce the number and length of footnotes. Each paragraph of text generally has no more than one footnote, and frequently the footnote includes multiple references pertinent to various concepts and quotations in the paragraph. I also have made extensive use of short titles, abbreviations, and repository symbols.

# Repository Symbols

CSmH     Henry E. Huntington Library, San Marino, California

Ct-Ar     Connecticut State Library, Hartford, Connecticut

CtHi     Connecticut Historical Society, Hartford, Connecticut

CtHUCC     United Church of Christ Connecticut Conference, Hartford, Connecticut

CtHT     Watkinson Library, Trinity College, Hartford, Connecticut

CtNlHi     New London Historical Society, New London, Connecticut

CtWOe     Oliver Ellsworth Homestead, Windsor, Connecticut

CtY     Yale University, New Haven, Connecticut

DLC     United States Library of Congress, Washington, D.C.

DNA     United States National Archives and Records Service, Washington, D.C.

MH-H     Harvard University, Houghton Library, Cambridge, Massachusetts

MHi     Massachusetts Historical Society, Boston, Massachusetts

MNF     Forbes Library, Northampton, Massachusetts

MPBA     Berkshire Athenaeum, Pittsfield, Massachusetts

Nc-Ar     North Carolina State Department of Archives and History, Raleigh, North Carolina

NcD     Duke University, Durham, North Carolina

NjHi     New Jersey Historical Society, Newark, New Jersey

NjP     Princeton University, Princeton, New Jersey

NN     New York Public Library, New York, New York

PHi     Historical Society of Pennsylvania, Philadelphia, Pennsylvania

RPB-JH     Brown University, John Hay Library of Rare Books and Special
           Collections, Providence, Rhode Island

R-Ar       Rhode Island State Archives, Providence, Rhode Island

# Short Titles and Abbreviations

The following list includes all short titles and abbreviations used in this book:

*Annals of Cong.* ✍ *Annals of the Congress of the United States*, 42 vols. (Washington, D.C.: Gales and Seaton, 1834–56).

*Bellamy's Works* ✍ Joseph Bellamy, *The Works of Joseph Bellamy*, 2 vols., ed. Tryon Edwards (Boston: Doctrinal Tract and Book Society, 1853).

*Brown's Ellsworth* ✍ William Garrott Brown, *The Life of Oliver Ellsworth* (New York: Macmillan, 1905).

*Bushman's Puritan to Yankee* ✍ Richard Bushman, *From Puritan to Yankee: Character and the Social Order in Connecticut, 1690–1765* (Cambridge, Mass.: Harvard University Press, 1967).

*Casto's Supreme Court* ✍ William R. Casto, *The Supreme Court in the Early Republic* (Columbia, S.C.: University of South Carolina Press, 1995).

*Christian Doctrine* ✍ Missionary Society of Connecticut, *A Summary of Christian Doctrine and Practice: Designed Especially for the Use of the People in the New Settlements of the United States of America* (Hartford, Conn.: Hudson & Goodwin, 1804) (Shaw-Shoemaker No. 6793).

Collier's "Sovereignty" ✍ Christopher Collier, "Sovereignty Finessed Roger Sherman, Oliver Ellsworth, and the Ratification of the Constitution in Connecticut," in *The Constitution and the States*, Patrick Conley & John Kaminski, eds (Madison, Wisc.: Madison House Publishers, 1988), 93–112.

*Colliers' Decision* ✍ Christopher Collier & James Lincoln Collier, *Decision in Philadelphia: The Constitutional Convention of 1787* (New York: Random House, 1986).

*Collier's Sherman* ✍ Christopher Collier, *Roger Sherman's Connecticut* (Middletown, Conn.: Wesleyan University Press, 1971).

*Combs' Jay Treaty* ✍ Jerald A. Combs, *The Jay Treaty Political Battleground of the Founding Fathers* (Berkeley, Calif.: University of California Press, 1970).

*Connecticut Acts* ✍ *Acts and Laws of the State of Connecticut in America* (New London, Conn.: Timothy Green, 1784) (Evans no. 18409).

*Connecticut Colonial Records* ❧ *The Public Records of the Colony of Connecticut, 1636–1776*, vols. 1–3 ed. J.H. Trumbull; vols. 4–15 ed. C.J. Hoadly (Hartford, Conn.: 1850–1890).

*Connecticut State Records* ❧ *The Public Records of the State of Connecticut*, Charles Hoadly, Leonard Labaree, Catherine Fennelly, Albert Van Dusen, & Christopher Collier, eds., 12 vols to date (Hartford, Conn.: Connecticut State Library, 1894–1986).

*Curry's First Freedoms* ❧ Thomas J. Curry, *The First Freedoms: Church and State in America to the Passage of the First Amendment* (New York: Oxford University Press, 1986).

*DeConde's Quasi-War* ❧ Alexander DeConde, *The Quasi-War: The Politics and Diplomacy of the Undeclared War with France, 1797–1801* (New York: Charles Scribner's Sons, 1966).

*Delegates Letters* ❧ *Letters of Delegates to Congress 1774–1789*, 24 vols. to date, ed. Paul H. Smith (Washington, D.C.: Government Printing Office, 1976–1996).

DHFFC ❧ *Documentary History of the First Federal Congress of the United States*, 12 vols. to date: vols. 1–3, ed. Linda Grant DePauw; vols. 4–6, ed. Charlene Bangs Bickford and Helen E. Veit; vol. 9, ed. Kenneth R. Bowling and Helen E. Veit; vols. 10–14, ed. Bickford, Kenneth R. Bowling, and Helen E. Veit (Baltimore: Johns Hopkins University Press, 1972–1995).

DHRC ❧ *The Documentary History of the Ratification of the Constitution*, 9 vols. to date: vols. 1–3, ed. Merrill Jensen; vols. 8–9 and 13–16, ed. John P. Kaminski and Gaspare J. Saladino (Madison, Wisc.: State Historical Society of Wisconsin, 1976–90).

DHSC ❧ *Documentary History of the Supreme Court of the United States 1789–1800*, 5 vols. to date: vol. 1, ed. Maeva Marcus and James R. Perry; vols. 2–5, ed. Marcus (New York: Columbia University Press, 1985–94).

*Farrand's Records* ❧ Max Farrand, ed., *Records of the Federal Convention of 1787*, 4 vols. (1937; reprint ed. New Haven: Yale University Press, 1966); 4th supplementary vol. ed. James H. Hutson, 1987.

*Goen's Revivalism* ❧ C.C. Goen, *Revivalism and Separatism in New England, 1790–1800: Strict Congregationalism and Separate Baptists in the Great Awakening* (New Haven, Conn.: Yale University Press, 1962).

Holt's "Judiciary Act" ❧ Wythe Holt, "'To Establish Justice': Politics, the Judiciary Act of 1789, and the Invention of the Federal Courts, *Duke Law Journal* 1989 (1990) 1421–1531.

*Levy's Establishment Clause* ❧ Leonard Levy, *The Establishment Clause: Religion and the First Amendment* (New York: Macmillan, 1986).

*Lettieri's Ellsworth*  |•  Ronald Lettieri, *Connecticut's Young Man of the Revolution: Oliver Ellsworth* (Hartford, Conn.: American Revolution Bicentennial Commission of Connecticut, 1978).

*Madison Papers*  |•  *The Papers of James Madison*, 17 vols. to date: vols. 1–7, ed. William T. Hutchinson and William M.E. Rachal; vol. 8, ed. Robert A. Rutland and Rachal; vols. 9–10, ed. Rutland (Chicago: University of Chicago Press, 1962–77); vols. 11–13, ed. Rutland and Thomas A. Mason; vol. 15, ed. Mason, Rutland, and Jeanne K. Sisson; vol. 16, ed. J.C.A. Stagg, Mason, and Sisson; vol. 17, ed. David B. Mattern et al. (Charlottesville, Va.: University Press of Virginia, 1977–91).

*Maclay's Diary*  |•  *The Diary of William Maclay*, Kenneth R. Bowling and Helen E. Veit, eds (Baltimore,: Johns Hopkins University Press, 1988).

*McLaughlin's New England Dissent*  |•  William McLaughlin, *New England Dissent 1630–1833*, 2 vols. (Cambridge, Mass.: Harvard University Press, 1971).

*Polishook's Rhode Island*  |•  Irwin H. Polishook, *Rhode Island and the Union* (Evanston, Ill.: Northwestern University Press, 1969).

*Stiles' Ancient Windsor*  |•  Henry Stiles, *The History of Ancient Windsor*, 2 vols. (Hartford, Conn.: Case, Lockwood & Brainard & Co., 1891).

*Valeri's Bellamy*  |•  Mark Valeri, *Law and Providence in Joseph Bellamy's New England* (New York: Oxford University Press, 1994).

*Swift's System*  |•  Zephaniah Swift, *A System of the Laws of the State of Connecticut*, 2 vols. (Windham, Conn.: John Byrne, 1796).

Verplanck's "Sketch"  |•  [Gulian C. Verplanck], "Biographical Sketch of Chief Justice Ellsworth," 3 *Analectic Magazine* (1814), 382–403. For Verplanck's authorship, see *Brown's Ellsworth*, 37 n.2.

*Oliver Ellsworth* (1792) by John Trumbull. In 1792 Ellsworth was a serious forty-seven-year-old senator at the height of his political powers.

### CHAPTER ONE

# Introduction

OLIVER ELLSWORTH IS, unfortunately, an obscure person to most twentieth century Americans—even to historians. But he was well-known and well-regarded in the late eighteenth century when our current system of government was created. James Madison wrote that he "always regarded [Ellsworth's] talents of a high order, and . . . they were generally so regarded." Ellsworth exerted so much influence in the Senate during its first years of operation that Aaron Burr joked, "if [Senator] Ellsworth had happened to spell the name of the Deity with two d's, it would have taken the Senate three weeks to expunge the superfluous letter." This short book is an exploration of Ellsworth's life and the role that he played in the creation of the federal republic. The story is told largely from his point of view and is sympathetic to his quest for order and to his support for emerging commercial interests.[1]

Ellsworth was an important participant in the creation and initial operation of the federal government under the Constitution. At the Constitutional Convention in Philadelphia, he was a significant contributor to the crucial compromises that shaped the Constitution. In the subsequent ratification process he was an influential polemicist and the leading speaker at Connecticut's ratification convention. From 1789 to 1796 he was the de facto majority leader of the United States Senate. He then became the third Chief Justice of the United States and subsequently ended his federal service as the leader of an important diplomatic mission to France in 1800. Although Ellsworth played an influential role in national politics throughout the 1790s, this book focuses primarily upon the creation of the federal government during the years 1787–1790.

The reason for the relative obscurity of Ellsworth's place in the pantheon of the Founding Era is related to the nature of his contributions. Although he was an intelligent man, he lacked the flashing, intellectual brilliance of men like Alexander Hamilton and James Madison. An early biographer, who knew him, candidly wrote that Ellsworth

> seems to have been rather practically well informed than profoundly or
> extensively learned. . . . He was formed by nature more for the discharge of
> active duties, than for contemplative study, or abstract science.[2]

The arena of practical politics—particularly legislative assemblies—was Ellsworth's preferred field of action. None of the Founding Generation was superior to and perhaps none even equaled him in the pragmatic art of effectively wielding political power in legislative bodies. Some two hundred years later, the brilliance of men like Hamilton and Madison is readily apparent in writings like the *Federalist Papers*, but the documentary evidence of Ellsworth's brilliant political maneuvering is more difficult to piece together.

Throughout the Founding Era, Ellsworth played an almost omnipresent role in forging what he called an "energetic" federal government. Little purpose would be served by retelling the whole story yet one more time. Ellsworth's participation in the Constitutional Convention in Philadelphia will be used to shed light upon his understanding of the art of political dealmaking rather than to rehearse the general meaning and significance of the Convention's labors. In particular the compromises on the states' representation in Congress and upon Congress's power to forbid the importation of slaves provide a laboratory for studying the nuances of Ellsworth's sophisticated political psychology and his consummate ability to craft effective political compromises.

Other episodes of the Founding Era are less familiar and will be addressed in more general scope. In particular, Ellsworth was the most effective and influential senator in the First Congress. He was the drafter and leading proponent of the Judiciary Act of 1789 that created the federal judicial system, and he had to bring all of his formidable political skills to bear on this complex and difficult task. In the Senate debates on the Bill of Rights, he was the floor manager, and he later was the Senate chairman of the Committee of Conference on the Bill of Rights and personally drafted the Committee's Report. Finally he was the architect of the Senate's Rhode Island Trade Bill that coerced that hold-out state into ratifying the Constitution and joining the Union. Rhode Island's ratification of the Constitution was the final step in the creation of the federal government. Ellsworth continued playing the premier leadership role in the Senate until 1796.

Ellsworth's exploits as a pragmatic politician are interesting, but what made him such a gifted political operative is more so. He had a clear, sophisticated, detailed, and ruthlessly analytical political philosophy and psychology that was quite consistent and never failed him in his quest for effective political solutions. His philosophy, however, was not that of the secular enlightenment. He was not like Madison, Jefferson, Hamilton, and many other Founders. He was a strict Calvinist who saw no difference between secular and religious life and whose entire world view of personal and political life was consciously based upon religion. His strict Calvinism provided him with a philosophical model that enabled him to make sense of the chaotic and occasionally tragic human condition. He viewed all human activity as a seamless web minutely predestined by an all-powerful God. Moreover he viewed himself as a "Righteous Ruler" chosen by God to rule on earth and elected by God for personal salvation.

In the late twentieth century, there is a tendency to compartmentalize religious belief short of the political realm—to separate secular decision making in public life from personal faith. Consistent with this tendency, the political leaders of the Founding Generation are frequently viewed as secular giants who either had little religion or whose religion was important in their private—but not their public—lives. For example, one capable and respected historian has written that "nearly all of the Founding Fathers claimed to be Christians; but, by virtually any standard of doctrinal orthodoxy, hardly any of them was . . . Quite possibly not a single delegate [to the Constitutional Convention] accepted Calvinist orthodoxy."[3] Even among today's historians, studies of religion in the eighteenth century almost always focus upon the ideas of ministers rather than those of public officials. Oliver Ellsworth stands in sharp contrast to this compartmentalized, secular vision, and his thoroughgoing integration of what today we call religious and secular life presents a valuable counterpoint to our inclination to separate the two.

In addition to shedding light on a largely unexplored aspect of the world view of the political leaders of the Founding generation, Ellsworth's understanding of the role of religion in society bears directly upon the religion clauses of the Bill of Rights. He played a significant role in framing these clauses and personally wrote the Establishment Clause. Therefore a thorough investigation of his complex and carefully elaborated views on the free exercise of religion and the governmental establishment of religion will provides fresh insights to the framing of the Constitution's religion clauses.

### CHAPTER TWO

# Ellsworth's Early Years
## *A Prelude*

*T*HE MOST INFLUENTIAL PERSONS in people's lives are generally their parents, and so it was for Oliver Ellsworth. Little is known about his mother and father, David and Jemima Ellsworth, but in retrospect each seems to have influenced him differently in his subsequent career in national politics. His mother, Jemima, assured that religion would occupy a central place in his life while his father, David, made a more secular contribution.

Oliver's oldest son, Oliver Jr., wrote that David Ellsworth, "had much cunning, or quick wit, and very sound judgment; was a selectman for nearly all his active life, and commanded a company of Conn. men at the Siege of Louisbourg, hence his title of Captain." In other words, when Oliver Ellsworth was born on April 29, 1745, his father was not in the Colony. He had sailed from Connecticut earlier that month as part of a colonial expeditionary force to lay siege to the massive, Vauban-style fortress of Louisbourg in Cape Breton in French Canada. This siege was the greatest feat of arms by a colonial army before the Revolutionary War. On May 11, the daring New England soldiers caught the French by surprise and conducted a successful amphibious landing that enabled them to invest the fortress. Meanwhile a squadron of the British Navy effected a tight naval blockade. For the next five and a half weeks, the New Englanders used more or less traditional European siege techniques to maintain continuous pressure on the fortress. Finally the French, who were cut off by land and sea and who despaired of reinforcement, surrendered on June 28.[1]

Oliver Ellsworth must have heard his father recount the story of the siege many times, and the expedition must have served as a dramatic paradigm for public service. The episode taught young Oliver that Connecticut's interests were linked with her sister colonies' concerns and that intercolonial cooperation was possible and could result in successful solutions. Moreover the expedition encouraged Oliver to think that he, like his father, could be an active participant in proto-national affairs and that national service might entail travel beyond Connecticut's borders. Finally the expedition served as proof that active inter-colonial cooperation was part of God's plan.

While Ellsworth's father served as a strong role model of successful public service in a proto-national cause, his mother, Jemima, played a far more significant role in shaping the course of her son's life. The same grandson who appreciated his grandfather's "cunning, or quick wit," described his grandmother as "a lady of excellent mind, good character, and pious principles."[2] These descriptions might, at first glance, be dismissed as mere platitudes, but they in fact provide valuable clues to Jemima Ellsworth's character. She was truly a lady of "pious principles," and her religion was to become the major spiritual and philosophical influence in her son's life.

David Ellsworth was described as a secular man with secular strengths like "cunning" and "wit." He engaged in secular feats like serving at Louisbourg. In contrast, his wife was described as a more complete person. Like David, she had an "excellent mind," but in addition to this secular strength, Jemima was a woman of "pious principles." Other factors also indicate that religion played a stronger role in Jemima's life than in her husband's. Although David had some standing within his church and was elected to various church committees,[3] surviving church records lend credence to the idea that Jemima was the source of religious strength in the Ellsworth family.

Until 1761, the Ellsworth family attended church in the First Society or parish of Windsor, but in the late 1750's a dispute arose with regard to the location of the Society's new meeting house. The problem was that the Society was divided by the Rivulet (renamed Farmington River in the nineteenth century) that was prone to flood. Those north of the Rivulet wanted the new meeting house to be built on their side, while the others contended for the south side. When the meeting house was finally built on the south side, David Ellsworth and others petitioned the colonial General Assembly to permit the formation of a new society north of the river, and eventually the North Society of Windsor was formed in 1761. Under the North Society's rules, only those members who could establish that they had had an actual and direct regenerating experience with God in which they came to know that God had elected them for salvation were entitled to communion. Although Jemima Ellsworth was almost immediately admitted to the new church as a member in full communion, her husband, David, never was.[4]

## ❦ THE GREAT AWAKENING

Like most people in Connecticut, Jemima Ellsworth was a Calvinist, but her Calvinism—and that of her son—cannot be understood without considering the Great Awakening that swept Connecticut (indeed, all of English-speaking North America) about five years before Ellsworth was born. In 1740 George Whitefield toured the Colonies in a series of revival meetings that utterly overwhelmed his audiences. Nathan Cole, who tilled a farm near Middletown, Connecticut, left a vivid account of one of those revivals. Cole related that as soon as he heard that Whitefield was coming to Middletown, "I dropt my tool that I had in my hand and ran home to my wife telling her to make ready quickly to go and hear Mr. Whitefield preach." He and his wife saddled their horses and rode as fast as they could toward Middlefield. As they approached, they noticed "a Cloud or fogg rising [and] heard a noise something like a

Nassau Hall (1764) drawn by W. Tennent, engraved by H. Dawkins.
At Ellsworth's *alma mater*, The College of New Jersey (later Princeton University), protestant
students were "left without any byas to their private judgments" in matters of religion.
COURTESY PRINCETON UNIVERSITY LIBRARY.

low rumbling thunder and presently found it was a noise of Horses feet coming down
the Road and this Cloud was a Cloud of dust made by the Horses feet." Everyone in
the area was rushing to Middletown "to hear news from heaven for the saving of
souls."[5]

When Cole finally arrived at the meeting place, some three or four thousand people
were there to hear the word. As Cole waited with trembling patience, he "saw Mr.
Whitefield come upon the Scaffold he Lookt almost angelical; a young, Slim, slender,
youth before some thousands of people with a bold undaunted Countenance." And
then he began to speak. Cole, who was in a state of "trembling fear," confessed with
trepidation that Whitefield

> gave me a heart wound; By Gods blessing: my old Foundation was
> broken up, and I saw that my righteousness would not save me; then I
> was convinced of the doctrine of Election . . . all I could do would not
> save me; and he had decreed from Eternity who should be saved and
> who not.

This experience was not uncommon, and even relatively sophisticated lay persons like
Benjamin Franklin were bowled over by Whitefield's message.[6]

Everywhere Whitefield went tremendous crowds of people came to hear his message of damnation and salvation. He strongly reaffirmed the traditional Calvinist val-

ues of the inherent depravity of man and salvation through God's grace alone. When he came to Windsor, he delivered a powerful sermon to an audience that undoubtedly included David and Jemima Ellsworth, who had married just a few months earlier. Whitefield noted in his diary that "the People of God seemed much revived in Windsor." As David and Jemima listened to Whitefield's powerful sermon, a young minister in the audience, who already had heard him several times, cried out that Whitefield "had kept the Good wine until now."[7]

Although Whitefield sparked countless personal revivals of faith, his ideas were unsettling to Connecticut's Standing Order clergy. In the beginning the Standing Order clergy were somewhat supportive of or at worst ambivalent about Whitefield, because he strongly reaffirmed traditional Calvinist values and was gathering many souls to Christ. Initially these conservative ministers made their pulpits available to Whitefield, but they quickly became hostile. Whitefield emphasized that salvation was based entirely upon a person experiencing saving grace by actually and personally feeling God's regenerating gift. This personal experience, however, was not based upon logic, good deeds, or social position.[8]

Whitefield's preaching smacked of enthusiasm and anarchy and was implicitly revolutionary. In emphasizing the importance of a personal regenerating experience, Whitefield "insisted much . . . upon . . . the necessity of a Minister's being converted before he could preach Christ right." Indeed, he proclaimed that unregenerate Ministers were "the bane of the Christian Church." After speaking at Suffield, Connecticut, Whitefield recorded in his journal that "the Word came with great Power . . . many ministers were present, I did not spare them—most of them thanked me for my plain dealing." But one of the ministers "was offended, and so would more of his stamp if I was to continue longer in New England."[9]

Whitefield's 1740 tour of Connecticut was followed by other evangelists from outside the Colony and inspired local evangelists as well. The Colony's Calvinists quickly split into two loose knit groups. The Standing Order disparagingly called the Whitefield-inspired camp, New Lights, with the conservative connotation that their ideas were new and therefore inherently suspect. In contrast, the Standing Order clergy referred to themselves as Old Lights because they stuck to tried and true ideas. The New Lights' particular emphasis upon an actual and personal regenerating experience from God was particularly disturbing to the Old Lights because it amounted to an implicit challenge to the Standing Order's spiritual authority.[10]

When local New Light evangelists began naming those in authority whom they viewed as unregenerate, the Old Lights responded with what amounted to a campaign of mild (which is to say bloodless) religious persecution. In 1742, the Connecticut General Assembly outlawed the New Light practice of itinerancy. This subtle legislation was based upon the New England tradition of congregationalism that defined a minister exclusively in terms of his relationship with his specific congregation. A minister without a congregation was no minister at all. Because the existing settled ministers were predominantly Old Light, New Light preachers could, as a practical matter, reach the masses only through itinerant preaching. Itineracy had been used by Whitefield and his successors with great effect, so the new act outlawed the practice and required the expulsion of itinerants who came from outside the Colony.[11]

In addition to muzzling New Light itinerants, the Old Lights attempted to deny higher education to men who might become New Light ministers. Yale College was dominated by its president, Thomas Clap, who mounted a relentless attack upon New Light enthusiasm within the college. In response, the New Lights opened an alternative school in New London called the Shepard's Tent, but the General Assembly immediately outlawed the establishment of schools not authorized by statute. This new law further provided that the Colony's tax laws that were used to pay ministers' salaries could be used only for the support of ministers educated at "Yale College, or Harvard College in Cambridge, or some other allowed foreign protestant college or University."[12]

The General Assembly's campaign against the New Lights continued in 1743 with a revocation of the Colony's thirty-five-year-old Toleration Act, which had originally been enacted for the benefit of Baptists. The previous year county courts in New London and New Haven had recognized New Light congregations as legitimate dissenting churches. To scotch this tactic, the Assembly rescinded the general toleration act and provided that henceforth the right to form a dissenting church would be decided by the Assembly on an *ad hoc* basis. Moreover, the Assembly advised that petitions to form a dissenting church would be granted only to sober dissenters having a "distinguishing character, by which they may be known from the presbyterians or congregationalists, and from the consociated churches established by the laws of this Colony."[13]

The revocation of the Toleration Act continued the Old Light campaign against New Light preachers but also had a significant impact upon lay persons. Because church attendance was required by law, New Lights in a parish with an Old Light church were required to attend the Old Light services. Moreover, this attack upon New Light lay persons was not coincidental. The 1742 General Assembly was officially commenced with an election sermon from an Old Light minister who urged the legislature to turn out of public office any government officials suspected of New Light sympathies. The General Assembly took heed and removed numerous New Lights from positions as judge or justice of the peace.[14]

Fortunately for the Ellsworth family they were spared from these Old Light persecutions. Their minister, Jonathan Marsh, was an old and respected clergyman who was at least sympathetic to the New Lights. Although the beginning of the Great Awakening usually is traced to Whitefield's fiery evangelism in 1740, a premonitory awakening occurred in the Connecticut River Valley in 1735. As part of this earlier awakening, Reverend Marsh's First Society in Windsor experienced a "remarkable pouring out of the Spirit of God [that resulted in] a great ingathering of souls to Christ." Moreover, Reverend Marsh, himself, had had a personal regenerating experience from God. In 1740, George Whitefield wrote in his *Journal* with pleasure that Reverend Marsh was "a true converted man."[15]

Although the Great Awakening occurred before Oliver Ellsworth was born, its spirit lived on in his mother, and she imparted it to her son. Life in Windsor was fairly basic. Ellsworth later told his son that when he was a boy, life was hard and manners were simple to coarseness.[16] There was only one carriage in Windsor, and most of the people ate from wooden trenchers. Evidently Ellsworth was a good student as a boy, and his parents were determined that he should become a minister. They were dissatisfied, however, with the education available in Windsor. This dissatisfaction should not be viewed as a rejection of Reverend Marsh. He had died in 1747, and there had followed a period of four years in which the Society had attempted to find a new pastor. Finally William Russell was selected in 1751 when young Oliver was six years old. Presumably Russell supervised Oliver's primary education, but for his college preparatory education, Oliver's parents sent him about 30 miles away to Joseph Bellamy's boarding school in Bethlehem. Evidently Ellsworth's parents either distrusted the quality of secondary education in Windsor, or perhaps Mr. Russell was an Old Light.

## ❦ THE NEW DIVINITY

Joseph Bellamy had a good reputation as a teacher who specialized in preparing young men to be ministers, but he was more than that. He was the intellectual and spiritual leader of Connecticut's New Lights. When George Whitefield has preached his fiery evangelism in 1740, Bellamy was a twenty-one-year-old minister with his own congregation, and Bellamy fully embraced Whitefield's preaching. Although Bellamy retained his position as a settled minister with a congregation of his own, he became one of the local itinerants who spread the New Light gospel throughout Connecticut in the early 1740s. But Bellamy was more than a preacher. He was an immensely analytical man who spent the rest of the decade working upon a careful and systematic explication of Calvinism. In 1750 he published his systematic analysis in a massive book entitled *True Religion Delineated*. Eight years later he published a carefully reasoned theodicy entitled *Four Sermons on the Wisdom of God in the Permission of Sin*, in which he provided an unbending Calvinist explanation of the existence of evil. Bellamy, along with Samuel Hopkins, was the leader of a thoroughgoing branch of Calvinism known as the New Divinity, which was inspired by the New Light ideas of the Great Awakening.[17]

We do not know when Ellsworth began his tutelage under Bellamy other than a brief statement in an early biographical note that it was "at an early age." When Ellsworth was seventeen, he left Bellamy in 1762 to attend Yale College. Perhaps he began his tutelage sometime around 1757, when he was twelve. We do know, however, that Bellamy was an extremely forceful, demanding, and dominating teacher and that his writings had an abiding influence upon Ellsworth. Some forty years later Ellsworth expressly used Bellamy's theodicy on *The Wisdom of God* as a model for urging Rhode Island's ratification of the Constitution, and Ellsworth expressly recurred to the theodicy in a 1799 grand jury charge. Moreover we will see that Ellsworth returned to the basic lesson of *The Wisdom of God* time after time in his political career.[18]

Because Calvinism—particularly New Divinity Calvinism—so utterly pervaded Ellsworth's life, some understanding of this unbending and radically absolute doctrine is essential to understand the man and the politician. Ellsworth was trained and believed in the strict tenets of the Westminster Confession of Faith that was written in 1648—the same creed that Max Weber posited as the purest basis of the Protestant work ethic. The Connecticut General Assembly officially adopted the Confession in 1708, and it remained the predominant creed of New England Calvinism throughout the eighteenth century. As a boy, little Olle Ellsworth was required by law to be taught the Confession, and he re-encountered it at Joseph Bellamy's boarding school. This consistent course was continued at Yale where "true religion . . . was Westminster Calvinism, and at every turn the students were exposed to the dogma of the orthodox faith." Indeed, all officers of the Yale corporation were required to assent in public to the Confession. Finally when Ellsworth was a mature adult, his church in Windsor formally adopted as their Confession of Faith the "assembly's Catechism" drafted by the Westminster Assembly of Divines.[19]

Because the Westminster Confession received a certain amount of gloss throughout the eighteenth century, the most reliable sources for a careful exploration of the substance of Ellsworth's religion are to be found in two bookends to his adult life. At the end of his life stands a New Divinity tract entitled *A Summary of Christian Doctrine and Practice*, written by a committee consisting of Ellsworth and some fellow members of the Connecticut Missionary Society. At the beginning of his life is the work of Joseph Bellamy, especially *The Wisdom of God*.[20]

The Westminster Confession, Joseph Bellamy, and Ellsworth's *Summary of Christian Doctrine* all envisioned a God who is eternal, infinite, unchanging, omnipresent, omnipotent, absolutely good, and absolutely wise. In stark contrast stands finite man who is in a state of original sin. God contracted with Adam, the representative of man, that if Adam would abide by God's commands, Adam would receive eternal life. But Adam broke this Covenant of Works, and after that breach all men have "become one with [Adam] in a universal revolt from God." Therefore, "[a]ll men as they come into the world are sinners; because they have a sinful nature or temper; and are destitute of holiness." They "are totally depraved; and, in themselves, utterly helpless." Man's helplessness or "impotency . . . consists in this, that [he] cannot effect a change of nature by his own acts or exercises, his reigning temper being wholly opposed to God and holiness; nor make satisfaction to divine justice, for his sins."[21]

Because man is helpless and God is all powerful, man's only hope of salvation lies in God's sole discretion. In contrast to the original Covenant of Works, after Adam's fall from grace, man became utterly powerless to effectuate or even influence his salvation. Fortunately, however, all-powerful "God, in his eternal counsels, has chosen a certain number of the human race to be heirs of eternal life." This "election of God is not grounded on good works fore-seen and fore-known of those who are called [i.e., the chosen or elect]; but is an act of sovereign goodness." The reason for God's decision to save some of mankind lies in the Covenants of Redemption and Grace in which Christ undertook to atone for man's sin and make satisfaction for man's violation of God's commands. Thus God's election of certain people for salvation is a unilateral pardon of the elect's sins. This pardon is undeserved and unearned "because the personal ill-desert of believers remains, because the satisfaction made [by Christ] is not of their own providing or making, and because faith itself, which interests them in it, is the gift of God."[22]

In analyzing this harsh doctrine, Max Weber surmised that a Calvinist like Ellsworth inevitably must have been deeply concerned to discover whether he, himself, was of the elect. Was he saved? *A Summary of Christian Doctrine*, like the Westminster Confession and the theology of Joseph Bellamy, provided a distressingly elusive answer to this vital question. The elect experience God's grace within themselves as a matter of "affections . . . known to be what they are, not by any process of reasoning, but by consciousness, or intuition." These affections, however, might be sinful and false. The proper test for judging one's affections is a "persevering and universal obedience to the will of God, as revealed in the scriptures." In theory, individuals could never know that they were saved; they could only hope.[23]

While Ellsworth was studying with Bellamy, Bellamy wrote and firmly taught that, "no honest man ought to believe his state to be good with more confidence than in exact proportion to his evidence; nor is there any evidence that will pass with our final judge, or that ought to be of any weight with us, but real holiness." This same ambivalence is present in the Confession of Faith of the Bloomfield Congregational Church where Ellsworth was a member in his early twenties when he briefly lived in that town. The Confession did not admit that Ellsworth could know that he was saved. It spoke only in terms of "hope."[24]

The Calvinist test of obedience to God's will did not require perfection. In a key passage, *A Summary of Christian Doctrine* explained:

> By persevering obedience is not meant sinless obedience; for to this none, in the present life, attain. What is meant is, a *general walk* with God. . . . The evidence of grace, therefore, must be in exact proportion to the regularity of our walk. . . . *Hence it is that full assurance of hope is often intermitted, and is usually, at any one time, of short duration.*

To Weber, "[t]he God of Calvinism demanded of his believers not simply good works, but a life of good works combined into a unified system," and this same systematic approach is found in *A Summary of Christian Doctrine*. A "general walk with God" was required, and "he alone shall be saved who endureth to the end."[25]

In addition to this general doctrine of predestined salvation, Ellsworth was particularly impressed by Joseph Bellamy's sermons on *The Wisdom of God in the Permission of Sin* in which Bellamy explained the existence of evil in a world created by a perfect God. This work was published in 1758 after Ellsworth entered Bellamy's tutelage, and Bellamy incorporated *The Wisdom of God* into his new student's education. Some fifty years later the thesis of *The Wisdom of God* was incorporated into Ellsworth's *Summary of Christian Doctrine*. Bellamy wrote this theodicy with a rigorous logic that remained ruthlessly true to Calvinist doctrine. The course of human events follows a perfect predestined plan conceived by a perfect God to craft the best possible world. Moreover, this plan is "as absolutely incomprehensible by us as it is by children of four years old." Although all the details are incomprehensible to finite and imperfect creatures, the broad outlines of God's plan were discernable to Bellamy: God in his infinite wisdom had decided that the permission of sin is the best method of instructing man in God's perfection and man's imperfection. Only individuals who thoroughly understand their sinfulness are fit to be saved by God. Bellamy's basic message was optimistic. We should not be disheartened by the presence of evil in the world. To the contrary, sin is actually a positive part of God's plan, and all will come right in the end.[26]

Although *The Wisdom of God* was a religious tract, its implications were not limited to what we today think of as the spiritual—as opposed to the secular—realm. Because Calvinists like Bellamy—and for that matter, Ellsworth—believed that all human conduct was predestined by God, any purported separation of spiritual from secular matters would have seemed dubious to them. Moreover Bellamy, himself, wrote his tract in significant part to address what today would be considered a secular crisis. In 1758 the French and Indian War was being fought, and the Catholic French seemed to be prevailing against the Protestant British. In the concluding sentence of Bellamy's preface, he exhorted his fellow colonists to persevere "let the present storm rise so high, and the time grow even so dark." In other words, one of his motivations was to provide a strong spiritual basis for Calvinists to bear up in the face of daunting military disasters.[27]

*The Wisdom of God* also had a subtle and quite useful lesson for Calvinist politicians. The idea that God has minutely predestined human history and that even evilness is part of God's righteous plan provides a powerful justification for political compromise. Because everything was part of God's plan, a Calvinist politician like Ellsworth could work enthusiastically with people whose principles he reviled. An interim compromise with evil would be acceptable as long as Ellsworth had faith in the general direction of politics. Such a compromise would not implicate Ellsworth's own principles because he could optimistically assume that the deal was part of God's plan. Whether Bellamy intended this subtle endorsement of pragmatic politics is unclear, but the message is there for the reader, and we will see that Ellsworth clearly embraced it.

The New Divinity's thoroughgoing doctrine of predestination had other secular implications. If, indeed, everything is predestined, there seems to be no basis for condemning anyone's actions as immoral, unethical, or wrongful. An accused wrongdoer could simply—to paraphrase an old saying—reply, "God made me do it." This objection was raised by Daniel Whitby and other eighteenth century thinkers who denied original sin and predestination and asserted that individuals are capable of controlling their own conduct. In turn Jonathan Edwards refuted Whitby, at least to the satisfaction of Calvinists, in Edwards' most important book, *Freedom of Will*. Edwards' attempted solution to this thorny problem was to reaffirm predestination and to emphasize that the wrongdoer's state of mind or internal disposition was the key to the merit or praiseworthiness of any particular act. Unregenerate sinners act with selfishness in their hearts while good people act with the love of God in theirs.[28]

Ellsworth's teachers, Joseph Bellamy and John Smalley, and his ministers at the First and North Societies in Windsor all followed Edwards on freedom of will. Moreover Ellsworth made a personal study of the issue in the late 1770s when he borrowed "Whitby on 5 points" from his minister. Finally, the Edwards analysis appears in passages from *A Summary of Christian Doctrine* that explain, "External action is not, by itself, either holy or sinful." Sin is entirely a function of the "temper of the heart" or internal disposition of a person. This doctrine probably had a subtle impact upon Ellsworth's approach to polemics and political debate. Under Edwards' freedom of will, the actions of Ellsworth's opponents were predestined by God, but their internal disposition was another matter. We will see that Ellsworth frequently resorted to *ad hominem* attacks that charged his political opponents with hypocrisy and selfishness.[29]

## ☞ THE NEW LIGHTS' "SUPERIOR ATTENTION TO CIVIL AFFAIRS"

In 1762 Ellsworth's studies under Bellamy were finished, and he entered Yale College at the age of seventeen. The Yale of the early 1760's, however, was not the same institution that had been so unfriendly to the New Lights twenty year earlier. The persecution of the New Lights had completely failed to stem the tide of their religious fervor, and the New Lights turned out to be unusually effective participants in the political arena. Their polemicists had from the beginning published a rich literature of toleration and religious freedom. At a more pragmatic level, the New Lights were careful to distinguish themselves from radical separatists and Baptists who deviated too far from Calvinism. In contrast, the New Lights made it clear that they were Calvinists who intended to work within the existing religious, social, and political order. In 1763 when Ellsworth was a freshman at Yale, William Samuel Johnson, who was an influential Connecticut Anglican, was bemused by the New Lights' political progress: "The N.L. within my short memory were a small party, merely a religious one." He continued, "they have acquired such an influence as to be nearly the ruling part of the government owing to their superior attention to civil affairs and close union among themselves in politics."[30]

Part of this "superior attention to civil affairs" was a comparatively benign attitude towards Anglicans. In 1762, as Ellsworth was leaving Bellamy's tutelage, the New Lights' political power was formally recognized when Bellamy was chosen to deliver the Colony's annual election sermon. Election sermons were an important political and social ceremony in New England. Each year, following the annual election for the General Assembly, an orthodox Calvinist minister would deliver a sermon to the Governor, the legislators, and an assembly of the colony's (later the state's) clergy. The sermon invariably dealt with some aspect of the proper relationship between religion and government. In his 1762 sermon, Bellamy continued the New Light rhetoric of religious tolerance by extolling the Colony's religious freedom. In particular, he expressly reassured Anglicans that if colonists "desire to declare for the Church of England, there is none to hinder them." Four years later, the Old Lights lost control of the Colony's governorship, lieutenant governorship, and upper house of the General Assembly in the 1766 election following the Stamp Act Crisis. As part of the 1766 maneuvering, the New Lights struck a deal with the Anglicans in which William Samuel Johnson became the first Anglican ever elected to the upper house. In return the Anglicans lent support for New Light candidates. The New Lights and their New Divinity successors retained this working political control of Connecticut throughout Ellsworth's life.[31]

Although New Lights were welcomed to Yale in the early 1760s, young Oliver Ellsworth's college career there was rocky to say the least. He was to be a pillar of the Standing Order in later life, but he evidently was a rebellious college student. Yale was not a happy college in the early 1760s. Its President, Thomas Clap, was a stern and imperious disciplinarian who ruled the college with an arbitrary hand. The students were so disgusted and angered by Clap's rule that the year before Ellsworth matriculated, they beat one of the tutors with clubs and broke into the monitor's office to steal the college's bills and accounts. These actions culminated in a riot in which the students used pistol fire to break all the tutors' and the president's windows.[32]

Student unrest continued unabated the next year, and eventually Clap was forced to resign in 1766. During the fall of Ellsworth's freshman year, the seniors went on strike rather than comply with a new system of examinations imposed by Clap. The freshmen and sophomores also had contributions to make, and Ellsworth apparently played a role in fomenting discord. In his first year he was disciplined on a number of charges. First he was charged with joining ten other students in the evening "to scrap and clean the college yard." This bizarre infraction seems rather harmless, but in the early 1760s, groups of Yale freshmen had developed a custom of staging disruptive demonstrations under the pretense of cleaning the College yard. Just a few months before Ellsworth matriculated, a formal rule was passed forbidding freshmen "to clean the College Yard" in order to "prevent the confusion and disorders which have heretofore happened." He was also disciplined with three other students who "after evening Prayers . . . put on their Hats and run and Hallowed in the College Yard in contempt of the Law of College." As a sophomore he was a minor ringleader at "a general treat or compotation of wine both common and spiced in and by the sophomore class." These offenses coupled with the general discord at the College were undoubtedly troubling to Ellsworth's parents. Perhaps the last straw was a vicious prank that was played at the end of Ellsworth's sophomore year. In order to discredit the college, some disgruntled students adulterated the commons' breakfast dough and caused "tremendous vomiting and purging" among virtually all the students who boarded at the college. At first everyone thought it was a case of poisoning, but after a thorough investigation President Clap concluded that the adulterating substance was "some strong physic and not any mortal Poyson." Whatever the cause, Ellsworth's parents had him dismissed from Yale a few months later.[33]

This dismissal, however, did not end Ellsworth's college career. After Yale, he continued his education at the College of New Jersey, which later became Princeton University. This choice was not coincidental. Like Yale, Princeton was a New Light institution. In the aftermath of the Great Awakening, it had been founded in significant part to educate men who planned to become New Light ministers, and its President,

Samuel Finley, was a well-known New Light who was a friend of Joseph Bellamy and who, as an itinerant preacher, had been expelled from Connecticut in 1743.[34]

But Princeton was significantly different from Yale. In the middle years of the eighteenth century when Ellsworth began his college education, 77% of Yale graduates came from Connecticut, 92% came from New England, and less than 1% from colonies below New York. During this same period, Princeton's graduates were drawn from eleven different colonies; including 28% from New England; 60% from New York, New Jersey, and Pennsylvania; and 12% from more southern colonies. This idea that men from many different colonies could come together to accomplish a common goal (in this case, education) had obvious implications for Ellsworth's subsequent participation in creating a national government.[35]

In addition, Princeton enthusiastically endorsed the principle of religious freedom for protestants. A college prospectus written under President Finley's supervision and published the year Ellsworth sailed south to New Jersey strongly reaffirmed this principle:

> To inculcate or even recommend the discriminating opinions of any one protestant denomination in preference to another, is carefully avoided. In those matters the students are left without any byas to their private judgments; and are always allowed, without restraint to attend the religious worship of any protestant society, whenever they have opportunity.

This model of tolerance in religious matters was to serve Ellsworth well in his later political career.[36]

Although the theoretical basis for religious tolerance was important, nineteen-year-old Oliver Ellsworth was probably most impressed by the managerial and teaching style of President Finley. In contrast to Clap at Yale, Finley got on well with his students, and the Princeton prospectus proclaimed that there had not "been above three or four fines imposed for upwards of three years last past; not even one, since DR. FINLEY hath presided." Ellsworth must certainly have preferred Princeton's amicable latitudinarianism to the zealous orthodoxy that had been ruthlessly imposed by Yale's obnoxious president.[37]

At Princeton Ellsworth continued to display the sophomoric opposition to authority that had gotten him into trouble at Yale. For example in later years he told of a clever ploy that he used to circumvent a rule that students were not to wear hats in the college yard. Ellsworth apparently intentionally violated this rule, but before he entered the yard he removed the brim of his hat. Upon being charged with the violation, he explained that the rule spoke only to the wearing of hats and that a hat, by definition, must have a brim. One can only imagine how President Clap at Yale would have received this impish plea, but President Finley evidently was amused, and Ellsworth's clever distinction carried the day.[38]

As the hat episode suggests, Ellsworth was developing a lawyerly ability to parse the written word and to discover subtle ambiguities in apparently clear language. As a scholar Ellsworth was an adequate student. An early biographer who knew him relates that he was "much more remarkable for his shrewdness and adroit management in all the little politics of the college, than for any uncommon proficiency in science or literature." In addition to playing at student politics, Ellsworth began developing his talent as a public speaker. In particular, he helped to found a debating society called the Well Meaning Club that was suppressed in 1769 but later reorganized as the Cliosophic Society. In these clubs students discussed literary matters and debated pressing issues of the day. This public speaking experience was valuable to future ministers and equally valuable to future lawyers.[39]

After Ellsworth left Princeton, his family insisted that he enter postgraduate theological studies with John Smalley in New Britain, Connecticut. Smalley had been a student of Joseph Bellamy and had a good reputation for preparing young men to be ministers. Ellsworth's postgraduate studies, however, did not last long. After a year he rejected his parents' plan for his career, quit his studies, and resolved to become a lawyer. The reason for this abrupt change is unclear, but there is no indication that the change was caused by a crisis of faith. At about the same time, he personally experienced his election by God for salvation and became a member of Windsor's North Society in full communion. There is an amusing anecdote that in preparing his first sermon for Smalley, Ellsworth devoted the first ten pages of his manuscript to defining his terms, which is supposed to have convinced Smalley that he was not suited to become a minister. A more plausible explanation of his switch from religion to the law lies in the New Divinity theology's emphasis upon intricate and obscure metaphysical analysis. In particular Smalley's work was "an avalanche of scholastic dogma." In contrast, Ellsworth's professional career was to be built on simple and direct analysis. Perhaps he simply could not abide the intricate metaphysical analyses required of New Divinity novices.[40]

❦ CHAPTER THREE ❦

# The "Righteous Ruler"

AFTER LEAVING SMALLEY, Ellsworth taught school and then studied law under two capable lawyers. He began his studies with Matthew Griswold who was to be Connecticut's lieutenant governor from 1769 to 1784 and governor from 1784 to 1786. Ellsworth completed his legal education under Jesse Root with whom he subsequently served in the Continental Congress and on the Connecticut Superior Court, the state's highest judicial court. Finally at the age of twenty-six, Ellsworth was admitted to the bar of Hartford County in 1771. From that year till 1774, he supported himself primarily by running a small farm that his father gave him and by practicing law on the side. In 1772 when he was still primarily a farmer, he virtually guaranteed his success as a lawyer when he married Abigail Wolcott. Ellsworth's wife was a member of the influential Wolcott clan that provided Connecticut with two different governors in the second half of the eighteenth century and a third in the first part of the next century. This marriage gave Ellsworth a firm toehold in Connecticut's Standing Order, and within ten years he had ascended to a position of significant political influence within the state.[1]

In 1773, a year after his marriage, he was elected from Windsor to the lower house of the General Assembly, and a year later was appointed a justice of the peace. At the same time, his earnings from the practice of law showed a substantial increase. In 1775 he gave up his Windsor seat in the General Assembly and moved to Hartford to become a lawyer in the Colony's capital. At about the same time, the Revolutionary War began, and Connecticut had to gear up its military to fight Great Britain. This move to a wartime economy entailed an enormous increase in expenditures, and the General Assembly created a special Committee of the Pay Table to supervise the spending program. Ellsworth was immediately appointed to this Committee.[2]

At first glance the position on the Committee of the Pay Table does not seem a very desirable appointment. The Committee did not make policy and played no role in the allocation of state funds. Instead Committee members were expected to travel throughout the state supervising the expenditure of already allocated funds, verifying that contracts had been performed, and settling claims. The overwhelming bulk of the work involved handling small claims by individual citizens. There was no glory here, nor was the pay particularly remunerative. There was just a lot of hard work that demanded painstaking attention to detail.

Ellsworth got the job because of his service in the General Assembly and his connection with the Wolcott clan, but he did not treat the job as a political sinecure. He reveled in his arduous responsibilities. As he later said, he "applied himself to the business of his appointment . . . with great cheerfulness." He spent the first few years of the war ceaselessly crisscrossing the state. For example on June 28, 1776 he directed the powder mill in Windham to deliver one hundred eleven & a half pounds of "Musquet Powder" to the Canterbury militia. On September 14, 1776, he was in New Haven approving the payment of twenty-eight pounds to the local militia for a march to Westchester, and on June 23 of the next year, he reviewed and approved a payment for "162 feet pine board best." There was no glamour or prestige to this mind-numbing bean counting. It was just a lot of hard work.[3]

Ellsworth used this apparently thankless task to make a reputation for himself as an extremely hardworking and reliable individual. In addition the work took him all over the state and enabled him to make personal contacts far beyond his home in Hartford County. As an auditor and adjuster of state accounts, he also worked closely with the small group of merchants who made a vast fortune providing supplies to the Revolutionary cause. By the end of 1777 he was known throughout the state as a capable, reliable, and hardworking man who had the imprimatur of the Wolcott clan.

In May of 1777, the General Assembly appointed Ellsworth State's Attorney for Hartford County. This office gave him considerable power over the enforcement of the state's laws and was "at that time of very considerable emolument." Just a few months after he became State's Attorney he was named a delegate to the Continental Congress. In 1779 he was elected from Hartford to the lower house of the General Assembly and appointed to the Council of Safety. Finally in 1780 he was elected to the General Assembly's upper house. At the same time, he retained his positions of State's Attorney, member of the Council of Safety, and delegate to the Continental Congress. This political advancement was extraordinary for a man who seven years earlier had been an unknown and inexperienced farmer who was practicing law on the side.[4]

Except for the governorship and lieutenant governorship, Ellsworth was now holding the most important executive and legislative offices in the state. As a delegate to the Continental Congress he and fellow delegates represented Connecticut's interests in Philadelphia and of necessity were kept abreast of and took part in shaping Connecticut's policies related to the War and other matters outside the state. Within the state, his positions on the Council of Safety and the Governor's Council were especially important. When the General Assembly was not in session, the twenty-three member Council of Safety had virtually plenary power to act for the state in governmental and military matters. When the General Assembly was in session, Ellsworth's position as one of the twelve elected members of the upper house, if anything, gave him even more power. The Governor's Council acted in secret, and as a coordinate branch of the General Assembly it could veto any bill and reject any political or judicial appointment. Moreover as a matter of practice only four Council members were necessary to block bills and appointments. Finally as state's attorney for one of Connecticut's most important counties, Ellsworth had enormous influence over the enforcement of the state's criminal laws.[5]

## ☙ THE CENTRALITY OF RELIGION IN ELLSWORTH'S PRIVATE LIFE

Although Ellsworth found his calling in law and government rather than the ministry, there is no evidence that his religious faith ever faltered. Zealous Connecticut ministers viewed him as a deeply religious man, and Ellsworth's actions confirm this judgment. Within the privacy of his home, he studied religion and presided over daily prayer meetings. He regularly attended church throughout his life and was an active lay participant in church governance. We will see that he frequently made religious allusions in his political essays, Senate speeches, and grand jury charges. Finally in later life he was a trustee of the Mission Society of Connecticut and a member of the committee that drafted the Society's *Summary of Christian Doctrine*.[6]

Ellsworth's faith was, in part, simply a matter of indoctrination. He probably listened to almost seven thousand sermons in his life, totaling almost fifteen thousand hours of instruction. In addition he used religion to make sense of personal tragedies in his life. A particularly revealing event was the death in 1778 of his nineteen-month-old first son, Olle. This death was a new and bitter experience for Ellsworth. At that time all but one of his grandparents, parents, uncles, aunts, immediate cousins, brothers and sisters were still alive or had lived at least to the age of 59. He had seen little Olle through the first year of infancy, seen him learn to feed himself, seen him crawl, seen him walk and begin to talk, and seen him in the wonderfully delightful months before toddlers develop their egos. He was a loving father who deeply mourned his "dear departed little son."[7]

For Ellsworth, the death of loved ones epitomized life's uncertainty and pain. A few years later in discussing the death of his brother's young son, he wrote, "This world is a scene of confusion mixed with disappointment & distress." He found solace in his religious faith that assured him "that all things will come right hereafter." The evils that we suffer seem inconsequential if we accept our life on earth as "but an embryo of our existence [that] derives its consequences only from its connection with future scenes." Ellsworth believed that departed loved ones were in heaven, and he looked forward to the time when he and his wife would "happily unite our little family, as well as those gone before as those that shall come after us, never to part again." Thus his religion reconciled him to and made sense of the death of loved ones and a "world . . . of confusion mixed with disappointment & distress." Any diminution of faith would have jeopardized this vital reconciliation.[8]

In addition to explaining the "world . . . of confusion mixed with disappointment & distress," Ellsworth's faith was crucial to his own personal salvation. In this regard his life was astonishingly similar to the model proposed by Max Weber in *The Protestant Ethic and the Spirit of Capitalism*. Weber did not present his theory as an absolute predictor of individual human conduct. Instead he based his model on a pure ideal-type seldom replicated in the real world. He used the Westminster Confession as the epitome of the protestant ethic and posited individuals who were utterly faithful to that harsh doctrine. Because Weber was concerned about the emergence of capitalism in the Western European society of the seventeenth century, the application of his model to Oliver Ellsworth's life in the second half of the next century may seem attenuated. In considering the New Lights of Connecticut, however, Weber's theory of a direct relationship between a protestant ethic and the spirit of capitalism seems equally applicable in the eighteenth century. The Great Awakening had dramatically renewed the New Lights' Calvinist faith in the fundamental tenets of the Westminster Confession. Therefore Weber's model of religiously inspired secular conduct in the seventeenth century is quite pertinent to New Lights like Oliver Ellsworth.

Oliver Ellsworth's New Divinity and the Westminster Calvinism analyzed by Weber were both based upon an omnipotent God who had predetermined the course of human events according to a preconceived plan beyond the comprehension of finite human beings. Similarly both Ellsworth and Weber's ideal Calvinist believed that God had preselected a comparatively small number of individuals for salvation and that human beings are utterly powerless to effect their own salvation. A logical strategy for coping with this rigorous predestination would have been simply to lapse into a passive, fatalistic withdrawal from worldly affairs. Why bother if God already has inexorably predestined each individual's fate? Weber reasoned, however, that an ideal Calvinist was desperately interested in his own salvation. This desire for salvation coupled with the ideal Calvinist's feelings of helplessness and uncertainty would produce a powerful psychological motivation to search for evidence of personal salvation.[9]

This vital search for evidence of one's own salvation was shaped by the concept of a calling, which presumes that man has been placed upon the earth solely for the glory of God and that all men's earthly endeavors are channeled to accomplish this divine objective. In particular, the elect who have been predestined by God for salvation pursue their calling according to God's rules. Therefore the vital evidence of salvation is to be found in good works performed in a calling. This analysis is self-evident in a passage from Ellsworth's *Summary of Christian Doctrine*:

> The end of all things is the glory of God. That conduct in rational agents which displays the glory of God is *fit and proper conduct*: and that which does not, is *unfit and improper conduct*.

This passage is a restatement of *The Shorter Catechism* of the Westminster Assembly, which was adopted by Ellsworth's church as its Confession of Faith.[10]

Weber described this pursuit of a calling as worldly asceticism by which he meant practicing a calling for the glory of God and not self-interest. In addition, predestined salvation was an all-or-nothing proposition in which the elect were consistent and the non-elect were not. "The God of Calvinism," wrote Weber, "demanded of his believers not single good works, but a life of good works combined into a united system." In this unforgiving model, any deviation from God's rules was frightening evidence of eternal damnation. Therefore Calvinists were required constantly to monitor their lives for a logical and consistent pattern of good works for the glory of God. Weber reasoned that this constant search for evidence inevitably modified the believer's behavior to conform to the model rules for secular conduct.[11]

Weber was addressing the emergence of capitalism, and his analysis of Calvinist doctrine and the details of a calling in the commercial sector neatly fits Oliver Ellsworth's Connecticut. The concept of worldly asceticism was expressly endorsed from the pulpit and explicitly linked to Calvinism. For example, in the last few months of Ellsworth's college preparatory studies, Joseph Bellamy wrote and delivered an election sermon that described a righteous nation during the coming millennium in which pious people would excel in their worldly callings. His description of the ideal, righteous merchant duplicates Weber's model.[12]

Ellsworth took to heart the idea of worldly asceticism of individuals steadfastly working at their calling and advised that "the best system of government cannot produce general happiness unless the people are virtuous, industrious, and economical." Conversely, he viewed "indolen[ce] and luxurious[ness]" as dangerous. Nor was this simply a secularized spirit of capitalism. Ellsworth expressly linked his advice to God: "Industry is most favorable to the moral virtue of the world; it is therefore wisely ordered by the Author of Nature, that the blessings of this world should be acquired by our application in some business useful to society."[13]

And Ellsworth ordered his private life according to this advice. Like Weber's ideal Calvinist, he was an extremely persistent individual who emphasized rational, systemic thought over undisciplined emotion. A colleague who worked closely with him wrote, "That man has a head of iron—just iron—that works with the precision of a mill, without its quickness and giddy manner. I profoundly admire the neatness and accuracy of his mind." Although Ellsworth became one of the richest men in Connecticut, "he lived in a plain and unostentatious style [, and] his economy was regular and systematic." He kept personal track of debts owed him down to a quarter of a penny, dressed simply, and despite his ownership of a handsome carriage insisted that his family walk almost two miles to church each Sunday.[14]

## ☙ THE RIGHTEOUS RULER

Weber wrote about the relationship between Calvinism and private commercial activities, and Ellsworth certainly conducted his private affairs with the worldly asceticism that Weber described. But Ellsworth was more than a merchant. His most visible calling was in government, and the New Divinity provided clear guidance for the practice of a calling in government. Government officials should be Righteous Rulers.

In the middle of the eighteenth century during Ellsworth's youth, the concept of public service was imbued with millennarianism. In 1758, Joseph Bellamy delivered a powerful message of millennarianism and the role of the Church Militant in preparing the way for Christ's rule on earth. He urged that true Christians should not passively await the Millennium when Satan would be bound and Christ would rule for a thousand years. He urged them to join the Church Militant:

> It therefore becomes all the followers of Christ, in their several spheres, and a firm belief of these things, to be of good courage, and exert themselves to the utmost, in the use of all proper means to suppress error and vice of every kind, and promote the cause of truth and righteousness in the world; and so be workers together with God.

In the concluding portion of the sermon, Bellamy wrote with a sense of urgency: "The time of the last general battle draws on, when a glorious victory is to be won; and . . . the army [of God] shall drive all before them at last."[15]

Four years later Bellamy returned to this theme in his election sermon. He reminded the General Assembly that when nations become righteous, the Millennium would be at hand: "Heaven would soon begin on earth." He emphasized the need for righteous rulers who would "promote a universal [religious] reformation" and thereby herald the advent of Christ's rule. Samuel Finley, Ellsworth's teacher at Princeton, also drew upon millennial ideas to urge Calvinists to be active servants in bringing about God's plan. This idea that righteous rulers would in some way effect or signal the longed-for commencement of Christ's rule was a powerful message and undoubtedly had a significant impact upon young Oliver Ellsworth.[16]

In retrospect, those who eagerly anticipated the immediate arrival of the Millennium were doomed to disappointment as the years passed and the anticipated event failed to transpire. This process of attenuation probably happened to Ellsworth. None of his extant writings look forward to the Millennium. Nevertheless, despite this inevitable attenuation, millennarianism persisted in North America throughout the eighteenth century and into the next.[17]

In addition to motivating conduct, millennarianism played a significant definitional role. The ideal of a ruler was defined at the outset of Ellsworth's adult life as an active participant in public affairs who is consciously motivated by Calvinist values. Thus, the definition created general categories of proper and improper conduct. To the extent that Calvinist leaders like Ellsworth wished to view themselves and be viewed as proper government officials, they would have been constrained to conform to these categories.

Millennarianism may have lent an air of urgency to the political process in the middle of the century and certainly provided a general definition of political leadership that emphasized activism. But the Golden Rule in the Book of Matthew provided more abiding encouragement and guidance for participation in government. From the middle of the century to the end, there was clear agreement among Connecticut Calvinists that the proper role of a good ruler was dictated by biblical revelation. In Bellamy's 1762 election sermon, he reduced all moral virtue to compliance with the two prime commandments from the Book of Matthew: "Thou shalt love the Lord thy God with all thy heart [and] Thou shalt love thy neighbor as thyself." He equated virtue with righteousness and expected secular rulers to be righteous. Bellamy exalted the righteous ruler because he attains "his high station merely on account of his merit [and therefore] is the wisest man in the province, and a father to all his subjects." As required by God's command to love thy neighbor, "all the influence his high station, superior wisdom, and goodness give him over [his subjects'] hearts, is wholly consecrated to make them a still holier and happier people." Bellamy likened this duty to serve the people to that of "a nursing father or mother towards an infant child." In contrast, sinful rulers are guilty of self-love. They "have no fear of God before their eyes, or regard to the public weal, and act an arbitrary and tyrannical part."[18]

Bellamy's emphasis upon the Book of Matthew and his explication of the righteous ruler was a continuing article of faith among Connecticut Calvinists. Some forty years later, Ellsworth's *Summary of Christian Doctrine* reiterated the primacy of the Book of Matthew. Although the absolute duty to love thy neighbor had become subtly attenuated, the duties of a ruler remained unchanged: "The Bible . . . teaches [that a ruler should do] whatever is essential to the common weal." Therefore rulers must "prefer . . . the true interest of the state to any partial interest." In particular, a public official's duty consisted "in providing good laws—in distributing impartial justice to the rich and to the poor—in protecting all in their rights and guarding the common interest and safety."[19]

This ideal of a righteous ruler is in many ways similar to the concept of republican virtue. We are told, however, that republican virtue was a secular notion that eighteenth-century Americans derived either directly or indirectly from the classical Greeks and Romans. The values of secular or classical republicanism undoubtedly were embedded in eighteenth-century New England political culture, but to emphasize this secular strand of thought ignores the realities of Calvinist culture. The Calvinist clergy were aware of classical republicanism and probably were influenced by it. But they explained their ideal of a righteous ruler exclusively in terms of biblical revelation, and they taught their fellow Calvinists that the ideal of a righteous ruler was dictated by the word of God. As a Standing Order minister explained in a 1776 election sermon, "In Scripture, we have the character of civil rulers decypher'd—the design of government pointed out—the duty of subjects enforced." Given their Calvinist faith in a world minutely predestined by an omnipotent God, the clergy could hardly explain such a key concept as being founded on the non-biblical writings and records of heathen Greeks and Romans.[20]

In addition to premising the concept of a righteous ruler exclusively upon the revealed word of God, Calvinists explicitly rejected secular virtue as a viable foundation for government. The classical ideal was fundamentally in conflict with the core Calvinist doctrines of original sin and election. Because human beings are inherently depraved, they have an inherent disability to conduct themselves according to the honorable rules found in the classics. The only hope of rising above this congenital depravity is through God's intervening election and bestowal of grace. Honor without election is little more than a facade that masks self-love and depravity. The Calvinist clergy were quite explicit in warning people to beware of individuals who professed to be virtuous but who did not have a righteous love of God and fellow man. The simple truth was that such an individual could not be trusted to eschew sinful self-interest. In contrast, a righteous ruler who had experienced God's grace understood the awesome significance of appearing before God on judgment day.[21]

Joseph Perry, Ellsworth's friend and neighbor, succinctly explained the matter in his 1775 election sermon:

> Other principles, such as *honor, public spirit, natural benevolence,* and *ambition,* it is true, in some instances have influenced men to do many worthy deeds for the happiness of the community they stood related to—many among the Greeks and Romans, from these principles, displayed noble instances of patriotism.—But such are not so sure, nor do they bind in the same way, nor to the same degree, as principles of religious virtue. —The good man has his mind impressed with a sense of future invisible objects—he lives and acts under a sense of the omniscient eye of God, remembers the solemn account we must give and the reward he shall receive for his conduct.

Thus the Calvinist clergy.[22]

This idea that a Righteous Ruler should do whatever is "essential to the common weal" is, on its face, so vague that it is virtually devoid of substantive content. The idea's Calvinist origins, however, had clear substantive implications for an officer's conduct of his public office. A Righteous Ruler's fundamental rules of governance were clear and simple. Above all else a Righteous Ruler would strive for an orderly society free of dissent. In this regard, a revealing passage in Ellsworth's *Summary of Christian Doctrine* provides, "The design of all government is to make every one feel the relation in which he stands to the community, and to compel him to conduct as becomes that relation." Similarly, the catechism of Ellsworth's church in Windsor provided, "The fifth commandment requireth the preserving the honour, and performing the duties belonging to everyone in their several places and relations, as superiors, inferiors or equals."[23]

This emphasis upon an orderly society is clearly present in the part of Joseph Bellamy's Election Sermon in which he describes a perfect society. In such a society, everyone would act in righteous concert. In religious matters, "there would be no sects, no parties, no divisions." Bellamy went on to affirm that in a perfect society, "the whole society [would be] in perfect love and harmony." In contrast, a perfectly unrighteous nation is one in which "peace and harmony are clear gone, and jarring, angry, passion reign . . . no government, civil, ecclesiastical, or domestic, all riot and confusion."[24]

The primary obstacle to creating this monolithic, righteous society was inherent in the people's basic character. The minister of Ellsworth's church in Hartford noted in an election sermon that "human nature must be taken by the civil governor as he finds it," and Calvinists who firmly believed in original sin viewed human beings as inherently depraved. In 1800 when Ellsworth was on a diplomatic mission to France, he explained his understanding of human nature in a revealing conversation with the

Comte de Volney, a French philosopher. After Volney outlined a comprehensive plan for reorganizing the government of France, Ellsworth remarked, "there is one thing Mr. Volney for which you have made no provision . . . *The Selfishness of Man*." This pessimistic view of human nature is little more than a restatement of the doctrine of original sin that pictured humankind as inherently depraved. Even the phraseology is taken from the New Divinity that defined sin exclusively in terms of selfishness. For example, Joseph Bellamy wrote in his principal work, "From this same root—this disposition to love ourselves supremely, live to ourselves ultimately, and delight in that which is not God wholly—proceeds all our evil carriage toward our neighbor."[25]

At first glance this doctrine of inherent depravity would seem to present an insurmountable obstacle to good government. After all, governors are themselves men. Therefore government would seem to be inevitably depraved. The Calvinists avoided this logical conclusion by invoking what was literally a *deus ex machina*. Government officials were not ordinary men. They were part of God's predestined plan, and they were selected by God to rule over men. This idea of divine selection was a common idea among Connecticut Calvinists and harmonized the apparent conflict between original sin and good government.[26]

That Ellsworth embraced this idea of divine rule is evident in a closed 1789 senate debate in which, according to a fellow senator:

> Ellsworth . . . got on the subject of Kings. Declared that the Sentence in the Primer of *Fear God and honor King* was of great importance that Kings were of divine appointment, that Saul the head & shoulders taller than the rest of the people was elected by God and anointed by his appointment.

This apparent reference to the divine right of kings should not be taken literally. If Ellsworth was a monarchist, he surely would not have espoused monarchy on the floor of the senate in 1789. He simply was too good a politician to commit such a gaffe. When Connecticut Calvinists used biblical verse to discuss government, they frequently used "king" as a generic word to signify government or government official. Therefore Ellsworth was saying that government officials—at least some of them—were "elected by God and anointed by his appointment."[27]

This Calvinist idea of a Righteous Ruler explains many aspects of Ellsworth's public character. He clearly was an elitist who undoubtedly viewed himself as having been handpicked by God. He clearly sought to foster a righteous Calvinist order, and he undoubtedly viewed his opponents as unregenerate sinners. At the same time, we will see that Bellamy's *The Wisdom of God* permitted him to accept compromises and to work with fellow politicians who, according to Calvinist theology, were depraved.

## ☙ A CALVINIST IN THE CONTINENTAL CONGRESS

An excellent example of the political flexibility inherent in *The Wisdom of God* is found in Ellsworth's attitude toward the alliance formed during the Revolutionary War between the rebelling protestant colonists and France, which of course was a Catholic power. In the late eighteenth century many New England Calvinists—probably most— were virulently biased against the Catholic Church. The extent of this bias is evident in a 1744 New Light pamphlet that strenuously objected to Old Light religious persecutions on the overtly Lockean idea that an individual's religion was strictly a personal matter between the individual and God. The pamphlet argued with much force that it would be presumptuous and officious for a government to purport to decide such inherently personal matters. The pamphlet, however, was—with unintended irony— entitled *The Essential Rights and Liberties of Protestants* and expressly stated that "*Popery*" is not a religion, "it is rather a conspiracy against it . . . the *Pope* being in Truth the Vice-Regent of the *Devil.*" Similarly Joseph Bellamy viewed the Pope as the Anti-Christ.[28]

Most of the New England clergy saw the obvious advantage of the French alliance and reined in their virulent anticatholicism. The minister of Ellsworth's church, however, had significant reservations and evidently wrote Ellsworth a letter complaining generally about the moral state of the world and specifically about the possibility that the French alliance would result in the spread of Catholicism. Ellsworth certainly did not approve of the Catholic Church, and his reply used the customary pejorative terms "popery" and "superstition." He was, however, not as concerned as his pastor and replied, "I am waiting, Sir, as well as you, tho' perhaps with less concern and more doubt, to see how the great events now taking place in the world will affect the moral state of it." Consistent with Calvinist theology, he noted that he did not know "the design of Providence in this respect." He then mildly rebuked his pastor by restating the central theme of *The Wisdom of God*: "But it is sufficient, dear Sir, that God governs the world, and that his purpose of Grace will be accomplished." Therefore the alliance with a Catholic power was acceptable.[29]

From this general analysis, Ellsworth turned to a pragmatic discussion of internal French politics and implicitly stated his understanding of the direct relationship between religion and civil order. Man's state of original sin and natural depravity was an immense impediment to civil order, and Connecticut Calvinists believed that religion played an important role in fostering order. Jonathan Trumbull, a leading minister who served with Ellsworth on the Committee that drafted *A Summary of Christian Doctrine*, later explained that when religion "is lost, and moral motives [therefore] have no influence, a people can be governed by severe laws and punishments only; by Newgates, swords and cannon."[30]

This same insight informed Ellsworth's analysis of internal order in France. He believed that the French leaders were essentially atheists and wrote that, "the court of France have themselves no religion at all; and care much less than in former reigns, what or whether any the nation [i.e., the populace] has." This change was a "shifting [of government] policy from superstition [i.e., the Catholic Church] to dissipation." This "shifting" was an explicit reference to the policy begun by Louis XIV of drawing the powerful nobility to Paris and furnishing them "with every amusement and gratification in the compass of nature." This strategy kept the nobility from "brooding" in the countryside where they "might be dangerous." The populace, however, could not be controlled in this fashion, and in the absence of religion—to use Trumbull's words—swords and cannons were necessary. Ellsworth agreed. Having neutralized the nobility, "[a] standing army does for the rest [i.e., the populace], and they have less occasion for popery."[31]

Throughout Ellsworth's service in the Continental Congress he had an abiding interest in the national government's fiscal stability and was a harsh critic of the policy of issuing paper currency that he believed would quickly and inevitably depreciate in value. Before the Revolution, the colonies of Massachusetts and Rhode Island had occasionally issued paper money called "old tenner" and after depreciation in the marketplace had replaced it at depreciated rates with new paper money called "new tenner." Even before Ellsworth became a delegate to the Continental Congress, he was criticizing the Congress's use of this old fiscal strategy. In 1777, he wrote William Williams, who was in the Continental Congress, about "the increasing anxiety for the publick credit & support of the paper currency which from its abundance & the criminal advantage taken by evil designing men is depreciating with a rapidity scarce known in the days of old Tenner." He believed that Congress needed to take steps to remedy this "alarming & notorious . . . evil."[32]

The next year Ellsworth was in Congress, and he wrote his brother that Congress was trying to remedy the problem of paper money. Although the "best time to have done this is indeed past," he continued, "I do not however despair of its being affected yet." The initial plan was to have the states enact substantial taxes to raise money to pay off the accrued national debt and to take "out of circulation some of the past Emissions [of paper money] to make way for future ones." He explained to a friend that this "heavy Tax" would be a "very cheap purchase for the prize [of independence] we have been contending for; & which, it seems to be the design of Heaven we shall soon have the full & peaceable possession of."[33]

Although Ellsworth contemplated replacing the old tenner with new tenner, he was at first adamantly opposed to replacing the old tenner at a deeply discounted rate. In a newspaper article, he insisted that the old tenner was a pledged faith and a failure to make good on the pledge would be the worst breach of faith. He believed that

> [America] could not violate her faith, without at once and forever los-
> ing all confidence of her citizens. She could not violate her faith with-
> out disgracing herself with all nations, and disqualifying herself for all
> treaties. She could not violate her faith without incensing the Almighty
> and daring his vengeance against her. She could not violate her faith
> and destroy her currency without effectually depriving herself of the
> means of defense. *In a word any violation of the public faith, on which her paper
> currency rests, would be madness, atheism and suicide.*

Unfortunately Ellsworth eventually had to eat these harsh words.[34]

All the while the depreciation of the Continental currency continued apace. In the beginning of 1780, Ellsworth was complaining to his wife that the market price in Philadelphia for an ear of corn was half a dollar. To his governor, he wrote that the "failure of that great resource the press [, which printed paper money], gives as was expected a violent shock." Nevertheless Ellsworth hoped that this shock would "prove a salutary one [because the] System of taxation urged by necessity is now establishing itself fast." But by March Ellsworth confessed to a friend that he had no idea what "the State of our finance will be three months hense." The fact was that he was coming to believe that the country could not or would not fully back its paper currency.[35]

At about the time that Ellsworth confessed to a friend that he was quite uncertain about the future state of national finances, he abandoned his firm opposition to the government's formal participation in the depreciation of the paper currency. As a member of a Congressional Committee charged with investigating the matter, he wrote a committee report proposing the issuance of new money that would replace the old money at a rate of 40 to 1. Then he drafted and voted for a formal resolution implementing his plan. Part of this plan was to secure firm guarantees from the states that they would provide sufficient funds to prevent further depreciation of the new bills that were to be issued.[36]

With this volte face, Ellsworth accepted the inevitability of depreciation. In an official letter to his governor, he and his mentor, Roger Sherman, explained:

> It has been judged impracticable to carry on the war another year with the present currency—and no other plan has been proposed that appeared So likely to relieve us from the Embarrassments of a frustrating currency as that which has been adopted by Congress.

At the same time, Ellsworth, writing as "a private citizen," told his governor that a crisis was at hand and that without the new measure "the Army must disband."[37]

In part Ellsworth reconciled himself to his pragmatic acceptance of depreciation by recurring to the lessons of *The Wisdom of God*. In urging the necessity of assuring that sufficient finances were available to support the Army, he argued:

> Can it, Sir, be the design of Heaven, that has roused us to exertions thus far, and armed mighty nations for our support and brought us within sight of the promised rest to leave us after all to destruction, and to lament also the best blood of our land as spilt in vain? I trust not.

Ellsworth trusted that the Revolution was part of "the design of Heaven" or God's plan and that all would come right in the end. Therefore the depreciation of the paper currency became a morally acceptable facet of God's plan.[38]

Although Congress managed to keep an army in the field, Ellsworth's plan to put the new paper currency—the new tenner—on a sound basis failed miserably. By the summer of 1781, he had completely given up on the idea of using paper money. He frankly wrote from Philadelphia that he wanted "to get rid of paper currency, it greatly Embarrasses our affairs; it is but little used here in any trade or dealing, and not at all, in the Market."[39]

The basic problem of financing the Revolution remained, and in 1781 the Congress formally requested the states to amend the Articles of Confederation to authorize the national government to levy a tax of 5% on all imported goods. Although every state save Rhode Island approved this amendment, Rhode Island first delayed its consideration of the proposal and finally rejected it. Because the Articles of Confederation required unanimity for any amendments, Rhode Island's action stopped the proposal in its tracks. Two years later in 1783, the Continental Congress again requested the states to grant a national taxing authority and again Rhode Island rejected the proposed grant.[40]

Ellsworth was firmly committed to the idea of giving the Continental Congress a taxing authority. He voted for the measure and served upon the Committee that drafted an extensive report designed to persuade the individual states to grant the requested authority. In a separate letter to his own state government, he urged:

> There must, sir, be a revenue somehow established that can be relied on and applied for national purposes as the exigencies arise, independent of the will or views of a single State, or it will be impossible to support national faith or national existence.

Massachusetts quickly voted to give the requested taxing authority, and he immediately wrote a friend in Massachusetts congratulating him on the action of "your wise and patriotick State."[41]

But all states were not so wise and patriotic. As a member of the Connecticut upper house, Ellsworth personally drafted legislation to grant the taxing authority, but the lower house—like Rhode Island—refused.[42] This was a mortifying defeat for Ellsworth, but his faith that all would come right as part of God's plan was to be vindicated when a new federal government was created at the end of the decade.

## ❦ ELLSWORTH'S STATE JUDICIAL SERVICE

Ellsworth's service in the Continental Congress ceased when the Revolutionary War ended in 1783. He returned to Connecticut where he continued his tenure in the state legislature's upper house and aspired to a seat on the Superior Court. But in 1784 the General Assembly restricted plural officeholding and forbade anyone to serve simultaneously in the Legislature and the Superior Court. The next year Ellsworth was again elected to the upper house and was appointed to the Superior Court. He resigned his seat in the Legislature and for the next four years served as a common-law judge.[43]

By a happy coincidence, the 1784 General Assembly also passed a statute requiring Superior Court judges to give written opinions in the cases they decided, and these opinions form the backbone of Ephriam Kirby's *Reports* that was published in 1789. After Kirby completed a final draft of his reports, he spent a few weeks at Ellsworth's house where Ellsworth—at the behest of his fellow judges—carefully read through the manuscript to verify its accuracy. Most of the opinions are reported by Kirby as being "By the Court," but this anonymity may be pierced in many cases by referring to the original manuscript opinions written by the judges themselves and scattered through the Connecticut Archives.[44]

Ellsworth and his brethren viewed themselves as common-law judges, and they had a general jurisdiction over civil and criminal disputes throughout the state. In resolving these disputes, the judges were inclined to defer to the rules and principles of the English common law. Later as Chief Justice of the United States, Ellsworth explained that the common law was "brought from the country of our ancestors [and] was the law of every part of the union." The common law, he continued, was "a known law, matured by the reason of ages, and which Americans have ever been tenacious of as a birth-right." On the Connecticut Superior Court, Ellsworth frequently relied upon the English common law in his written opinions.[45]

The English common law, however, was not absolutely binding in Connecticut. The courts of Westminster in England administered a common law for England, and English law was not necessarily suited to changed conditions in the New World. The best example of changed conditions is an opinion by Chief Judge Law in which he refused to apply an English rule that the value of land was fixed by the purchase price. Law explained:

> The diversity in this respect, between the British practice and ours, is undoubtedly founded in the permanent worth of their lands, as an old country, and the increasing worth of ours, as a new country.

Ellsworth agreed with this changed circumstances rational.[46]

In addition to the changed circumstances rationale, Ellsworth felt free to reject English precedent that he viewed as simply unreasonable. A good example is his opinion for the whole court in *Wilford v. Grant*. The case involved a judgment against six men for assault and battery, and two of the men appealed on the basis that they were minors who had not been represented in the litigation by guardians. Ellsworth and the rest of the court concluded that there was reversible error regarding the two minors but not in respect of the four remaining adult defendants. The English common law provided that in such a case there had to be a complete reversal as to all defendants. To make matters worse the victim had died, and therefore the action could not be recommenced.[47]

Although the facts in *Wilford* did not seem to implicate any changed conditions between England and Connecticut, Ellsworth had no trouble firmly rejecting the English rule forbidding a partial reversal. He explained:

> The common law of England we are to pay great deference to, as being a general system of improved reason, and a source from whence our principles of jurisprudence have been mostly drawn: The rules, however, which have not been made our own by adoption, we are to examine, and so far vary from them as they may appear contrary to reason or unadapted to our local circumstances, the policy of our law, or simplicity of our practice.

Ellsworth believed that the English rule was unreasonable in a tort action where there was no right of contribution and any of the individual defendants might be obliged to pay the entire judgment. He also sought to avoid the "unnecessary expense and delay of justice" that would be occasioned by retrying the case. Finally there was the sad fact that the victim's death apparently precluded a retrial.[48]

Of the many opinions that he wrote, Ellsworth viewed *Adams v. Kellogg* as the most significant. The case involved the will of Mary Kellogg in which she left her husband a large piece of real estate. Mary's brother challenged the will on the ground that a *feme covert* or married woman was not competent to make a will, and Ellsworth, speaking for a unanimous court, ruled in 1786 that a married woman was indeed incompetent to make a will in respect of realty. The husband subsequently appealed the case to the upper house of the General Assembly, which like the House of Lords in England, exercised an appellate jurisdiction over the common-law courts. In October, 1788, the upper house was "nearly equally divided on the question" but reversed Ellsworth's opinion.[49]

Ellsworth was miffed by the reversal and set about writing a detailed opinion justifying the original opinion that he had given two years earlier. He candidly wrote Ephriam Kirby that his new opinion was written after the fact and asked Kirby to include the new opinion in Kirby's soon-to-be published *Reports*. Ellsworth jocularly explained, "The doctrine of Relation [i.e., a technical legal doctrine allowing certain acts to relate back in time], a very precious one to a lazy man, I suppose I have a right to avail myself of." Kirby complied with the request and published the more elaborate opinion at the end of his *Reports* under the title "Judge Ellsworth's Notes."[50]

Ellsworth's opinion was comprehensive and methodical. Evidently some of the small majority in the upper house that voted to reverse his earlier decision were swayed by a new argument that all human beings have a natural right to dispose of property by will. Ellsworth had not addressed this argument in his earlier opinion, but he began his elaborate opinion with a natural rights analysis. Following Blackstone, Ellsworth noted that not all legal rights are inherent in nature. The Divine reason of the natural law does not provide an answer to every conceivable problem and is indifferent to many subjects of human law. He viewed the right to will property as a mere municipal right rather than a natural right. Ever the careful lawyer, Ellsworth went on to opine that even if the power to will property were a natural right, it could be "controlled by long use and custom [or] by the reason of the case." Everyone knew that married women could not will personal property or make contracts. Therefore custom and reason dictated that any putative natural right to devise real property had been modified.[51]

From natural law he turned to an analysis of the English common law and traced the English common law of wills back to "Abraham's time." In his historical explorations, he explained that the notion of a woman being allowed to will real property came from the Romans, which he condemned as a "heathenish source." He conceded that the Roman law "has been absurdly adopted by some Christian nations," but attributed the adoption to the despised Catholic Church whose "clerical influence has been sufficient to shackle [Catholic countries] with the civil law." Ellsworth then pro-

New Haven County,
1ᵗ Augᵗ Term 1786.

Wilford vˢ Grant —

— Error. Judgment reversed in part only. —

The Judgment complained of is against minors
& adults, as joint trespassers. Minors are presumed want-
ing in discretion to manage their own causes, or to
appoint & instruct attornies; guardians are therefore
to be assigned who shall take care for them & be accountable. In this case none were assigned, & Judgment
went against the minors by default; thro' the neglect
of the plaintᵗ in the action to inform of their infancy,
which he ought to have done before he took judgment
against them by default or otherwise. But the principal question is, can the judgment be reversed as to
them & stand good against the rest? No reason
appears rerum natura, why it should be reversed
as to the adults also. They were fairly tried & con-
victed, & they might have been taken alone at first,
or the Plaintᵗ might have entered a nolle prosequi
as to the others & proceeded against them. Nor could
any one in the execution, if levied upon for the whole
compel a contribution, it being for a tort. — If a
judgment must be reversed as to all merely to give
relief to one who may be entitled to it, there will
be unnecessary expence, & a delay of Justice &, in cases
circumstanced like the present, a failure of it;

for

Page one of Ellsworth's manuscript opinion in Wilford v. Grant (1786).
Ellsworth and his fellow judges believed that the common law of England should be
adopted in Connecticut but not so far as it "may appear contrary to reason or unadapted
to our local circumstances."

for the right of action here being merely personal
& the original plaint dead, the action cannot be
commenced again de novo. The common law rule
of England is indeed against a reversal in part
only. But it doth not appear that this rule has
been adopted in our practice here, so as to have become
authoritative. The common law of England, we
are to pay great difference to, as, in general, a system of
improved reason & a source from whence
our principles of jurisprudence have been
mostly drawn. It's rules however which have
not been made our own by adoption, we are
to examine, & so far as they may appear contrary
to reason, or unadapted to our local circumstances, the policy of our law, or simplicity of
our practice, to vary from. Which, for the
reasons above suggested, we do in this case; &
reverse the judgment as to the minors only.

Law
Dyer
Sherman
Pitkin
Ellsworth

Page two of Ellsworth's manuscript opinion in Wilford v. Grant (1786).

ceeded to prove beyond doubt that under the common law of England a woman could not will real property.[52]

Of course the English common law did not automatically apply in Connecticut, but "by practice or resolutions of our own" common law, the English principle had in fact been adopted in Connecticut. "It certainly was not the understanding," Ellsworth explained, "in the early settlement of this country, that a *feme covert* had power to devise lands." This understanding was based upon firm religious principles: "The Christian ideas of matrimonial union, and of the power of the husband over the wife, were pursued so far as not to suffer her to hold lands."[53]

Having established that married women had neither a natural law nor common law right to will lands, Ellsworth turned to the applicable Connecticut statute, which was ambiguous. He capably parsed the statute and explained precisely how the words could be interpreted to continue married women's common-law disability to will land. The thrust of his argument was that if the legislature intended to overturn such a well-established rule, clearer language would have been used.[54]

Ellsworth concluded his opinion with a lengthy paragraph addressing "the policy of extending such a power to *feme coverts*." His previous analyses had been devoted to ascertaining and applying the applicable law, but in this final paragraph he wrote of what he believed was best for Connecticut. Earlier in his opinion he had referred to the "Christian ideas of matrimonial union, and of the power of the husband over the wife," and he recurred to Christian ideas or values in his conclusion. Ellsworth believed that

> the general reasons urged for the institution of wills [do not] seem to extend to the case of a *feme covert*. That of their use in aiding family government does not; because the government is not placed in her hands.

By family government, Ellsworth meant the model of government found in the Bible. The New Divinity was quite clear in this regard. According to *A Summary of Christian Doctrine*, a husband "is bound to act as a king, and as a priest, in his own house, according to the will of God." Although the wife had some concurrent authority, "Still, as the husband is the head of the wife, it does not become her to contend with him, by direct opposition to his will, even for her rights."[55]

In addition Ellsworth believed that denying married women the power to make a will of realty would protect them from "endless teasing and family discord." Needless to say, he did not explain why men did not need this protection. Continuing in this vein, he pragmatically noted that women are "placed in the power of a husband, whose solicitations they cannot resist, and whose commands, in all things lawful, it is their duty to obey." Again, the source of this wifely duty was the Bible. Some fifteen years later, *A Summary of Christian Doctrine* commanded "Wives, to reverence our husbands; to obey them, in all things lawful." Ellsworth believed that this duty of reverence and obedience opened wives "to coercions imperceptible to others, and dangerous for them to disclose."[56]

Ellsworth's idea of explaining the policy in support of his decision seems com-

monplace in the late twentieth century but was somewhat adventurous for an eighteenth century common-law judge. Judges were supposed to decide cases according to
the law. They were not supposed to consider matters of policy, and Ellsworth knew
that his excursion into policy was questionable. He concluded his analysis with an
equivocal statement that "Political considerations, therefore, so far as they can be of
weight, serve to confirm the opinion, that a *feme covert* has not power to dispose of her
estate by will." In all likelihood, Ellsworth delved into political considerations because—notwithstanding the upper house's judgment of reversal—he did not view the
case as over. A few months after Ellsworth wrote his elaborate opinion, the issue was
presented to the entire General Assembly. He may well have known about this planned
legislative strategy and may have penned his opinion with an eye to this last-ditch
strategy. Although the General Assembly refused to enact legislation reaffirming
Ellsworth's views, he eventually had the last laugh. About twenty years later Ellsworth
was again a member of the upper house and participated in a decision overturning the
original decision of the upper house and reinstating his original Superior Court decision that a married woman could not will realty.[57]

While Ellsworth was serving as a judge in the latter half of the 1780s, Connecticut
called upon him once more to perform a national service. A Constitutional Convention was called to be convened in Philadelphia in 1787, and Ellsworth was chosen as
one of his state's delegates. In Philadelphia he was to play a significant role in creating
a stronger framework for a lasting federal republic.

Oliver Ellsworth and Abigail Ellsworth (1792) by Ralph Earl.
In this picture of Ellsworth and his wife, he is holding a copy of the
United States Constitution. The house outside the window is Elmwood, his home.

COURTESY WADSWORTH ATHENAEUM, HARTFORD. GIFT OF THE ELLSWORTH HEIRS.

### CHAPTER FOUR

# The Constitution of the United States

I N 1787, THE CONSTITUTIONAL CONVENTION was convened in Philadelphia to create a new system of government, and Ellsworth was one of the delegates. Ellsworth and his fellow Connecticut delegates to the Constitutional Convention reflected the pragmatic reality of Connecticut politics. The state's General Assembly initially selected Ellsworth, William Samuel Johnson, and Erastus Wolcott as delegates to the Convention, and each of these men were members of and obviously represented a specific faction within the state. Wolcott was a leading member of the state's anti-federalist agrarian faction that emphasized local interests and distrusted the idea of a stronger national government. Ellsworth was a member of the federalist faction that dominated the state's Standing Order and was particularly solicitous to commercial interests and the state's Calvinist religious establishment. Johnson was the state's most prominent Anglican and some twenty years earlier had played a significant role in the New Lights' ascension to power during the Stamp Act Crisis.[1]

The old division between New Lights and Old Lights had been effectively ended by the need for political unity during the Revolution, but following the Revolution new divisions had emerged. In the fall of 1786, a few months before the Constitutional Convention was called, Noah Webster wrote in the *Connecticut Courant*:

> There are two parties in the state—jealous of each other; *federal men and anti-federal*. The federal men suppose the anti-federal to be knaves, designing artful demagogues. The anti-federal suppose the federal to be ambitious tyrannical men, who are aiming at power and office at the expense of people at large.[2]

Although Webster exaggerated the state's polarization, his description was not entirely inaccurate. Given this atmosphere, Connecticut's delegation seemed destined to conflict between Ellsworth and Wolcott with Johnson serving as a mediator.

This seemingly inevitable conflict, however, never came to pass because Wolcott refused to serve as a delegate, and Roger Sherman was selected as his replacement. Sherman, who was 65 years old, was a highly respected elder statesman in Connecticut politics, and his selection must have delighted Ellsworth because the two men had much in common. Sherman was a New Light who had first been elected to the Governor's Council during the Stamp Act Crisis. During the Revolution, Ellsworth had served with Sherman in the Continental Congress and on the Council of Safety and the Governor's Council. At the time of their selection as delegates to Philadelphia, the two men were fellow judges on the Superior Court. Like Ellsworth, Sherman was a federalist who was sympathetic to commercial interests and who agreed on the need for a stronger national government. In addition to having so much in common, Sherman and Ellsworth were close personal friends, and Sherman was Ellsworth's political mentor. In later years, Ellsworth candidly told John Adams that "he had made Mr. Sherman his model in his youth." After Sherman died in 1793, Ellsworth seldom visited New Haven without paying his respects at his old friend's grave.[3]

Many historians have suggested that Ellsworth was little more than Sherman's yes-man at the Constitutional Convention or at best Sherman's able lieutenant, but these suggestions are implausible. Although Sherman clearly had been Ellsworth's mentor and remained his dear friend, the notion of a subservient relationship between the two men is quite inconsistent with their conduct before and during the Convention. In the Continental Congress, Ellsworth usually voted with Sherman, but twenty percent of the time he voted contrary to his mentor's judgment. Later both men were judges on Connecticut's Superior Court, and on a number of occasions Ellsworth wrote formal judicial opinions dissenting from his older friend's position. Similarly in the Convention itself Ellsworth and Sherman deadlocked Connecticut's vote on at least two occasions.[4]

Moreover Ellsworth was a former pupil who had surpassed his master in political power within the state's Standing Order. Both men were ready, willing, and able to serve as delegates to the Constitutional Convention, but Ellsworth was the first choice to represent the state's federalists. Sherman was a second choice. Similarly after the Constitution was ratified both men wished to serve in Congress, but Ellsworth was chosen for the more prestigious seat in the Senate, and Sherman was elected to the House. Sherman did not become a senator until the state's other senator, William Samuel Johnson, resigned in 1791.[5] Ellsworth's position of superior political strength does not mean that he rather than Sherman was the leader. Instead the two men were strong-willed, intelligent, and capable political allies who were close friends. They had worked together for a number of years as co-equals, and they continued this effective partnership at the Convention.

Sherman, Ellsworth, and Johnson were in more or less agreement on the need to enhance the national government's powers to deal effectively with matters of national interest. Nevertheless when they arrived in Philadelphia, they were appalled by the Virginia delegation's proposal for a sweeping change that would create a powerful national government. Ellsworth and his colleagues were not so frightened of the proposed extent of the new government's powers as they were of those powers being exercised contrary to Connecticut's interests. Moreover their concern about

Connecticut's fate was not merely hypothetical. The Virginians' plan was consciously drafted to vest the larger states with control over the new and powerful government.

The Virginia Plan's principal architect was James Madison, and the government he designed would facilitate rather than limit the exercise of national power. In addition to the powers already exercised by the Continental Congress, Madison's proposed federal legislature was to have power "to legislate in all cases to which the separate States are incompetent or in which the harmony of the United States may be interrupted by the exercise of individual Legislation; [and] to negative all laws passed by the several States, contravening in the opinion of the National Legislature the articles of Union."[6] These openended concepts of state incompetence, harmony of the Union, and a congressional right to negative all state laws were obviously ambiguous and susceptible to broad interpretations.

The Virginians repeated this openended approach to governmental power when they called for the creation of a powerful national judiciary. In addition to "one or more supreme tribunals," a system of "inferior tribunals" was to be established throughout the nation. This extensive system of national courts was to have specific power to try all sorts of cases that arose on the high seas, cases in which foreigners or citizens of more than one state might be interested, and cases involving the collection of the national revenue. The new national courts were also to have a general power to examine "questions which may involve the national peace and harmony."[7]

This proposal for a powerful national government with openended powers created the specter that those powers would inevitably be exercised contrary to some of the states' interests. Madison and his fellow Virginians trusted, however, that the new government would not act contrary to Virginia's and other large states' interests because under their plan representation in both branches of the national legislature was to be based solely upon state populations. Madison candidly explained in private that, from the viewpoint of the large states, this proportional representation would assure that the general government would exercise its new powers in a wise and trustworthy manner. Proportional representation, he wrote, would "obviate the principal objections of the large states to the necessary concessions of power [to the new government]."[8]

Madison's analysis was persuasive to the three states with the largest populations, Virginia, Pennsylvania, and Massachusetts. In addition the three Deep South states of North Carolina, South Carolina, and Georgia initially aligned themselves with the three largest states for reasons that are not entirely clear. Perhaps the three southernmost states believed that through population growth they were destined to become large states. The delegates from these slave states also probably trusted that Virginia's leadership of the large state bloc would prevent a constitutional modification of slavery.

Delegates from the small states were quite dissatisfied with the Virginia Plan's provision for proportional representation because they feared that the large states would exercise their consequent control over the new national government in ways detrimental to the small states. This dissatisfaction surfaced almost immediately. On May 30, the second day of the Convention's consideration of the Virginia Plan, James

Madison moved that the Convention reject the existing rule of one state/one vote that prevailed in the Continental Congress under the Articles of Confederation. Madison assumed that his motion was "generally relished [and] would have been agreed to," but George Read of Delaware quickly took the floor and threatened that if this radical change were adopted, the Delaware delegation might leave the Convention. Rather than force such a crisis at this early date, the Convention then agreed to postpone its consideration of proportional representation.[9]

Although the issue was temporarily postponed, proportional representation continued to loom large in the various delegates' minds. A little over a week later on June 9, William Paterson of New Jersey moved that the Convention formally revisit proportional representation. In the process, he emphatically warned that

> N. Jersey will never confederate on the plan before the Committee [i.e., proportional representation]. She would be swallowed up. He had rather submit to a monarch, to a despot, than to such a fate.

In response, the large state delegates were equally adamant in insisting upon proportional representation. James Wilson of Pennsylvania insisted that, "if the small states will not confederate on this plan, Pena. & he presumed some other States, would not confederate on any other.[10]

This heated and potentially catastrophic exchange took place on a Saturday, and when the delegates returned the next Monday, a number of compromises were offered. In particular Roger Sherman recalled an idea that he had first proposed eleven years earlier in the Continental Congress. He reminded the Convention that the national legislature was to have two branches. Why not have representation in the first branch be in proportion to population but retain the one state/one vote rule in the second branch? The large states, however, firmly believed as a matter of principle that they were right, and in retrospect reason seems to have been on their side. The large states also knew they had sufficient votes to impose their will upon the Convention and simply were not interested in a compromise. In a series of votes on June 11, Sherman's proposal was rejected, and proportional representation was adopted for both branches of the legislature.[11]

These votes and subsequent votes provide valuable insights into Oliver Ellsworth's and the Connecticut delegation's understanding of the art of political deal-making. In some people, a willingness to compromise is simply a symptom of the absence of firm convictions coupled with an aversion to confrontation. This type of malleable individual essentially conforms to outside pressure. In contrast, Sherman, Ellsworth, and Johnson did not view political compromise as a process of passively abdicating principle in the face of necessity. Rather they actively sought an alternative solution that could accommodate apparently conflicting interests. They sincerely believed that Sherman's idea was a sound compromise that protected the interests of both the large and the small states. Having determined upon this alternative solution, they stubbornly clung to it for the rest of the Convention.

In the June 11 voting when Sherman first broached his idea, the Connecticut delegates were rigorously true to their compromise solution. They sided with the larger states on representation in the first branch, and the vote was 9–2, with only New Jersey and Delaware insisting upon a monolithic rule of one state/one vote. Conversely when the Convention took up representation in the second branch, Sherman moved, with Ellsworth's second, that the old rule of one state/one vote should be retained. The Convention, however, or more precisely the large states, was not yet prepared to accept the Connecticut Compromise, and proportional representation was adopted for the second branch by a close but firm vote of 6–5, with the three largest and three southernmost states in the majority.[12]

Following these votes the Convention proceeded to other matters while the small state delegates digested their defeat. The Connecticut delegates were not discouraged. After all, their proposed compromise had come within one vote of prevailing, and they knew that there would be other votes. Nor were the New Jersey and Delaware delegates unduly discouraged. Almost as soon as the June 11 vote was lost or perhaps earlier, William Paterson and some other delegates began drafting a new, free-standing plan that they planned to submit as an alternative to the Virginia Plan. By June 14 this new plan was almost finished, and William Paterson asked for a one-day adjournment to prepare a plan that would be presented the next day. Of course, his requested adjournment was granted.[13]

The next day Paterson presented his plan, and the Convention agreed to consider it as an alternative to the Virginia Plan. Under the Paterson Plan the national legislature would have only one chamber, and representation would be based upon the idea of one state/one vote. In addition, the national government would not be as powerful as the one embodied in the Virginia Plan. Instead of providing a general openended grant of legislative powers, the Paterson Plan provided for specific, comparatively narrow grants of legislative authority. Instead of a single chief executive, multiple executives would be appointed, and the state governments would be given a limited power to effect the removal of federal executive officers. Finally under the Paterson Plan, state—rather than federal—trial courts would be used to enforce federal laws with a limited right of appeal to a federal appellate court.[14]

James Madison believed and most modern historians have agreed that the Paterson Plan was "concerted among the deputations or members thereof, from Cont. N.Y. N.J. Del. and perhaps Mr. Martin from Maryd." Although the Connecticut delegates almost certainly participated in drafting the Plan, their participation does not mean that they were in favor of it. There is no surviving evidence that any of the Connecticut delegates ever spoke in favor of the Plan that they had helped to draft. Nor did any of the Connecticut delegates speak against the Plan. Except for a single technical comment by Ellsworth, the Connecticut delegates stood mute during the debate.

Just four days after Paterson presented his plan, the Convention formally adopted the Virginia Plan and rejected the Paterson Plan by a vote of 7–3–1. In this head-to-head competition, Connecticut voted for the Virginia Plan and was the only small state that sided with the large-state bloc.[15]

At first glance, this decision to participate in drafting the Paterson Plan, but not to support it in debate, and finally to vote against it smacks of double dealing. There is no evidence, however, that any of the other delegates viewed Connecticut's conduct in this light. Indeed, two months later William Paterson was corresponding with Ellsworth in terms of warm friendship and high respect.[16] The Connecticut delegates' obvious success in simultaneously working with and rejecting Paterson is further evidence of their enormous abilities to effect political compromises.

Although the Connecticut delegates clearly were in sympathy with Paterson's insistence upon a monolithic rule of one state/one vote, they decided relatively early that the large states would never agree to a complete small-state victory and accordingly committed themselves wholeheartedly to a compromise. Undoubtedly they told Paterson in private that they would not support his Plan because they believed that their compromise was the right way to go. At the same time they probably viewed Paterson's Plan as an excellent device for clarifying the large and small states' intransigence and paving the way to an adoption of the Connecticut Compromise.

On June 11, the crucial small states of New Jersey and Delaware and the dominant large state bloc had rejected the Connecticut Compromise. The large states had insisted upon proportional representation in what was to be the Senate, and New Jersey and Delaware had insisted on one state/one vote in what was to be the House. The Paterson Plan was basically the last chance for the small states to achieve a monolithic rule of one state/one vote. After it was decisively rejected, the New Jersey and Delaware delegations' options were drastically narrowed to three choices: either embrace the Connecticut Compromise, accept the Virginia Plan's unacceptable proportional representation, or walk out of the Convention. At the same time, the debate over the Paterson Plan inevitably demonstrated the depth and sincerity of the small states' opposition. Although the large states prevailed in this vote, they had to know that some of the small states were ready to walk, and this knowledge could not help but enhance the Connecticut Compromise's viability.

The head-to-head confrontation between the Virginia Plan and the Paterson Plan was beneficial to the Connecticut Compromise in another way. Such a full scale debate was likely to generate hard feelings and solidify opposition. These feelings and opposition, however, would be centered upon the plans before the Convention and not upon the Connecticut Compromise. The Compromise was not formally in play, and the Connecticut delegation, by standing mute, remained above the fray.

Another consideration guiding the Connecticut delegates' actions was their certain knowledge that after the vote on the Paterson Plan they would have a full opportunity to present their compromise. Virtually all of the Convention's deliberations up to and including the head-to-head vote on the Paterson and Virginia plans took place under a parliamentary procedure called the Committee of the Whole House. In England the King or his representatives had a right to be present when the House of Commons was in session, and to counteract this right the Commons had developed a practice of forming a Committee of the Whole House and excluding all but members of the Commons on the basis that the work was being done in a committee meeting rather than a session of Parliament. The effect in Philadelphia of this Committee of the

Whole House procedure was to render all Committee votes preliminary and nonbinding. After the Committee chose the Virginia Plan over the Paterson Plan and reported it to the Convention, the Connecticut delegation knew that they would have a chance to present their compromise to the Convention as an alternative to the Virginia Plan.

Finally on June 27, the Convention itself rather than a Committee of the Whole House formally took up the issue of representation in the House of Representatives. Most of this debate was given over to an interminable diatribe by Luther Martin of Maryland, who all that day and much of the next spoke in favor of the one state/one vote rule. The last day of debate was on June 29, and there probably was a general understanding that the large state block was not going to budge. That day's debate began with a temperate speech by William Samuel Johnson in which he calmly reviewed the small states' need for protection. Johnson concluded his speech by noting that the large states' position was not entirely without merit. He therefore urged the Convention to consider the Connecticut Compromise. Later in this debate, Ellsworth stated, "I do not despair but that we shall be so fortunate as to devise and adopt some good plan of government."[17]

When the first vote was taken on representation in what was to become the House of Representatives, the large states prevailed by a close but firm vote of 6–4–1. In this vote, the Connecticut delegation chose to vote for one state/one vote. This vote is somewhat puzzling because it was contrary to the Compromise that they clearly advocated. Perhaps the New Jersey and Delaware delegations still were not convinced that the Connecticut Compromise was the best solution. By showing solidarity with the small states, the Connecticut vote may have demonstrated that the rule of one state/one vote in the House simply was not going to come to pass. The stage was now set for a vote on the Connecticut Compromise. The Connecticut delegation had carefully planned for this last-best opportunity to present their Compromise and had agreed that Ellsworth would take the lead in this crucial debate. After the vote on proportional representation in the House, Ellsworth moved that the delegates proceed immediately to representation in what was to become the Senate. After the Convention agreed, Ellsworth moved that a one state/one vote rule be adopted for the Senate. He then took the floor as the primary speaker for his motion and continued during the succeeding debate to be the primary advocate of the Connecticut Compromise. Except for one brief speech by Sherman, his Connecticut colleagues made little contribution to this debate.[18]

Ellsworth's speech in support of his motion may or may not have changed any of the delegates' minds. Nevertheless, it is worth studying in some detail as an example of Ellsworth's powers as a public speaker. Ellsworth began in a constructive vein. He "was not sorry on the whole . . . that the vote just passed, had determined against [the one state/one vote] rule in the first branch." The vote was not a defeat for the small states. It was an opportunity for the Convention, and he "hoped it would be a ground of Compromise with regard to the 2d branch."[19]

After this optimistic beginning, he turned to the merits of the controversy. In the back of everyone's mind were the veiled and occasionally not so veiled threats of the small states to walk out of the Convention and destroy the entire process. But Ellsworth did not immediately reiterate this threat. He emphasized sound principle over raw political power. He wanted the Convention to embrace the compromise—not to be forced into it. In a very common sense way, he "confess[ed] that the effect of [his] motion is, to make the general government *partly federal and partly national*." By this mixed language he meant that on national matters the government would represent the entire people of the United States, but the states also had interests to be represented. He continued:

> The proportional representation in the first branch was conformable
> to the national principle & would secure the large States agst. the small.
> An equality of voices [in the Senate] was conformable to the federal
> principle and was necessary to secure the Small States agst. the large.

He was in effect urging that the small and large states be treated equally—that each be "secure . . . agst." the other.[20]

Only after noting the principled basis and fairness of the Connecticut Compromise did Ellsworth turn to the small states' raw political power to destroy the Convention. He warned, "if no compromise should take place, our meeting would not only be in vain but worse than in vain." The simple fact was that all the New England states, save Massachusetts, "would risk every consequence rather than part with so dear a right." If the Convention foundered upon this issue of representation, he believe that "we will be forever separated." He warned that the states would eventually form into two separate nations—one north of the Delaware River and one south.[21]

After making this not so veiled threat, Ellsworth immediately pointed out some advantages that the large states would have under the Connecticut Compromise. As a practical matter, even under a one state/one vote rule the large states would inevitably have more power. In support of this point, he noted that in the "Dutch Confederacy" the province of Holland had a "prevailing influence." In addition, he assumed that the large states inevitably would have more power over the Executive. This assumption proved to be remarkable accurate when the first ten presidential elections were won by candidates from the large states of Virginia and Massachusetts.[22]

After noting the advantages that the large states would enjoy under the Connecticut Compromise, Ellsworth returned to the reasons that the small states feared proportional representation. Here his thoughts were influenced by his Calvinist faith in original sin and consequent pessimism about human nature. He believed that the large states would inevitably combine. "They will like individuals find out and avail themselves of the advantage to be gained by it." Moreover, he noted, the self-evident and pragmatic fact that "three or four States can more easily combine, than Nine or Ten States."[23]

Ellsworth's final argument was somewhat akin to resorting to legal precedent. He reminded the Convention that the existing Articles of Confederation had formed a "perpetual" union on the basis of the one state/one vote rule. He viewed the Articles, however, as more than a legal precedent. The Articles were in the nature of a wedding vow. They were, to use Ellsworth's words, an "antecedent plighted faith" under which the states had solemnly engaged to form a perpetual union. The implication was that a complete abandonment of the one state/one vote rule would be akin to a breach of honor.[25]

Ellsworth concluded his speech by reminding the Convention of the chief value of compromises. He agreed that a "strong Executive, a Judiciary & Legislative power [should] be created," but he urged caution. Ellsworth concluded by stating that, "He was not in general a half-way man, yet he preferred doing half the good we could, rather than do nothing at all."[26]

Some modern historians have suggested that this "half-way man" comment was at best ironic and perhaps even hypocritical. For example one historian has described Ellsworth as "the 'half-way man' of the century."[27] Ellsworth, however, cannot possibly have intended to project an image of irony or hypocrisy. He was too adept a politician to indulge such a self-destructive inclination. Instead his comment should be viewed as one more bit of evidence of the extent to which he incorporated religious faith and political action into a seamless web.

Ellsworth's "half-way man" comment had an overtly religious meaning. All New England Calvinists would have understood his comment as a reference to the Half-way Covenant that liberalized the rules for membership in Calvinist churches. Traditionally only people who had a personal regenerating experience with God and had made a credible public confession of their experience could be admitted to church membership and have their children baptized. The Half-way Covenant allowed for a kind of conditional membership if an unregenerate person would profess belief in God's word and agree to live a life according to His word. The Covenant also allowed these unregenate persons' children to be baptized. The conditional members or half-way men, however, were not entitled to take communion or vote on church matters. Ellsworth's church in Windsor followed this custom until 1776 when the church voted to admit half-way members to communion.[27]

In other words, when Ellsworth said that he was not "in general a half-way man," he was speaking the literal truth. He was not a unregenerate person. In 1768 he had had a personal regenerating experience with God and had been admitted to church membership in full communion.[28] He knew he was one of God's elect, and this self-knowledge must have lent credibility to his arguments in favor of the Connecticut Compromise. He sincerely believed that the plan that his mentor, Roger Sherman, had conceived was a fair and equitable resolution of the problem. Indeed, his Calvinist faith whispered to him that Sherman's idea came from God.

Ellsworth's speech and those that followed echoed all the arguments and counterarguments that already had been presented on the Convention's floor and in numerous private discussions. With one small exception, the large state delegates remained intransigent. That one exception was Abraham Baldwin, the leader of the Georgia delegation. After Ellsworth's speech, Baldwin said that although he planned to vote against Ellsworth's motion, he believed that the "second branch ought not to be elected as the first." He would prefer that representation in the second branch be based upon wealth. He also stated that he "thought it wd. be impossible for the Gen. Legislature to extend its cases to the local matters of the States." At least Baldwin was open minded on the issue of representation in the Senate.[29]

Ellsworth made his motion on June 29, a Friday, and debate continued the next day. In this subsequent debate Ellsworth spoke again and addressed some of the points made by large state delegates. The details of his rebuttal are not so important as the reasonable tenor of his remarks. He began his rebuttal by assuring the Convention, "I have the greatest respect for the gentleman who spoke last [James Wilson of Pennsylvania]. I respect his abilities, although I differ from him on many points." He closed by reminding his fellow delegates that his "remarks are not the result of partial or local views. The state I represent is respectable, and in importance holds a middle rank." By this he meant that in terms of population Connecticut was either the smallest of the large states or the largest of the small ones.[30]

At the end of the Saturday debate, Ellsworth drew on an idea suggested the day before by Abraham Baldwin. Ellsworth recognized that a strong national government was necessary to preserve national security, but insisted that domestic happiness would have to depend primarily upon local or state government. A national government representing the people generally would not be able to

> descend to the local objects on which [domestic happiness] depended. It could only embrace objects of a general nature. He turned his eyes therefore for the preservation of his rights to the State Govts.[31]

Because the state governments inevitably would be performing vital functions at a local level, they needed protection from the national government, and the Connecticut Compromise would secure this protection.

After the Saturday debates concluded, the delegates did not rest. The small state delegates knew that they had the votes of Connecticut, New Jersey, Delaware, and New York. There was, however, some doubt about Maryland because on Friday Maryland had divided on the issue of representation in the House. Even if they could bring Maryland into the fold, the big state bloc would still have six votes. The only apparent chance of breaking this solid six-vote bloc was to lobby Abraham Baldwin, who had at least expressed some ambivalence about proportional representation in the Senate.

On the next Monday, the convention voted on the Connecticut Compromise without debate. The Maryland delegation previously had been split between Daniel of St. Thomas Jenifer who thought proportional representation would provide the fairest basis for representation and Luther Martin who did not. Jenifer, however, delayed his attendance till immediately after the vote was taken, and his temporary absence gave Maryland's vote to Martin. As a result, five votes were cast in favor of the Compromise. As was customary, the vote began with the northeasternmost state of New Hampshire and terminated with the southernmost state of Georgia. With Maryland now in favor of the Compromise, the count was an even 5–5 when Georgia was polled. Until this moment Georgia had consistently voted with the big state bloc, but something had changed over the weekend. The individual Georgia delegates could not agree; they split their votes evenly. Georgia was divided, the solidarity of the big state bloc was cracked, and the final vote was 5–5–1.[32]

The reasons for the change in the Georgia delegation's vote are complex and probably will never be entirely understood. Until the weekend preceding the vote, Georgia had four delegates. Two of the Georgia delegates, however, were also members of the Continental Congress, which was sitting in New York. The day before the vote on the Connecticut Compromise, these two members went to New York to enable the Continental Congress to form a quorum with a temporary southern majority that would press hard for free navigation on the Mississippi River. As a result of this absence, Georgia was left with only two delegates, and one of them, Abraham Baldwin, voted for the Connecticut Compromise.[33]

If the small states lobbied Baldwin over the weekend—and it is inconceivable that they did not—Ellsworth was the man for the job because he happened to be a personal friend of Baldwin. Two years later in the first Congress the two men boarded together, and Baldwin was describing Ellsworth as his "chum." In fact, Ellsworth and Baldwin had much in common. Baldwin was born and raised in Connecticut and was a Yale graduate who, like Ellsworth, had originally planned to become a minister. He subsequently, however, had turned to the law and had emigrated to Georgia in 1784.[34]

From Baldwin's speech on Friday, Ellsworth knew that his "chum" was opposed to a uniform rule of proportional representation for both the House and the Senate, and Ellsworth attempted to address some of Baldwin's concerns in the Saturday debate. There is no record of the private conversations that undoubtedly occurred between the two men, but Luther Martin subsequently reported that Baldwin voted "from a conviction that we [the small states] would go home, and thereby dissolve the convention before we would give up the question."[35]

This fear that the Convention would be dissolved was an especially significant consideration for Georgia, which was a fairly weak state bordering on hostile forces to the South and West. About a half a year later, Georgia Washington was confident that Georgia would ratify the Constitution. He explained, "if [Georgia], with powerful tribes of Indians in its rear, the Spaniards on its flank, do not incline to embrace a strong *general* Government there must, I should think, be either wickedness, or insanity in their conduct." Ellsworth fully understood the precariousness of Georgia's situation, and in a private, heart-to-heart meeting, he evidently was able to convince Baldwin that the small states would, indeed, go home if the Connecticut Compromise failed.[36]

This tie vote was the turning point for Ellsworth and for the Convention. After the vote, the Convention elected a committee to revisit the issue of representation. In recognition of Ellsworth's leadership on this issue, he rather than Sherman was elected to this committee. Ellsworth, however, became ill, and Sherman was substituted as Connecticut's representative. Some have suggested that Ellsworth feigned his indisposition as a ploy to put Sherman on the Committee. There is, however, no evidence to support this suggestion other than the implausible belief that Ellsworth was subservient to Sherman. In contrast, James Madison believed that "Ellsworth . . . was kept away by indisposition," and after the Convention Ellsworth noted in his expense account that he had been ill during the Convention and had to retain the services of a doctor.[37]

This committee on representation was loaded in favor of the Connecticut Compromise and predictably reported in favor of the Compromise. Although the large states fought a rear-guard action, the Convention eventually adopted the Compromise by a slight majority. Finally a caucus of large state delegates, along with a few small state delegates, met about two weeks after the crucial July 2 tie vote. The large state delegates were in disarray. They could not agree on the importance of proportional representation in the Senate, and they worried about "the policy of risking a failure of any general act of the Convention by inflexibly opposing [the Connecticut Compromise]." In the end they tacitly agreed to acquiesce in the Compromise. Ellsworth undoubtedly attended this caucus, and James Madison subsequently related that, "from the day when every doubt of the right of the smaller states to an equal vote in the Senate was quieted. . . . Ellsworth became one of the [the general government's] strongest pillars."[38]

After the Connecticut Compromise was adopted, Ellsworth continued to play an active and influential role in the Convention. For example, he served on the five-man Committee of Detail that wrote the rough draft of the Constitution. He also played a morally dubious role in shaping the Convention's compromise on the issue of slavery. In the dispute over representation in the House and Senate, Ellsworth fought for a compromise that was on its own terms was fair and just. But when the issue of slavery arose, he espoused a resolution that on its own terms was morally repugnant to him.

The Connecticut Compromise's solution to the problem of representation embodied a compromise that was entirely positive and quite principled. Both sides of the controversy had legitimate interests to be protected, and this ingenious scheme was a fair compromise between the extremes. In contrast, a subsequent compromise that the Connecticut delegation forcefully pushed was not so principled. Towards the end of the Convention, the issue of slavery arose, and the Connecticut delegation proved willing to espouse a compromise that would bolster the institution of slavery. They embraced this compromise despite the fact that they personally believed that the institution was evil.

After the Connecticut Compromise was securely in place, the Convention appointed a five-man Committee of Detail to put together a rough draft of the Constitution. The Committee included Ellsworth, John Rutledge of South Carolina, and James Wilson, who was a friend and business ally of Rutledge. After about two weeks of work, the Committee reported a rough draft of the Constitution that forbade the national government to lay any import tax on slaves or any export tax of any kind. The government was also positively forbidden to prohibit the importation of slaves. Finally no navigation acts restricting trade were to be allowed unless passed by a supermajority of $2/3$ in each House.[39]

These provisions were not the coincidental result of the Committee of Detail's principled effort to provide the best government possible. Thomas Jefferson, who was our ambassador to France at the time of the Convention, later wrote that George Mason informed him that initially the question of "the importation of slaves . . . was left to Congress." South Carolina and Georgia, however, believed "that Congress would immediately suppress the importation of slaves [and] therefore struck up a bargain with the three New England states."[40] Part of this bargain involved a similarity in the economies of South Carolina and Connecticut. They were the only two states, a major part of whose economies depended entirely upon the direct export of their own commodities. South Carolina exported rice and indigo, and Connecticut exported livestock, lumber, and food to the West Indies. After the Connecticut Compromise was accepted, the Connecticut delegation was basically satisfied with the direction that the Convention took. They worked together with the southerners on the issue of export taxes. On the issue of slavery, however, the two Deep-South delegations made it clear that they would walk from the Convention if the Constitution were written to permit the national government to prohibit the further importation of slaves. Having used this same threat in the big state/small state dispute, the Connecticut delegates were sensitized, and in order to save the Constitution they were inclined to support the southern demands.

Although the Connecticut delegates willingly entered into a pact that would protect the states' right to continue importing slaves, other delegates were not so solicitous towards this evil. When the Convention turned to the portions of the Committee of Detail draft that dealt with slavery, a number of delegates spoke out on this evil. George Mason of Virginia wished to halt the "infernal traffic" of importing slaves. He prophetically argued that

> slaves . . . produce the most pernicious effort on manners. Every master of slaves is born a petty tyrant. They bring the judgment of heaven on a Country. As nations can not be rewarded or punished in the next world they must be in this. By an inevitable chain of causes & effects providence punishes national sins, by national calamities. He lamented that some of our Eastern brethren had from a lust of gain embarked in this nefarious trade. . . . He held it essential in every point of view, that the Genl. Govt. should have power to prevent the increase of slavery.

Similarly Luther Martin had previously insisted that slavery "was inconsistent with the principles of the revolution and [it was] dishonorable to the American character to have such a feature in the Constitution."[41]

Ellsworth agreed with Mason's insistence that a continuation of slavery would bring God's judgment on the nation. New Divinity Calvinists emphatically condemned slavery. Only a year earlier, Ellsworth had listened to Levi Hart deliver an election sermon back in Connecticut condemning slavery in the strongest possible terms. Hart was deeply disturbed by the continued existence of slavery after the revolution and distainfully described slaveholders as "returning, 'like the dog to his vomit,' to that dreadful infraction of the law of nature and of God, the practice of stealing their brethren of the human race, and selling them." Ellsworth and the Connecticut Standing Order agreed that slavery was utterly wrong, and after the Convention Ellsworth wrote that "all good men wish the entire abolition of slavery."[42]

Needless to say, Ellsworth would not countenance slavery in his own house. In early 1790, he and his wife bought a "negro girl" who would be a servant and possibly a companion to his daughters. Six years earlier, the Connecticut legislature had enacted a law that no child subsequently born into slavery within the state could be held as a slave past the age of 25. Therefore because the girl was born before this law was enacted, her legal status was that of perpetual slavery. Ellsworth had no compunctions about buying the girl, but he refused to "take her as a slave for life." Instead he contemplated emancipating her and agreeing, as required by Connecticut law, to be chargeable for her support should she ever "come to want." Consistent with these plans, the first national Census taken later that year lists one nonwhite, free person and no slaves in the Ellsworth household.[43]

Given Ellsworth's firm opposition to slavery, it must have been infuriating to listen to George Mason, who was himself a slaveholder, preach against the evils of Ellsworth's proposal to allow the continuation of the slave trade. As soon as Mason finished his speech, Ellsworth jumped up to address Mason's statement that slavery had "the most pernicious effect on manners [and made every slaveholder] a petty tyrant." With syrupy irony, Ellsworth noted that because "he had never owned a slave [, he] could not judge of the effects of slavery on character." Having implied in the clearest way that Mason was lacking in character, Ellsworth proceeded to suggest that Mason was a hypocrite. Everyone in the room knew that Mason was not an advocate of abolition. Playing off this knowledge, Ellsworth matter-of-factly noted "if it was to be considered in a moral light we ought to go further and free those already in the Country." In other words Mason was a hypocrite who was willing to preach about character and morality but who was unwilling to follow the logic of his preaching.[44]

These gut punches did not end Ellsworth's *ad hominem* attacks. Notwithstanding Mason's allusions to character and morality, Ellsworth explained that Mason's insistence upon a power to bar the importation of slaves was based upon cunning selfinterest. The simple fact was that slaves "multiply so fast in Virginia & Maryland that it is cheaper to raise them than import them."[45] In other words, Mason was on his moral high horse about importing slaves because his state did not need to import slaves.

That these fierce charges of moral hypocrisy came from Ellsworth's mouth seems ironic. At first glance Ellsworth was an even bigger hypocrite. He was at least as opposed to slavery as Mason and probably more so. At the same time, his position in the Convention was more supportive of slavery. Either Ellsworth had a principled basis for reconciling the disjunction between his principles and his actions, or he was the grand hypocrite of the Convention.

Ellsworth's position on banning the importation of slaves was obviously influenced by the South Carolina and Georgia delegations' insistence that they would never accept such a grant to the federal government. Just a few weeks earlier he had used precisely such a threat when he convinced his friend Abraham Baldwin to vote in favor of the Connecticut Compromise. When the Convention subsequently took up the importation of slaves, the shoe was on the other foot, and Baldwin was the one who was making the threat. Ellsworth was willing to give in to the Deep South demands in order to keep them in the fold. As his friend Roger Sherman explained, "it was better to let the S. States import slaves than to part with them, if they made that a sine qua non."[46]

In addition, Ellsworth's attitude toward the deal with the Deep States was influenced by Bellamy's *The Wisdom of God*. Ellsworth believed that the Constitution was part of God's plan for humanity. As he later said, "national laws [under the Constitution] are that means by which it pleases heaven to make of weak and discordant parts, one great people." Joseph Bellamy had taught him that God's plan was not always intelligible to mortals and that even sin was part of His plan. Because slavery was an evil, the eventual elimination of slavery was inevitable. In supporting the Deep South's right to import slaves, Ellsworth explained and his friend Roger Sherman agreed that

> As population increases; poor laborers will be so plenty as to render slaves useless. Slavery in time will not be a speck in our Country. Provision is already made in Connecticut for abolishing it. And the abolition has already taken place in Massachusetts.

If the Constitution was indeed part of God's plan, there could be no wrong in supporting even those parts of the plan that would temporarily continue a known evil. In the end, slavery would be abolished according to God's predestined schedule.[47]

In stating that Connecticut had already commenced the abolition of slavery, Ellsworth was referring to the legislation that abolished slavery for children born after 1784 but that continued slavery for those already born. This tentative law seems inconsistent with an absolute opposition, but Connecticut Calvinists did not believe in an immediate and complete abolition of slavery. Even Levi Hart, who had described slaveholders as dogs returning to their vomit, was ambivalent about the process of abolition. He called for a "gradual . . . abolition of slavery [that would] protect the friendless Africans among us from abuse, on the one hand, and, on the other, secure society from injury by improper and ill-timed manumissions." Ellsworth agreed with this graduated approach. He wished for "the entire abolition of slavery as soon as it can take place with safety to the public, and for the lasting-good of the present wretched race of slaves."[48]

This gradual approach to abolition does not mean that the Connecticut Calvinists were insincere in their opposition to slavery. The 1784 legislation actually did serve its intended purpose. During the years 1790 through 1820, the number of African Americans in the state gradually increased from about 5500 to about 8000. At the same time, there was a constant and dramatic decrease in the number of slaves. In the 1790 national census, 50% of African Americans were slaves, but by 1820 only 1% were slaves.[49]

So Ellsworth was a sincere opponent of slavery who nonetheless could sincerely support the Deep South's desire to continue the importation of slaves. The secret lay in the extreme Calvinist notion of predestination that saw everything as part of God's plan. There is, however, another aspect of Ellsworth's conduct that smacks of hypocrisy. In a sense Mason's and Ellsworth's positions on the importation of slaves were the opposite sides of the same coin. Ellsworth was a sincere opponent of slavery who supported importation, and Mason was a slave holder who opposed importation. There seems to be a moral contradiction in both men's positions. Thus Mason was in a sense doing exactly what Ellsworth was doing. Yet Ellsworth pointed out the readily apparent conflict in Mason's position and viciously attacked him as a hypocrite whose character had been diminished by slavery.

In part the viciousness of Ellsworth's attack was probably caused by a visceral anger that a slaveholder would be preaching about the morality of slavery when Ellsworth was forced to defend the Deep South states' rights to import slaves. Ellsworth's Calvinism also played a role in his attack. Ellsworth believed that his support of the Deep South states was morally justified because it was part of God's plan. Given his faith in predestination, he also would have had to have conceded that Mason's actions were also part of God's plan. Nevertheless under Calvinist doctrine, Ellsworth was acting righteously and Mason was deeply sinful.

According to the Edwardsean/New Divinity model of moral accountability, all human actions were predestined by God. What a man actually did was neither righteous nor sinful—neither good nor bad. What counted was the man's internal disposition—whether he acted with a love of God.[50] From a New Divinity perspective, Ellsworth was supporting a Constitution that was part of God's plan for the general benefit of the community. In sharp contrast, Ellsworth charged that Mason was motivated by the partial economic concern of Virginia rather than the general good of the whole, and this kind of selfishness was the essence of sinfulness under the Edwardsean/New Divinity model. Therefore Ellsworth was righteous, and Mason was sinful.

Although the Edwardsean/New Divinity model of free will inclined Ellsworth to attack the personal character of his opponents, he did not rigorously follow the model. Throughout his life he advanced arguments based on an assumption that men could control their actions. For example later on in the Convention, Ellsworth took the position that members of Congress should be eligible to serve in other federal offices after they left Congress. He believed that this possibility of reward would serve as a partial encouragement "for obtaining the services of the ablest men in the Legislature."[51] This idea that men could modify their conduct to obtain a good is in flat contradiction to the Edwardsean/New Divinity model.

As a matter of ordinary logic, predestination cannot coexist with an individual's ability to control individual conduct, but human beings have never been completely governed by ordinary logic. Ellsworth's *a priori* faith in predestination was central to his entire understanding of the world, and he accepted the Edwardsean/New Divinity explanation of free will because it harmonized predestination with moral accountability. But Ellsworth also was an effective participant in political society and part of him intuitively believed that men could control their actions. Intellectual dissonance like this may be unacceptable in a philosopher, but it is commonplace in gifted politicians—even in honorable politicians.

Ellsworth's position on slavery at the Convention was the moral nadir of his career, and his overdetermined attack on George Mason suggests that he had personal doubts about his position. He personally believed that slavery was evil, and yet he allied himself with the Deep South states to support the institution's continuation. To make matters worse, he clearly was willing to give the Deep South states more than they were willing to settle for. Other delegations drew the line on a complete Constitutional prohibition against barring the importation of slaves and insisted upon a compromise. Ellsworth, however, had locked himself into a morally dubious position in order to secure the Deep South's approval of the Constitution and would not budge from his firm support of the Deep South's position. Finally the Convention agreed, over Ellsworth's objection, to empower Congress to prohibit the importation of slaves after 1808.[52]

## ☙ RATIFYING THE CONSTITUTION

After the Convention, the Constitution was submitted to the individual states for ratification, and in Connecticut Ellsworth played the leading role in the ratification process. The opening shot in this campaign was a letter that Ellsworth and Roger Sherman wrote to Governor Huntington enclosing a copy of the proposed Constitution and urging its ratification. This letter clearly was written as a political document and was published in seven newspapers within the state and sixteen newspapers in other states.[53]

Ellsworth and Sherman very briefly summarized the compromise on representation in the Congress and also noted some restraints that the Constitution would place on state governments. The bulk of the letter, however, discussed the powers that the new federal government would have. Ellsworth and Sherman reassured their readers that the federal government's powers would "extend only to matters respecting the common interests of the Union, and are specially defined, so that the particular states retain their *Sovereignty* in all other matters." Specifically, the federal government would have an independent taxing authority, and its money would be spent "for the common defense and general welfare, and for payment of debts incurred for those purposes."[54]

Ellsworth followed up with a series of thirteen essays published under the pseudonym "A Landholder." He addressed the Constitution's merits in a plain, straightforward, and easily understood style. Although the decade of the 1780's had witnessed almost a constant clash in Connecticut between agrarian and mercantile interests, Ellsworth characteristically strove for unity and harmony rather than conflict. He described himself as a merchant who had retired from trade to become a farmer—a man of both camps. His theme was that the livelihood of both farmers and merchants were tied to trade and that a stronger national government would provide for a "good national regulation of trade" that would benefit everyone. In his final essay, he returned to the common interests of merchants and farmers and portrayed a society in which farmers and manufacturers would work within the state for the common good. He concluded, "The sources of wealth are open to us, and there needs but industry to

become as rich as we are free."[55]    Ellsworth's Calvinism is evident in virtually every one of his "Landholder" essays. In the last essay in which he extolled the glories of being industrious and rich, he was careful to note that he was not talking about personal gain for personal gain's sake. He explained that, "Industry is most favorable to the moral virtue of the world, it is therefore wisely ordered by the Author of Nature, that the blessings of this world should be acquired by our own application in some business useful to society." In "Landholder II," Ellsworth expressly broached an abiding theme of his essays. The Constitution's opponents were morally corrupt individuals who, consistent with Calvinist doctrine, acted with "selfish motives," and Ellsworth used the overtly religious concept of "unrighteousness" to describe the selfish schemes of men who lack virtue.[56]

Ellsworth's general insistence that the opponents of the Constitution were selfish men is related to the Edwardsean/New Divinity doctrine of Freedom of Will that influenced his virulent personal attack on George Mason at the Constitutional Convention. As the ratification process continued, Ellsworth frequently reverted to *ad hominem* attacks on some of the Constitution's prominent opponents outside the state. Ellsworth charged that Elbridge Gerry of Massachusetts was an incompetent liar who sought to protect his "state dignities or emoluments" and who opposed the Constitution because it would adversely affect his speculation in old Continental Money. Richard Henry Lee of Virginia was a man of "artful . . . scurrility" who was motivated by an "implacable hatred to General Washington." In addition to labeling George Mason as a dissembler in the same class with Elbridge Gerry, Ellsworth reiterated his belief that Mason was a hypocrite on the subject of slavery who was motivated always to benefit Virginia "regardless of every disadvantage to the other states." Ellsworth went on to name five specific antifederalists in New York who opposed the idea of a federal impost because their salaries were "paid by the state impost."[57]

These were truly venomous attacks whose flavor is epitomized by Ellsworth's charge that

> In Virginia the opposition wholly originated in two principles; the madness of Mason, and the enmity of the Lee faction to General Washington. Had the General not attended the convention nor given his sentiments respecting the constitution, the Lee party would undoubtedly have supported it, and Col. Mason would have vented his rage to his own negroes and to the wind.

Ellsworth, however, insisted that the great mass of people who had doubts about the Constitution were "as honest and brave as any part of the community.[58]

Sophisticated politicians of the time viewed Ellsworth's essays as effective polemics. In New York, Rufus King believed that "'the Landholder' will do more service our way than the elaborate works of Publius." Over the centuries, however, the wisdom of Publius, or the Federalist Papers, has withstood the passage of time, and Ellsworth's efforts have faded into obscurity. One reason that Ellsworth's efforts have not been so memorable is his emphasis upon *ad hominem* attacks. Although these attacks fit neatly into Ellsworth's Calvinist understanding of moral accountability, they come across as mean-spirited and were in some details unjustified. In addition the relevance of such charges are inexorably limited to the specific politics of the late eighteenth century and have no relevance to either politics or the Constitution some two hundred years later.[59]

A more important reason for the failure of Ellsworth's polemics to withstand the passage of time stems from his particular understanding of the political process. He had a monolithic view of human society. Everything was structured according to God's perfect predestined plan, and the end of God's plan was harmony and order. In order to foster this harmonious order, God selected righteous rulers who would do the right thing with a love of God in their hearts. This monolithic view of society was adequate to explain the workings of a small, homogeneous state like Connecticut, but it was quite inadequate to explain the workings of a large, pluralistic country like the United States.

The United States has always been a pluralistic society in which serious political discord has been inevitable. Ellsworth's understanding of the political process explained serious discord as sinful conduct that was predestined by God for some heuristic purpose. His solution to serious discord was to have a government of righteous rulers who would have a monolithic—and of course proper—view of proper policy. In a pluralistic society, this harmonious model might work in the short run, as it did throughout the 1790's when a Federalist coalition more or less controlled the federal government, but in the long run it was doomed to failure. In contrast, the *Federalist Papers* embraced conflict and advanced a system of separated powers in which competing interests would balance against each other.

When the Connecticut Ratifying Convention finally was convened, Ellsworth was the Constitution's leading advocate. An eyewitness to the proceedings related that, "Mr. Ellsworth was a complete master of the subject [, and] he was armed on all points." Pierpont Edwards, who delivered a speech immediately before one of Ellsworth's speeches, was embarrassed to report that after Ellsworth finished talking, he, Edwards, felt "like a lighting bug in broad daylight."[60]

On the opening day of the debates, Ellsworth was chosen to deliver the first speech, which he obviously had prepared in advance. His basic theme was the necessity of creating a strong national government that could deal effectively with military and economic threats from abroad. He opened his speech by bluntly declaring, "A union is necessary for the purposes of national defense. United we are strong; divided, we are weak." He went on to embroider his argument with numerous allusions to the lessons of classical civilization and contemporary Europe, but he never strayed far from his theme that the existing national government under the Articles of Confederation was simply too weak and relied too much on the individual states. Ellsworth urged:

> A more energetic system is necessary. The present is merely advisory. It has no coercive power. Without this, government is ineffectual or, rather, is no government at all.

Ever the practical politician, Ellsworth particularly emphasized the need to place the new government on a sound fiscal footing.[61]

Throughout the Connecticut Convention's deliberations, Ellsworth "took a very active part in defending the Constitution; scarcely a single objection was made but what he answered." When James Wadsworth, the leader of the opposition, complained that giving the federal government both "the power of the sword and purse is despotic," Ellsworth immediately rebutted the charge with a carefully organized and elaborately detailed argument. Ellsworth's basic defence was to return to the need for an adequate national defense, and in the process he revealed a quite modern understanding of warfare. Drawing upon the lessons that he had learned during the Revolutionary War, he explained:

> Wars have now become rather wars of the purse, than of the sword. Government must therefore be able to command the whole power of the purse.

Ellsworth's basic debating style was to rely upon what he judged to be indisputable facts and to insist that his positions flowed ineluctably from these indisputable facts. "[H]is energetic reasoning bore down all before it," and the Convention voted to ratify the Constitution by an overwhelming vote of 128 to 40.[62]

# A BILL

## TO ESTABLISH THE

## JUDICIAL COURTS of the UNITED STATES.

BE IT ENACTED by the senate and representatives of the United States of America in Congress assembled, That the supreme court of the United states shall consist of a chief justice and five associate justices, any four of whom shall be a quorum, and shall hold annually at the seat of the federal government two sessions, the one commencing the first Monday of February, and the other the first Monday of August. That the associate justices shall have precedence according to the date of their commissions, or when the commissions of two or more of them bear date on the same day, according to their respective ages.

AND BE IT FURTHER ENACTED by the authority aforesaid, That the United States shall be, and they hereby are divided into eleven districts to be limited and called as follows, to wit, one to consist of the state of New-Hampshire, and that part of the state of Massachusetts, which lies easterly of the state of New-Hampshire, and to be called New-Hampshire district; one to consist of the remaining part of the state of Massachusetts, and to be called Massachusetts district; one to consist of the state of Connecticut, and to be called Connecticut district; one to consist of the state of New-York, and to be called New-York district; one to consist of the state of New-Jersey, and to be called New-Jersey district; one to consist of the state of Pennsylvania, and to be called Pennsylvania district; one to consist of the state of Delaware, and to be called Delaware district; one to consist of the state of Maryland, and to be called Maryland district; one to consist of the state of Virginia, and to be called Virginia district; one to consist of the state of South-Carolina, and to be called South-Carolina district; and one to consist of the state of Georgia, and to be called Georgia district.

AND BE IT FURTHER ENACTED by the authority aforesaid, That there be a court called a district court in each of the afore-mentioned districts to consist of one judge, who shall reside in the district for which he is appointed, and shall be called a district judge, and shall hold annually four sessions, the first of which to commence as follows, to wit, in the districts of New-York, and of New-Jersey on the first, in the district of Pennsylvania on the second, in the district of Connecticut on the third,

The printed Senate Judiciary Bill.
Ellsworth's Senate Judiciary Bill epitomized his consummate ability to craft effective political compromises.

CHAPTER FIVE

# The Judiciary Act of 1789

$T$HE FIRST CONGRESS UNDER THE CONSTITUTION was to convene in 1789, and in early March the senators and representatives, one of whom was Oliver Ellsworth, began to converge on New York (the first seat of the federal government). Ellsworth was quite committed to an effective implementation of the Constitution that he had helped create and ratify, and he arrived in New York on March 4. Unfortunately, however, there were not enough senators to form a quorum until April 6. Ellsworth, however, did not while away this month on frivolous pursuits. With characteristic seriousness, he wrote his wife, "I employ my time as I presume a number of others do, in looking into and preparing for the business we are soon to enter upon." When Congress finally was convened in April, he was fully prepared for the business at hand.[1]

Clearly Ellsworth's fellow senators were impressed with his abilities and his energy. As soon as formalities were completed regarding the electoral college's election of George Washington and John Adams to the Presidency and Vice Presidency, the Senate elected Ellsworth chairman of a Grand Committee consisting of a senator from each state to prepare a bill for organizing the judiciary of the United States. This committee drafted the legislation that was to become the Judiciary Act of 1789. That same day he also was elected to chair a committee to draft procedural rules for the conduct of business in the Senate. This pattern of extensive participation in and leadership of Senate committees continued for the next seven years. During this time, all Senate committees were *ad hoc* select committees. Ellsworth was elected to and served on more than three times as many committees as the average senator and was, in effect, the de facto Senate majority leader throughout his service in Congress.[2]

## ☙ DRAFTING THE JUDICIARY ACT

Ellsworth's single most remembered service was to draft the Judiciary Act of 1789. The Constitution had created only the barebones of a federal judiciary and left some immensely important and quite controversial questions unanswered. Ellsworth's job was to flesh out those barebones and to answer those questions. His selection to chair the drafting committee was fortunate and in no way coincidental. He was the perfect man for the task. Indeed, no one in the United States was as qualified to implement the

Constitution's judicial article. Ellsworth had been a successful and skilled litigator and a respected state judge. At the time, some in the nation's capital believed that he should be considered for appointment as the first Chief Justice of the United States, and seven years later he became the third Chief Justice. In addition to his extensive courtroom experience on both sides of the bench, he had served with distinction in the Connecticut General Assembly and the Continental Congress. As a Continental legislator, he had drafted the ordinance that created the national appellate court under the Articles of Confederation for the review of state court prize decisions. He had also been a leading participant in the framing and ratification of the Constitution. Finally, Ellsworth, as we have seen, was an immensely practical politician who thoroughly understood the art of political dealmaking.[3]

In addition to being the formal chairman of the Committee, his fellow senators viewed him as the "leading projector" of the judiciary measure.[4] It was Ellsworth's bill. He was, however, ably assisted by his Calvinist friends, William Paterson of New Jersey and Caleb Strong of Massachusetts. Ellsworth and Paterson had known each other since college days at Princeton and had developed a personal friendship at the Constitutional Convention. Ellsworth and Strong were also close friends. All three senators wanted to create a strong federal judicial system.

## ç OPPOSITION TO THE FEDERAL COURTS

Others, however, did not want a strong federal judicial system. This issue had first been joined at the Constitutional Convention before the compromise was reached on representation in the Congress. All the delegates to the Convention had agreed that there should be a national Supreme Court with appellate authority to review judicial cases affecting national interests. The conflict had concerned whether federal trial courts should be created for these cases. Many of the delegates insisted that the existing state courts should be used to try all cases with a limited right of appeal to the Supreme Court. Other delegates did not trust the state courts and wanted to create an extensive system of federal trial courts. This serious disagreement had been resolved with a masterful compromise. The Constitution authorized Congress to create federal trial courts but not to require their creation. This solution, which was proposed by James Madison and James Wilson, has come to be known as the Madisonian Compromise. Similarly Congress also was given significant power to limit the kinds of cases that the Supreme Court could hear on appeal.[5]

The opposition to an extensive system of federal courts was based in part upon general or theoretical concerns. During the ratification process, George Mason warned the public in a widely circulated statement that the proposed federal courts would "absorb and destroy the judiciaries of the several states." In addition to this almost visceral objection, the opponents of the federal courts were deeply disturbed by the absence of any Constitutional guaranty of the right to trial by jury. These two objections were particularly troubling in the case of small claims against relatively poor defendants. For example, Richard Henry Lee of Virginia, who served on Ellsworth's Senate drafting committee, was worried about "the vexatious and oppressive calling of citizens from their own country . . . to be tried in a far distant court, and as it may be without a jury, whereby in a multitude of cases, the circumstances of distance and expense may compel numbers to submit to the most unjust and ill-founded demand."[6]

These more or less general objections were directly implicated by one of the most serious domestic and foreign policy problems of the new republic. During the Revolutionary War, the rebelling states had adopted an array of legislative strategies that successfully prevented British creditors from recovering debts owed by American debtors. To remedy this problem, the negotiators of the Treaty of Paris that ended the war agreed in Article IV of the Treaty that "creditors on either side shall meet with no lawful impediment to the recovery of the full value in sterling money of all debts heretofore contracted." Notwithstanding Article IV, many American debtors—particularly in the South—continued refusing to pay their British debts, and some state legislatures and courts overtly cooperated with them. Years later, Chief Justice Marshall candidly recalled, "The fact was notorious that it was the general opinion of [Virginians] and of the juries that a British debt could not be recovered."[7]

Professor Wythe Holt[8] has pointed to one aspect of the debt problem not readily apparent to late-twentieth-century minds steeped in a commercially oriented and individualistic society. Many Americans of the Founding Era viewed themselves primarily in terms of their relationship to society rather than as individuals seeking to maximize individual goods. Particularly among nonmerchants, this communitarian outlook extended to contractual relations. In addition, the endemic refusal to pay was probably motivated in part by simple dishonesty.

These communitarian Americans viewed their contracts with British creditors as just one aspect of their overall relationship with Great Britain. Another aspect was a long and costly war caused, in the opinion of many Americans, by British overreaching and oppression. Great Britain's blatant misconduct must have appeared to communitarian Americans as a hideous rent in the fabric of society. When the British contracts are seen as part of the overall relationship between American and Great Britain, the notion of honoring those contracts in the face of Britain's misdeeds becomes outrageous. Immediately after the war, people complained, "If we are now to pay the debts due to British Merchants, what have we been fighting for all this while?"[9] This combination of communitarian principle and personal greed was a potent political force, and it was enhanced by an economic depression in the 1780s. As a result, British creditors were unable to obtain a remedy in the courts of some states, particularly Virginia. As long as local debtors had significant control over the courts, there was no real possibility that the debts would be paid.

This status quo was threatened by the Constitution's provision for federal courts. In a close and hard-fought political struggle, the Virginia Ratification Convention eventually approved the proposed Constitution—but only after recommending amendments for a drastic curtailment of federal judicial power. These proposed amendments would have authorized only two kinds of federal courts. Congress could create inferior admiralty trial courts whose power would be limited to maritime cases. In all other cases except maritime proceedings in the inferior admiralty courts, trials would be conducted in state courts. The Supreme Court's appellate authority over state court litigation would have been restricted to cases arising under treaties, controversies in which the United States itself was a party, and litigation between parties claiming lands under grants from different states. Even within this narrow scope of federal appellate jurisdiction, the Supreme Court was to have no power to review the state trial court's determinations of facts except in cases of equity and admiralty jurisdiction, in which by tradition juries were not used and evidence was given by deposition. Finally—and clearly with an eye to claims of British creditors—the Virginians proposed that no federal court should have any power over cases in which the claim originated before the ratification of the Constitution. A Connecticut friend and political ally of Oliver Ellsworth subsequently wrote that the "obvious effect of these restrictions would have been to divest the general government of *all control* not only over *many* questions arising under the *Constitution and Laws of the United States*, but over *all questions* relative to *infractions of the fourth article of the treaty of peace.*"[10]

## ⦿ SEEDS OF A COMPROMISE

This firm opposition to federal courts presented an immense problem for Ellsworth, and the problem was exacerbated by the fact that the people of the United States were as yet comparatively unattached to the new federal government that he was helping to create. Because the issue of federal courts was controversial, a judiciary act that would garner only a bare majority vote in each house of the Congress would be a pyrrhic legislative victory. In terms of real-life politics, he had to fashion a system that would be acceptable to Americans in every significant region of the country. As a practical matter, a close and controversial vote on his bill would detract from the political legitimacy of the new government. In particular, a Judiciary Act favored by a large majority of northern members of Congress but only a minority of southern members would have been a catastrophe. He needed large margins of victories in both houses of Congress in order to assure the public that the new federal judiciary was organized on sound and uncontroversial principles. Obviously a compromise solution was called for, and obviously Ellsworth was the ideal man for the task.

Ellsworth clearly believed that an extensive system of federal courts was essential to the Union. In characteristically Calvinist terms he had written a year earlier that a "perfect uniformity must be observed thro' the whole union or jealousy and unrighteousness will take place; and for a uniformity one judiciary must pervade the whole."[11] Nevertheless, he did not see the creation of federal courts as an ultimate objective. In retrospect he clearly saw his proposed judicial system as a means to achieve several discrete and important national security objectives. This concern for national security cannot explain all of his bill's contours, because the measure was a human endeavor involving a mishmash of conflicting, supporting, and interlocking purposes. Therefore a purely monolithic explanation of his legislative agenda is implausible.

Nevertheless, national security clearly was a major—probably the primary—motivation of Ellsworth and his fellow Federalists who created a new nationwide system of federal courts. Ellsworth's bill vested this extensive system of courts with plenary power over prize cases, suits to enforce federal revenue laws, and prosecutions for violations of federal criminal law. In exchange, the federal courts' jurisdiction over other cases was severely restricted.

During the initial month of his Committee's work, Ellsworth presumably tried to broker a compromise within the Committee. If he did, he failed because three of the ten committee members eventually voted against the judiciary bill's passage. This failure to reach a consensus within the Committee complicated his task. Instead of directly negotiating an accord with fellow Committee members, he had to make a unilateral offer of a compromise that he judged would be acceptable to the Congress at large.

Fortunately there was a limited but significant consensus within the Congress on the need for a federal judicial system. Everyone—even the Virginians—agreed that there had to be a Supreme Court with some appellate jurisdiction. Likewise, all agreed that federal admiralty courts should be established on each state's seaboard to deal with maritime disputes. This consensus begged the fundamental questions of whether there should be a Supreme Court and a system of federal trial courts spread throughout the nation. Therefore Ellsworth's basic task was to draft acceptable statutory language that would define and limit the power of the federal trial courts and of the Supreme Court over specific types of cases.

## ☙ LIMITING THE SUPREME COURT'S POWER

The most significant aspect of the Supreme Court's jurisdiction was its appellate authority to review the decisions of state courts and inferior federal courts. The Constitution itself vested the Court with broad authority over cases involving federal law, admiralty cases, and cases of diversity and alienage jurisdiction. Within these categories there was no constitutional limitation to the Court's authority to overturn the judgments of the state and federal courts. The Constitution also expressly provided for Supreme Court appellate review "both as to law and fact."

The potential reach of the Supreme Court's appellate authority may be illustrated by an opinion written by Ellsworth when he was a state judge in Connecticut. In *Huntington v. Chaplin*,[12] Ellsworth held that under the common law, a person interested in the payment of a debt may not testify as to the plaintiff's acceptance of the payment. But Roger Sherman, Ellsworth's good friend and political mentor, dissented. Judge Sherman thought this general common-law rule was subject to equitable exceptions. If the same issue were to arise in a British creditor case, Ellsworth's strict view of the issue would prevent an American debtor from presenting evidence of his partial payment of the debt. A state court might therefore adopt Sherman's more lenient view and—depending upon the equities of the case—allow the debtor to testify.

If a state court adopted Sherman's more lenient view in a British creditor case, the

Constitution's broad grant of appellate authority authorized the Supreme Court to overrule the state court on this simple common-law issue of the admissibility of evidence. The Court's appellate authority under the Constitution extends to controversies between an alien and an American citizen and draws no distinction between obviously federal issues like the meaning of a treaty and simple common-law issues like the admissibility of evidence. Under the Constitution, the Court is literally vested with appellate jurisdiction over entire cases and controversies, not merely over discrete legal issues that may arise within cases and controversies.

This notion that the Supreme Court of the United States may correct a state court's common-law decision rings strange to modern ears, but an eighteenth-century attorney would have been hard-pressed to deny the Court's constitutional jurisdiction over such issues. Today virtually all American attorneys are more or less legal positivists, but eighteenth-century Americans were natural lawyers. A closer look at the eighteenth century's predominant natural-law philosophy will help to clarify this fundamental shared understanding among Americans in the Founding Era.

The most influential written example of natural-law thinking in the Founding Era was Blackstone's *Commentaries*, published in 1765. Blackstone emphatically denied that judges made law, and in the case of statutes this model of the judicial process was easily applied. Statutes were preexisting laws that judges simply read and applied in particular cases. Blackstone's model was more complicated in common-law cases because the common law was unwritten. Blackstone and virtually all eighteenth-century English-speaking lawyers believed that the common law preexisted judges and was independent from them. The metaphysical problem was, who made the common law— where did it come from? In the case of statutes, this question was easily answered by reference to Parliament. But in the case of the common law, the answer was not so simple.

Blackstone, Ellsworth, and late-eighteenth-century common lawyers believed the common law existed independently from the state. Neither kings nor legislators nor even judges were necessary to create the common law. Instead, it was part of the law of nature. But by "nature" they did not mean a godless system organized by Darwinian striving. Nietzche's announcement of God's death was more than a century into the future. In eighteenth-century America, virtually everyone still believed that nature was God's creation and was ordered by him. This vision was especially strong in the case of Calvinists like Ellsworth who believed that God had absolutely and minutely predestined human existence.

Consistent with this vision of God's nature, Blackstone wrote that God had ordained a system of "external immutable laws of good and evil." Human laws—especially the common law—"derive all their force, and all their authority" from this universal natural law and are invalid if they are contrary to it. Turning specifically to England, Blackstone defined the common law as a body of unwritten customs that receive "their binding power, and the force of laws, by long and immemorial usage, and by their universal reception throughout the kingdom."[13]

Under this theory, judges do not make laws. They are not legislators. They are, to use Blackstone's phrase, "the living oracles" of a common law that preexists in nature. Reasoning in humans was a process bestowed by God that enabled them to detect the subtleties of God's preexisting natural law; judges, through their education, talent, experience, and wisdom, were supposed to use their reasoning to discern the law in the cases that came before them. A judge's task was thus to discover rather than to create common law, and Blackstone wrote that "the principal and most authoritative evidence" of the common law is the corpus of judicial decisions. Blackstone was quite conservative and firmly believed in the doctrine of stare decisis, the idea that prior judicial decisions should be followed. But he admitted an "exception, where the former determination is most evidently contrary to reason." A prior decision that is clearly contrary to reason should not be followed. In these exceptional situations, "the subsequent judges do not pretend to make a new law, but to vindicate the old one from misrepresentation." He did not think that a clearly unreasonable decision was "*bad law*" but rather insisted that it was "*not law*" at all. When Ellsworth later sat on the Connecticut Supreme Court of Errors, the court, in a per curiam opinion, adopted this precise analysis.[14]

Natural-law thinking had enormous consequences for the Supreme Court's appellate jurisdiction over state court judgments. Obviously the Court could correct an erroneous application of a federal statute, a treaty of the United States, or the federal constitution. But the Court's appellate authority over cases presumably also gave it authority to correct erroneous applications of the common law on the basis that a state court had departed from proper common-law principles.

In practice, the Supreme Court's appellate power over the state courts' administration of the common law obviously would have arisen in any state court litigation involving citizens of different states or aliens. But the power was also inherent in the Court's appellate jurisdiction over cases arising under federal law. In 1789 no one could predict the scope of this ambiguous "arising under" jurisdiction. The specific wording of the Constitution extended the Court's jurisdiction to "cases" rather than to discrete issues of federal law that might arise in particular cases. Therefore the constitutional language "cases . . . arising under" federal law might reasonably be interpreted to include any case that might be decided by a rule of federal law. Thus the language could clearly extend to nonfederal issues in a case. In the event, the Supreme Court under Chief Justice Marshall settled on this reasonable but expansive interpretation in 1824.[15]

Fortunately, the Constitution provided a mechanism for limiting the Supreme Court's potentially immense appellate power. The Court's appellate jurisdiction was subject to "such exceptions, and under such regulations as the Congress shall make." Ellsworth had been a member of the Committee of Detail that added this clause to the Constitution, and he fully understood the clause's potential reach. He made extensive use of this grant of legislative authority. Ellsworth proposed limiting the Supreme Court's appellate jurisdiction to specific situations in which there was an obvious and direct interest in assuring a federal court review of a particular issue. Under his bill, the Court's appellate authority over state courts extended to specific issues governed by positive, written federal laws—specifically to "the constitution, treaties or laws of the United States . . . or [a federal] commission." To clarify this limitation, he expressly provided that "no other error shall be . . . regarded as a ground of reversal in any such case as aforesaid, than such as . . . immediately respects the before mentioned questions of validity or construction of the said constitution, treaties, statutes, commissions, or authorities." These words cannot reasonably be expended to permit the review of common-law determinations of state courts.[16]

Ellsworth also limited the Court's appellate authority over the lower federal courts. Insofar as legal issues were concerned, the Court's power over litigation originating in federal courts was both broader and narrower than its authority over state courts. His bill gave the Court no appellate authority over federal criminal trials. But in civil cases coming from the lower federal courts, it was given a general authority to review all legal issues regardless of whether they were controlled by written federal law, written state law, or the unwritten common law.[17]

In addition to crafting precise limitations to the Supreme Court's power to review issues of law, Ellsworth had to deal with the Court's power over issues of fact. This technical legal distinction between issues of fact and issues of law may be illustrated by the issue that sparked the disagreement between Ellsworth and Sherman in *Huntington v. Chaplin*. Whether the debtor in that case should have been allowed to testify as to his partial payment was an issue of law, and the court did not allow the testimony. But if the debtor had prevailed on this legal issue, he would not necessarily have won. A debtor's bald assertion of a partial payment does not mean that the payment actually was made. There would still have been an issue of whether there was an actual transfer of money from the specific defendant to the specific plaintiff. The resolution of this kind of factual issue requires a trial in which a jury hears conflicting evidence and decides what in fact happened.

The Supreme Court's potential authority under the Constitution to review and overturn a jury's determination of factual issues was controversial and had obvious implications for the general right to trial by jury and specifically in the trial of British creditor cases. Ellsworth resolved the potentially explosive issue of the Court's appellate review of facts by limiting its appellate power to review by "petition in error" (later changed to "writ of error"). This subtle limitation effectively preserved litigants' traditional right to have factual issues determined finally by a jury. In Connecticut and all other common-law jurisdictions, "in the case of issues in fact tried by Courts or juries, let the judgment be ever so erroneous [a writ of] error will not lie." A writ of error could be used only to obtain the review of a legal issue.[18]

In crafting the Supreme Court's appellate jurisdiction, Ellsworth astutely used the Constitution's exceptions and regulations clause to defuse all possible objections. On legal issues he expressly and drastically limited the Court's power over state courts to a narrow range of clearly defined federal issues. On factual issues he completely eliminated the Court's power of review. This concession on the review of facts turned a major fairness issue into a nonissue, but it also made the creation of federal trial courts crucial. Cases are frequently won or lost on the basis of the fact finder's resolution of the pertinent factual issues, and Ellsworth's concession gave trial courts a virtual plenary power over the resolution of facts. If federal trial courts were not created for the trial of cases impressed with a federal interest, the cases would have to be tried in state courts.

### ❦ THE FEDERAL TRIAL COURTS' ADMIRALTY POWERS

When Ellsworth turned to federal trial courts, he was greatly assisted by another fortunate consensus. Virtually every member of the first Congress agreed on the necessity of creating federal trial courts with an admiralty jurisdiction over maritime disputes.[19] This specialized head of jurisdiction is worth exploring because admiralty courts epitomized Ellsworth's legislative agenda for the lower federal courts' general trial jurisdiction. In addition, the reason for creating federal admiralty courts has been significantly obscured by the passage of two hundred years and a radical change in the nature of admiralty cases tried by federal courts.

Today the federal courts' jurisdiction over maritime cases is dedicated almost entirely to private disputes between private litigants. But there is no evidence that the Founding Generation thought of admiralty litigation primarily in terms of private disputes. Eighteenth-century Americans understood that admiralty courts adjudicated some types of private claims, but this understanding was irrelevant to their decision to move maritime litigation from the existing state admiralty courts to federal admiralty courts. Surviving records indicate clearly that the admiralty clause was placed in the Constitution and the federal admiralty courts were subsequently created to assure complete federal jurisdiction over three specific categories of litigation: prize cases, criminal prosecutions, and cases arising under federal revenue laws. The Founding Generation's paradigm of federal admiralty jurisdiction was not private dispute resolution but maritime cases that implicated a direct sovereign interest of the United States—cases involving the regulation of maritime warfare, the collection of revenues, and the prosecution of criminals. The Founding Generation's basic concept of federal admiralty jurisdiction is best described as public, not private, litigation.

Crimes on the high seas were the least significant of the three types of cases that epitomized admiralty litigation. One reason for vesting the federal courts with special criminal jurisdiction related to the technical transfer of sovereignty from the states to the federal government. Because crimes on the high seas are committed outside of individual states' borders, there was some concern that the states lacked authority over them. In contrast, the federal government, with its general sovereign power over international transactions, clearly had authority. Moreover, crimes on the high seas—especially piracy—had traditionally been viewed as a proper subject of admiralty jurisdiction, so there was an unexamined assumption that the federal admiralty courts would try them.

In contrast to jurisdiction over crimes on the high seas, admiralty jurisdiction over revenue cases was vital. An adequate and reliable stream of revenue was essential to the federal government's operations, and virtually all of the government's revenue was expected to come from import duties upon goods brought in by sea. In fact, during the first eleven years of the federal government's operation, 87 percent of its revenue came from customs duties. In North America, the pre-Revolutionary imperial vice-admiralty courts and the subsequently created state admiralty courts, with their traditional authority to seize ships and cargoes, had always been used to enforce import and navigation laws. Most people therefore assumed that federal admiralty courts with jurisdiction over revenue cases would be a fiscal necessity for the new government. While the Judiciary Act was being drafted, a knowledgeable observer deeply interested in revenue matters insisted that "it is indispensably necessary that Courts of Admiralty be immediately instituted [because] without them no system of Revenue can be put in Execution."[20]

A federal jurisdiction over prize cases was also of vital concern to the federal government. The United States was a maritime nation separated from Europe by the Atlantic Ocean, which isolated the nation from European land powers. At the same time, the ocean provided a great highway for commerce. Because the United States was a maritime nation, naval warfare was central to national security, and prize courts played a critical role in supporting the nation's ability to wage naval war. A major objective of naval warfare has always been to capture or disrupt the enemy's commercial shipping, and in the eighteenth century captured vessels—known as prizes—were sold for the benefit of the capturing vessel. The prize money served as a reward to the crews of regular navy vessels. Even more significantly, the prize system was used as a quick and inexpensive method of increasing effective naval strength. During times of war, private merchants would be commissioned as privateers and authorized to prey on enemy shipping. In return, the privateers were allowed to keep their lawful captures.

During the Revolutionary War, the vast majority of American armed vessels were privateers, and they captured some two thousand British vessels and cargoes worth an estimated eighteen million pounds sterling.[21] The resulting injury to British commercial interests is obvious. Moreover, this privateering activity required the British to commit a significant number of naval units to the protection of their merchant marine. The ability to launch a host of maritime raiders without direct financial cost and at the mere stroke of a pen was an invaluable asset to a maritime nation that could not afford the enormous expense of a significant naval establishment.

After taking a prize, the privateers would sail the captured vessel and cargo to a friendly port, where the capture would be reviewed by a prize court. If the court determined that the captured vessel was a lawful prize, the court would condemn the vessel and give the privateer lawful title. This use of prize courts to regulate captures was one of the primary characteristics that distinguished privateering from piracy, and judicial condemnation obviously facilitated the sale of prizes. In addition, efficient and effective prize courts were a necessary inducement for encouraging privateering ventures. During the Revolutionary War, James Wilson and a group of Philadelphia merchants urged the creation of efficient prize courts because, they said, "In the privateering trade in particular, the very life of which consists in the adventurers receiving the rewards of their success and bravery as soon as the cruise is over, the least delay is uncommonly destructive."[22]

Besides encouraging the privateering trade, prize courts played an essential role in regulating privateers' activities. Given that these raiders were officially commissioned by the national government to wage maritime war on the nation's enemies, the government had a compelling interest in assuring that privateers did not venture beyond the scope of their commissions into piracy. This regulation was accomplished through the determination of the key issue in all prize cases—prize or no prize? In making this determination, the prize court inevitably considered the nature of the privateers' conduct toward foreign vessels and the status of the United States' foreign relations with other countries involved in particular captures. When Alexander Hamilton urged ratification of the Constitution, he explained that admiralty cases, especially prize cases, "so generally depend on the laws of nations, and so commonly affect the rights of foreigners, that they fall within the considerations which are relative to the public peace."[23] These obvious national security concerns, coupled with the need to provide for effective enforcement of revenue laws and the need to punish crimes on the high seas, made the existence of federal admiralty courts inevitable.

## ☙ SHAPING THE COMPROMISE ON FEDERAL TRIAL COURTS

The consensus on admiralty jurisdiction had enormous implications for the creation of a nationwide system of federal trial courts. The potentially daily administration of prize laws during times of war and of revenue laws during both war and peace required an admiralty court in each major seaport. The option of restricting federal judicial power to a simple and relatively inexpensive Supreme Court in the nation's capital was therefore not a realistic possibility. There was definitely going to be a system of lower federal courts, and the only issue was what sort of cases—in addition to admiralty matters—would be committed to the lower courts' jurisdiction.

To a significant degree, the lower courts' nonadmiralty jurisdiction presented the same problems that had confronted Ellsworth in working out the Supreme Court's appellate jurisdiction. When Ellsworth turned to this nonadmiralty lower court jurisdiction, he drew heavily on the same insights that had informed his approach to the Supreme Court's appellate jurisdiction and the district courts' admiralty jurisdiction. He made no serious effort to track the jurisdictional language of the Constitution but instead limited the lower courts' jurisdiction to discrete and unambiguous categories of cases that were obviously essential. In addition, he added a few more unambiguous categories that—like admiralty cases—were both noncontroversial and impressed with an obvious national interest. The Constitution's provision for a general jurisdiction over cases arising under federal law was by far the most troubling issue. The problem was that this particular head of jurisdiction had no clear limits. The "arising under" language could be reasonably construed as encompassing any case whose resolution might require the application of federal law, and this broad construction was eventually placed on the Constitution's "arising under" clause.[24] Under such an expansive interpretation, a case predominantly governed by nonfederal law would nevertheless be deemed to arise under federal law as long as even a single substantive aspect of the dispute might be governed by federal law.

Given this potentially broad sweep, the Constitution's "arising under" clause played directly into the generalized visceral fear that the federal courts were ideally suited to "absorb and destroy the judiciaries of the several states." Moreover, the Constitution's ambiguous language also directly implicated the specific fear that the federal courts would be used to effectuate Article IV of the Treaty of Paris. British creditors' suits always involved the enforcement of a debtor's promise to pay money. These promises, like most legally enforceable promises, were actionable as a matter of common law, not federal law. But some states provided American debtors with defenses based either upon arguably misapplications of the common law or upon specific state statutes. To the extent that these defenses violated the Treaty, they could be trumped by the Treaty. Thus even though virtually all of the legal issues in the case would not be governed by specific federal law, the case would nevertheless "arise under" a treaty of the United States. To make matters even worse, thousands of the British creditors claims against individual debtors were for relatively small amounts. Therefore the "arising under" clause also directly implicated the fear that defendants would be unfairly and at great expense hailed to distant federal courts to defend against small claims.

Although some of Ellsworth's contemporaries, including Attorney General Edmund Randolph, believed that Congress should vest the federal trial courts with a general jurisdiction over all cases arising under federal law,[25] the Constitution did not require a plenary vesting of jurisdiction. The entire purpose of the Madisonian Compromise was to authorize a more flexible approach, and Ellsworth ably wielded this authority. Perhaps there were sufficient votes in Congress to pass a general grant of federal question jurisdiction, but Ellsworth chose not to gamble. He made no reference whatsoever to a general jurisdiction over cases arising under federal law, and he thereby preempted the argument that the federal courts would absorb and destroy the state judiciaries.

Ellsworth's basic approach to delimiting the lower courts' trial jurisdiction is evident in an obscure but specific provision for alien tort claims. Ellsworth proposed and the Congress enacted his proposal that the lower courts would have jurisdiction over "all causes where an alien sues for a tort only in violation of the law of nations or a treaty of the United States." This provision has little intrinsic importance, but it is worth considering as a clear illustration of Ellsworth's conscious decision to draft around the political problems implicated by the British debt cases. In drafting this obscure clause, Ellsworth undoubtedly had in mind prior incidents in which torts had been committed against diplomats and their servants in violation of the law of nations.[26]

Of course, the primary sanction for this kind of misconduct was a criminal prosecution, and Ellsworth's bill gave the federal courts criminal jurisdiction over attacks on diplomats.[27] But these attacks also might cause property damage or personal injury. Ellsworth's alien tort claim provision empowered the federal courts to try civil actions seeking private compensation from defendants who committed torts in violation of international law.

The alien tort claim provision is interesting because it is, to a significant degree, open-ended. If violations of diplomatic immunity were the sole concern, the statute could easily have been drafted to apply only to foreign embassies. But Ellsworth chose to open the federal courts to any alien who may have suffered from any tortious violation of international law. Quite possibly he also had in mind the continuing problem of American citizens' mounting private military expeditions against the Spanish territories in Florida. In addition, he may have contemplated torts by American citizens against aliens who, under United States treaties, were entitled to the free exercise of religion or to safe passage through the country.[28]

The idea that the federal courts should be open to any alien who had suffered tortious injuries in violation of international law was similar to the national consensus on the need for federal admiralty courts. The clear national interest was so obvious that Ellsworth felt free to use broad, open-ended language to vest the courts with complete power over these cases. At the same time, however, he chose to exclude the most flagrant, significant, and ongoing breaches of international law. The British creditors, who clearly were aliens, could not use the alien tort claims act because their claims were contract actions and not tort actions.

This strategy of carefully carving out discrete and clearly defined categories of federal question jurisdiction is repeated in more important portions of Ellsworth's bill. Although duties on goods imported by sea were to be the federal government's primary source of revenues, Ellsworth anticipated that taxes unrelated to maritime commerce would also be levied, and he therefore provided an open-ended jurisdiction over nonadmiralty revenue collection cases. In the eighteenth century, revenue laws were typically enforced through the seizure of property and the imposition of penalties and forfeitures. Accordingly, Ellsworth's bill also vested the federal district courts with "exclusive original cognizance of all seizures on land, or ... waters [not otherwise subject to Admiralty jurisdiction] and of all suits for penalties and forfeitures incurred under the laws of the United States."[29]

Another clear example of a case arising under federal law was a criminal prosecution, and within this discrete category of cases Ellsworth again resorted to open-ended language. In addition to their plenary jurisdiction over admiralty cases, aliens' tort claims, and revenue cases, the federal trial courts were given "cognizance of all crimes and offenses that shall be cognizable under the Authority of the United States."

Although Ellsworth was clear that the federal trial courts should have a complete jurisdiction over any and all crimes, his bill called for the creation of two separate types of lower federal trial courts. The district courts, whose primary job was to adjudicate admiralty cases, also were authorized to try minor crimes involving moderate punishment. In the case of whipping, fines, and imprisonment, punishment could not exceed thirty stripes, one hundred dollars, and six months. In practice, these ceilings proved so low that the district courts almost never tried criminal cases.[30] For punishments in excess of these limits, a case had to be prosecuted in a federal circuit court.

Federal circuit courts were a major innovation. Each district court was staffed by a federal district judge who was required to reside in the district for which he was appointed. Ellsworth's Bill called for the creation of thirteen districts that followed state borders, except that separate courts were created for the districts of Maine and Kentucky that were then parts of the states of Massachusetts and Virginia. In contrast to the one-judge district courts, the circuit courts were originally envisioned as three-judge courts consisting of the resident district judge and two circuit-riding Supreme Court Justices.

The basic purpose of the circuit courts was to provide Supreme Court participation in important categories of litigation without requiring expensive and inconvenient appeals from the local federal trial courts to the national capital. Instead, circuit-riding Justices would in effect make Supreme Court decision making more accessible to litigants throughout the country. As Senator Paterson explained, the circuit courts would "carry Law to [the People's] Homes, Courts to their Doors."[31] The Supreme Court Justices' participation in criminal trials in the circuit courts was especially important because a criminal conviction was traditionally not subject to appellate review. Following this tradition, Ellsworth's bill did not authorize appeals in criminal cases and vested the circuit courts with sole jurisdiction over major federal crimes.

The circuit courts were also given an important trial jurisdiction over civil cases in which an alien is a party or in which a citizen of one state sues a citizen of another. In defense of these provisions, Ellsworth forcefully explained that the Constitutional convention

> had in view the condition of foreigners when they framed the judicial of the U. States. The Citizens were already protected by [state] Judges & Courts, but foreigners were not. The Laws of nations & Treaties were too much disregarded in the several States. Juries were too apt to be biased against them, in favor of their own citizens & acquaintances: it was therefore necessary to have general Courts for causes in which foreigners were parties or citizens of different States.[32]

The basic problem with this alienage jurisdiction was that the British creditors' claims were the prototypical civil action in which an alien was a party, so alienage jurisdiction flew straight in the teeth of the strongest objections to federal trial courts.

Ellsworth had stated and restated in the Continental Congress and the Connecticut ratification convention that Americans' failure to repay the British created serious foreign policy problems.[33] But he also understood that his proposed alienage jurisdiction would engender powerful opposition. He therefore agreed to compromise the nation's need to provide for effective enforcement of Article IV of the peace treaty. He limited the circuit court's alienage and diversity of citizenship jurisdiction to cases in which the amount in controversy exceeded five hundred dollars.

In the late twentieth century, five hundred dollars does not seem a very significant limitation, but it was a substantial sum two hundred years ago. During the secret

Senate debates on the Judiciary Bill, one Senator noted that "[t]he Farmers in the New England States [are] not worth more than 1,000 Dr. on an Average." The five-hundred-dollar amount in controversy limitation effectively denied these farmers—and, more importantly, their out-of-state creditors—the protection authorized by the Constitution's diversity provision. It also effectively barred a vast number of common-law tort actions from the federal trial courts. During the closed Senate debates, the point was made that the circuit courts' jurisdiction would extend to "Money, Merchandize, Land bought and sold." Tort actions are notably absent from this list, and Ellsworth fully understood that the limitation would be a significant barrier to tort claims. He had served on the highest judicial court in Connecticut for four years and knew that tort judgments in excess of five hundred dollars were virtually nonexistent.[34]

The five-hundred-dollar limitation would have its most significant impact upon the British debt cases. Although the total debt owed to British creditors was high, the great majority (for some British firms, over 90 percent) of the individual debts was for sums of less than five hundred dollars. Moreover, the technical legal rules that regulated the joinder of claims (common-law pleading) did not permit a plaintiff to try multiple claims in one lawsuit. Therefore, as a practical matter, the amount in controversy limitation barred the great majority of British claims from the new federal courts.[35]

Because of its impact upon the British debt cases, the five-hundred-dollar limitation was the most significant compromise in Ellsworth's bill. In theory, Supreme Court appellate review was available to correct errors in the tremendous number of British claims relegated to the mercy of the state judiciaries. In practice, however, an appeal all the way to the Supreme Court would have been prohibitively expensive in comparison to the size of the claim. Therefore the limitation must be viewed as a conscious decision to compromise one significant national security interest to achieve another—the need to gain acceptance of the new federal government.

This compromise could easily be described as a raw political deal designed to acquiesce in continued violations of the peace treaty, but such a view would be too simplistic. During the ratification process, Senator Lee and others had forcefully and persuasively pointed out the unfairness of forcing a local farmer to defend against a small and possibly invalid claim in a distant federal trial court, and Ellsworth agreed with this criticism. Some seven years later he acknowledged in a different context the immense "difficulty of bringing [witnesses] from the remotest parts of the union to the seat of government."[36] An amount in controversy limitation was thus almost inevitable on the simple basis of fairness. In any event, this compromise was clearly legitimated by *The Wisdom of God*.

## ☙ THE CONGRESS ACCEPTS ELLSWORTH'S COMPROMISE

When the Senate took Ellsworth's bill under consideration, the proposed compromise on the Supreme Court's appellate jurisdiction was readily accepted with some minor tinkering but no known objection. The lower courts, however, proved more contro-versial. The issue that had sparked significant debate at the Constitutional Convention and whose resolution was postponed by the Madisonian Compromise was finally to be resolved. On the first day of the Senate's debates, Senator Lee moved to restrict the lower courts' jurisdiction to admiralty cases.

In the ensuing debates, Lee, his fellow Virginian William Grayson, and Pierce Butler of South Carolina bluntly explained their conviction that the creation of federal trial courts would cast a "Stigma upon State Courts [by implying] that [they would] not do what is right." More significantly, they charged that "the ultimate tendency of [the Bill was] manifestly . . . to destroy, to cut up at the Root the State Judiciaries, to annihilate their whole system of Jurisprudence and . . . finally swallow up every distin-guishing mark of a distinct [state] government." These strong words were not mere political posturing for the public. The Senate debates were closed and forbidden to be published. We know the debates only from the surviving private records of individual senators.[37]

These southern objections had been more or less persuasive two years earlier at the Constitutional Convention, but in Philadelphia the federal courts' potential jurisdic-tion was not clearly demarcated. Quite to the contrary, the proposals for subject-matter jurisdiction at the Convention were virtually open-ended. Ellsworth's bill, however, almost completely reversed this situation. He was fully aware of the concern that the federal courts might swallow up the state judiciaries. All of his jurisdictional proposals were impressed with a clear and direct federal interest and, with the possible exception of admiralty jurisdiction, were subject to precise and easily recognizable limits.

In the Senate debates, Ellsworth responded to the southern senators' arguments with characteristic bluntness. He warned that "there will be attacks on the General Government that will go to the Very Vitals of it [and that state] Judges may Swerve."[38] Unfortunately, no one recorded the details of Ellsworth's argument, but he clearly saw federal trial courts as vital to the defense of the federal government. From earlier speeches that Ellsworth delivered in his successful efforts to achieve the Constitution's ratification, it is reasonable to assume that he portrayed federal trial courts as essential to the effective enforcement of federal criminal and revenue laws.

During the ratification process, Ellsworth had stated that the proposed Constitu-tion was necessary to create an "energetic" government that could act directly to vin-dicate the national interest. In his words, "A more energetic system is necessary. The present [under the Articles of Confederation] is merely advisory. It has no coercive power. Without this, government is ineffective or, rather is no government at all." He emphasized that an energetic government especially needed the power of "raising and supporting armies [to] protect the people against the violence of wicked and over-grown citizens, and invasion by the rest of the mankind." Although Ellsworth empha-sized the need to raise and support armies, he was not a soldier. Reasoning from his wartime service in the Continental Congress, he equated military power with fiscal power. "Wars," he explained, "have now become rather wars of the purse, than of the sword." In fighting a war, a government without revenue "has [not] the means to enlist a man or buy an ox."[39]

An effective military establishment was necessary also to deal with domestic rebellion, but Ellsworth did not view armed force as the optimal solution to internal discord. Given that "a coercive principle [is] necessary for the Union," he reasoned, "the only question is, shall it be a coercion by arms?" The answer was obvious: "I am for coercion by law [that] singles out the guilty individual and punishes him for breaking the laws of the Union."[40] Obviously an extensive system of federal courts would contribute directly to effecting Ellsworth's coercion principle by punishing crimes and enforcing revenue laws.

In the closed Senate debates on the Judiciary Bill, William Paterson, who had also played a significant role in drafting the bill, forcefully explained the need for federal trial courts to enforce criminal laws and revenue laws. Picking up on Ellsworth's imagery of attacks on the vitals of the general government, Paterson saw criminal jurisdiction as a matter of "Self-Preservation." He asked, "If Offenses be committed against this Union, will you put it in the Power of State Judges to decide thereupon-to acquit or to condemn- I hope not-You put your Life in their Hands." The problem was that there was no appeal in criminal cases, especially when a jury had acquitted the defendant. To deprive the federal courts of jurisdiction to punish crimes was to present the states "with a Sword to destroy" the union. Similarly, Paterson urged the Senate not to "give up the Power of collecting your own Revenue . . . you will collect Nothing." The problem was that "State Officers will feel it their Interest to consult the Temper of the People of the State in which they live rather than that of the Union." Ellsworth agreed with his friend's analysis. During the ratification process, he had warned that if no federal trial courts were created, "It will at any time be in the power of the smallest state by interdicting their own judiciary, to defeat the measures, defraud the revenue, and annul the most sacred laws of the whole empire."[41]

Paterson's and Ellsworth's arguments undoubtedly were particularly persuasive because their fellow senators knew that these two forceful men were sensitive and attentive to state interests. Today the federal government—even Congress—is frequently viewed as divorced from the individual states. The primary concerns of a member of Congress are his or her individual constituents and national interests, with the interests of state governments playing a distinctly secondary role. This comparative lack of concern for state interests, however, did not exist in the first Congress.

Ellsworth and his fellow senators were not elected by the people; they were chosen by their state legislatures. In preparing the Judiciary Bill, Ellsworth specifically sought the advice of Connecticut's Governor, Lieutenant Governor, and Chief Judge. All three of these officers approved his plan and recommended the creation of a comprehensive system of lower federal courts. In a letter to his friend the chief judge of Connecticut's Superior Court, Ellsworth emphasized his concern for the interests of state courts.

> Without [a system of federal trial courts], there must be many appeals
> or writs of error from the Supreme Courts of the States, which by

> placing them in a subordinate situation, and subjecting their decisions
> to frequent reversals would probably more hurt their feelings and their
> influence, than to divide the ground with them at first, and [establish a
> system of federal trial courts].

These thoughts were not penned for public consumption. They were private and intended for a personal friend.[42]

Ellsworth's concern for a fair balancing of national and state interests was undoubtedly apparent to his fellow senators and must have added great credence to his forceful advocacy of federal trial courts. Most significantly, by defusing the explosive issue of British debt, Ellsworth succeeded in splitting the potential southern bloc and actually gained a slight majority of southern votes. His bill passed the Senate by a vote of 14 to 6.[43]

Ellsworth's strategy was equally successful in the House of Representatives. The bill was not entirely acceptable to the southern representatives, but neither was it an anathema. For example, there was an initial belief that James Madison would lead the fight against the judicial bill in the House of Representatives, and Madison did not especially like the measure. Nevertheless, he apparently decided not to take an active role in opposition to it and maintained a low profile in the House's consideration of the bill. The House debates more or less parallel the Senate's deliberations, and the bill passed the House by a comfortable majority of 37 to 16. The southern representatives—like their fellow southern senators—approved the measure by a slight majority.[44]

Perhaps Ellsworth should have gritted his teeth and pressed for a broader federal jurisdiction adequate to enforce the Treaty of Paris. If he had, he might have prevailed, albeit by a closer vote. He chose, however, not to gamble, and the Senate's treatment of a process bill that he drafted that same year suggests that his concessions to localist concerns in the Judiciary Act were wise. In the process bill, Ellsworth sought to establish technical procedural rules regulating the commencement of common-law actions in federal court and the enforcement of judgments. He saw no pressing political need to compromise on this technical issue. Instead he took a thoroughgoing nationalist view and proposed uniform rules for all the federal courts. The Congress, however, gave the back of its hand to this proposal. Instead of enacting uniform rules, Congress provided that the institution of common-law suits and the enforcement of judgments would be regulated by the local rules of the state in which the federal court was located. If Ellsworth had pressed harder in the Judiciary Act to enforce rights under the Treaty of Paris, the localist sentiment that gutted his process bill might have jeopardized the Act's passage.[45]

Even if Ellsworth had narrowly prevailed on the enforcement of treaty rights, the victory might have been pyrrhic. He undoubtedly understood that a close and controversial vote would have detracted from the political legitimacy of the new government. As it happened, the large margins of victory that his judiciary bill received in both chambers had the practical effect of assuring the public that the new federal judiciary was organized on sound and uncontroversial principles.

### CHAPTER SIX

# The Bill of Rights and
# Its Religion Clauses

While the senate was working on the Judiciary Act, the House of Representatives was working on a number of proposed amendments to the Constitution that came to be known as the Bill of Rights. During the ratification process, many of the Constitution's opponents complained that the Constitution did not include a declaration and preservation of substantive rights like the right to trial by jury, freedom of the press, or freedom of religion. In response to this criticism, the Constitution's advocates in many states tacitly agreed that if the Constitution were to be ratified, the first Congress would propose a declaration of substantive rights that would be added to the Constitution as amendments. In accordance with this informal understanding, when the first Congress was convened, the House of Representatives, under the able leadership of James Madison, turned to this task.[1]

Although Ellsworth was to play the leading role in the Senate's consideration of the Bill of Rights, he was not particularly enthusiastic about the task. During the ratification process, he had actively opposed requests that a declaration of substantive rights be added to the Constitution. In part his opposition stemmed from pragmatic political concerns. He believed that in talking of amendments, the Antifederalists' "design is to procrastinate, and by this carry their own measures." Other Connecticut Federalists also believed that the issue of Constitutional amendments was being raised in part simply to stall the proposed Constitution's ratification. Therefore Connecticut's ratification convention rejected all proposed amendments because the convention "deemed it too dangerous to hazardous delays under a tottering Constitution" based upon the Articles of Confederation.[2]

In addition to this passing political concern, Calvinist political psychology provided little if any support for adding a declaration of substantive rights to a constitution. Connecticut's Standing Order ministers constantly preached that Righteous Rulers were the *sine qua non* of good government. Therefore, even a "bad constitution, under the direction of wise and pious rulers . . . may become a blessing. . . . But the best constitution, committed to rulers of a contrary description, may be subverted; or so abused, as to become a curse." Consistent with this idea, Connecticut's Declaration of Rights and Privileges, which was the state's primary constitutional document, contained no substantive declaration of rights and simply guaranteed a rudimentary form of equal protection and due process of law. The source of substantive constitutional rights was explained in the Declaration's preamble. Because "the Legislature depends on the free and annual Election of the People, they [the People] have the best Security for the Preservation of their civil and religious Rights and Liberties."[3]

The overriding importance of having good, which is to say righteous, rulers, led Ellsworth's mentor, Roger Sherman, to dismiss the idea of a Bill of Rights as insignificant. "For," wrote Sherman, "guard such privileges by the strongest expressions, still if you leave the legislative and executive power in the hands of those who are or may be disposed to deprive you of them—you are but slaves." Oliver Wolcott, Sr., another Connecticut friend and political ally of Ellsworth, was of much the same mind. Ellsworth undoubtedly agreed with this analysis. "It is good government which secures the fruits of industry and virtue; but," he reminded Connecticut, "the best system of government cannot produce general happiness unless ["both public and private citizens"] are virtuous, industrious, and economical."[4]

In addition to the pragmatic argument based upon human nature and Connecticut tradition, Ellsworth offered a somewhat arid lawyer's argument against the need for a Bill of Rights. The idea of a Bill of Rights derived from the English *Magna Charta* in which the King granted his subjects certain rights. This approach made sense under the English political theory that all political power rested with the King, but in the United States the people were the font of all power. Therefore "to have inserted in this constitution a bill of rights for the states, would suppose them to derive and hold their rights from the federal government, when the reverse is the case."[5]

Ellsworth was dubious about the need or efficacy of a declaration of substantive rights, but he did not ignore the political reality of amending the Constitution. When the constitutional amendments proposed by the House of Representatives were presented to the Senate, he paid careful attention to them. The Senate debated the House proposals for a week, and numerous *ad hoc* amendments were considered. At the conclusion of these debates, there was some confusion regarding the net effect of the various motions that had been approved or rejected. Throughout the debate, Ellsworth had kept careful track of the ebb and flow of motions, and at the end he was able to resolve the confusion by proposing a single, omnibus amendment keyed to the original House proposals. His consolidated motion passed by the required 2/3 majority. In effect Ellsworth was the Senate floorleader for the Bill of Rights, and his fellow senators formally recognized his leadership when they selected him to chair the Committee of Conference that worked out the differences between the House and Senate versions of the Bill of Rights.[6]

As chairman from the Senate for the Committee of Conference, Ellsworth wrote the committee report that established the final wording of the Constitution's Establishment Clause.[7] Moreover, he had a sophisticated understanding of religious freedom that he elaborated in essays published before and after the Bill of Rights was drafted. His understanding of religious freedom is particularly interesting became his fellow senators clearly chose him as their leader in shaping the Bill of Rights.

## ☙ ACCOMMODATIONISTS AND SEPARATIONISTS

Americans never have and never will reach a consensus on all aspects of the proper relationship between government and religion. Virtually everyone agrees with the general propositions that government should not prevent people from freely exercising their religion and that government should not establish a religion. At the same time virtually everyone agrees that government should impede or prevent some forms of admittedly religious conduct and that some forms of government support for religion is permissible. The question is where to draw the lines. Many Americans are accommodationists who are more inclined to permit significant governmental intrusions into the religious sphere, but many other Americans are separationists who are inclined to a much stricter separation of church and state.

In the first Congress, James Madison is generally and accurately viewed as the champion of separationism.[8] In addition to being a separationist, he clearly was the progenitor of the Bill of Rights, and he was the chairman from the House of the Committee of Conference on the Bill of Rights. Therefore we may reasonably believe that his separationism influenced the drafting of the First Amendment's religion clauses. In terms of leadership in the creation of the Bill of Right's, Ellsworth was Madison's analog in the Senate, but unlike Madison, Ellsworth clearly was an accommodationist. Although much has been written on Madison's views on the proper relationship between church and state, Ellsworth's views present unexplored territory.

## ☙ RELIGION AND ORDER IN EIGHTEENTH-CENTURY CONNECTICUT

Ellsworth's views on church and state were deeply influenced by the fact that throughout the eighteenth century his home state of Connecticut was ruled by Calvinists for Calvinists. At the beginning of the century, the General Assembly formally recognized the colony's de facto religious establishment by enacting the Saybrook Platform, which included a Confession of Faith based upon the Westminster Confession. The Platform also established a kind of presbyterian system of church governance in which county consociations dominated by the ministers were given authority to resolve local church disputes and to license ministers. This superstructure of church governance was a deviation from the traditional congregationalism of the Cambridge Platform that left the resolution of disputes and licensing of ministers exclusively to individual congregations. The General Assembly also expressly and formally established Westminster Calvinism by providing that, "all the Churches within this government

The Committee of the two Houses appointed to confer on their different votes on the Amendments proposed by the Senate to the Resolution proposing Amendments to the Constitution, and disagreed to by the House of Representatives, have had a conference, and have agreed that it will be proper for the House of Representatives to agree to the said Amendments proposed by the Senate, with an Amendment to their fifth Amendment, so that the third Article shall read as follows "Congress shall make no law respecting an "establishment of Religion, or prohibiting the free ex- "-ercise thereof; or abridging the freedom of Speech, or "of the Press; or the right of the people peaceably to "assemble and to petition the Government for a redress "of grievances"; — And with an Amendment to the fourteenth Amendment proposed by the Senate, so that the eighth Article, as numbered in the Amendments proposed by the Senate, shall read as follows "In all criminal prosecutions, the accused shall enjoy the right to a speedy & publick trial by an impartial jury of the district wherein the crime shall have been committed, as the district shall have been pre-viously ascertained by law, and to be informed of

the

Committee of Conference Report on the Bill of Rights.

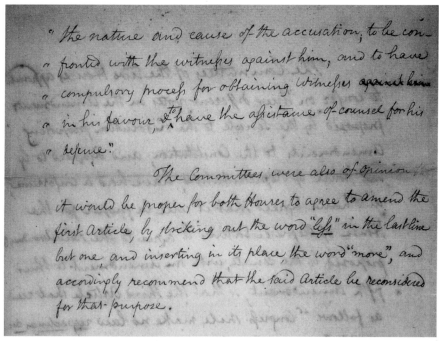

"the nature and cause of the accusation, to be confronted with the witnesses against him, and to have
compulsory process for obtaining witnesses against him
in his favour, & have the assistance of counsel for his
defence."

The Committees were also of opinion
it would be proper for both Houses to agree to amend the
first Article, by striking out the word "less" in the last line
but one and inserting in its place the word "more", and
accordingly recommend that the said Article be reconsidered
for that purpose.

Committee of Conference Report on the Bill of Rights.
Ellsworth was the floor leader of the Senate's deliberations on the Bill of Rights and as
chairman from the Senate for the Committee of Conference wrote the report resolving the
differences between the House and the Senate.
COURTESY NATIONAL ARCHIVES.

that are, and shall be thus united in doctrine, worship and discipline, be, and for the
future shall be, owned and acknowledged, established by law."[9]

As part of this formal establishment, every person in the state was required to
attend the established Calvinist churches and to pay a tax that was dedicated to the
payment of the Calvinist ministers' salaries and other religious purposes. As the century progressed, a series of exemption or toleration acts were passed to allow Baptists,
Anglicans, and Quakers to attend churches of their own persuasion and to have their
taxes paid over to ministers of their own persuasion. Connecticut's exemption acts,
however, applied only to individuals who could prove that they actually attended a
dissenting church of one of the three specified denominations. Therefore, the general
requirement of church attendance was maintained, and all Calvinists and many dissenters who lacked a dissenting church in their town continued to be taxed for the
support of the established church. The basic system of taxation, tilted in favor of the
Calvinists, continued throughout the century and into the next.[10]

The last quarter of the century witnessed significant expansions of toleration for
dissenters. In 1770 the legislature extended religious toleration to all persons "professing the Christian protestant religion, who soberly and conscientiously dissent from
the . . . established [religion]." Then in 1784, Ellsworth's close friends and political

allies, Roger Sherman and Richard Law, edited a complete revision of the laws of Connecticut that eliminated the Saybrook Platform. Their revision was approved by the legislature, which included Ellsworth in the upper house. Under the Saybrook Platform, Connecticut Calvinists had had a presbyterian form of church governance and many Calvinists in Connecticut called themselves presbyterians for this reason. The elimination of the Saybrook Platform officially permitted individual churches to revert to the pure congregationalism of the Cambridge Platform.[11]

Although these changes were noteworthy advances in religious toleration, Connecticut's late eighteenth century Standing Order had a narrow, concept of the separation of church and state. For example, Zephaniah Swift, who was a deist and converted to Anglicism and who also was one of Ellsworth's friends and political allies, celebrated these changes as "a complete renunciation of the doctrine, that an ecclesiastical establishment is necessary to the support of civil government."[12] This insular or perhaps wishful thinking ignores the fact that toleration was extended only to those "professing the Christian *protestant* religion." Roman Catholics need not apply. Moreover the state continued to tax its citizens for the specific support of the protestant religion, and the Calvinist churches retained their place of preference.

Connecticut also used criminal law to punish certain types of public religious dissent. Blasphemy was a crime at common law and by statute regardless of the blasphemer's religion, and the blasphemy statute was drafted with a specific eye to protect two of the central tenets of Calvinism. Individuals were forbidden to deny either the Holy Trinity or God's "Government of the World." The latter provision affirmed the doctrine of predestination, and the former was directed toward Unitarianism. Another statute required all persons to attend some public worship even if against their conscience. In 1793, Jesse Root, who was a judge on the Superior Court and who had taught Ellsworth the practice of law, explained that this provision did not violate a person's freedom of conscience because "no man can plead as an excuse, for not worshiping his Maker, in some way or other, that it is against his conscience." Two years later, however, Zephaniah Swift claimed that the mandatory public worship law had fallen into desuetude.[13]

A final criminal statute, technically limited to persons educated in Christianity, went far beyond the blasphemy laws. The statute criminalized the espousal of atheism or polytheism "by writing, printing, teaching, or advisedly speaking." The people were further forbidden to "deny the *Christian* Religion to be true." More specifically, unitarians and others were forbidden to deny the Holy Trinity and to deny "the Holy Scripture of the Old and New-Testament to be of Divine Authority." Although the statute was technically limited to christians and individuals educated in Christianity, the limitation was irrelevant because virtually everyone in the state was a christian. Moreover, parents and masters were required by law to have children memorize "some short orthodox catechism without books, so as to be able to answer to the Questions that shall be propounded to them out of such Catechism, by their Parents, Masters, or Ministers." In practice this requirement was implemented by having schoolmasters "catechise the children weekly, and have them read daily in the Bible." Because the state was so uniformly christian, latitudinarians like Zephaniah Swift believed that these laws verged on being superfluous. Nevertheless, even Swift agreed that, "To punish the open, public, and explicit denial of the popular religion of a country, is a necessary measure to preserve the tranquility of government."[14]

In addition to mirroring the utter dominance of christianity, Connecticut's laws mirrored the utter dominance of Calvinism. The discrimination against unitarians is one example though perhaps only of theoretical significance during Ellsworth's life. An especially petty example of Calvinist manipulation of a superficially neutral law was based upon a 1791 statute requiring all persons to comply with days of public fasting and thanksgiving proclaimed by the Governor. Because the Governor was always Calvinist, these days were proclaimed according to Calvinist wishes. To make things worse, however, during the first four years of the statute, feasts frequently were proclaimed on Episcopalian fast days and fasts on Episcopalian feast days. This obnoxious practice was not stopped until a Calvinist governor was elected who happened to be a friend of the state's episcopalian bishop.[15]

## ❦ OLIVER ELLSWORTH AND THE BAPTIST PETITION MOVEMENT

The most pervasive manipulation of state laws in favor of the predominant Calvinists was found in Connecticut's tax system. Notwithstanding the Calvinists' steadily increasing tolerance of different strands of protestantism, dissenters—particularly Baptists—remained quite dissatisfied with the state's fiscal support of religion. This dissatisfaction resulted in the Baptist Petition Movement at the beginning of the first decade of the nineteenth century in which the Baptists petitioned the Connecticut General Assembly to bring about a complete disestablishment of religion. The movement is significant contemporary evidence of the extent of Connecticut's remaining establishment of religion and also provides valuable insight into Ellsworth's understanding of the propriety of state support for religion.[16]

The Baptists' initial petition was presented to the General Assembly in 1802. The following year they lodged a second petition reiterating their basic complaint but including a more detailed account of specific grievances. Their fundamental complaint was that the existing laws of Connecticut constituted "the Presbyterian [i.e., Calvinist] denomination an established religion." In addition to objecting generally to laws establishing a particular mode of worship, the Baptists objected to all laws that compelled the payment of a tax to support religion or that in any way subordinated one Christian sect to another. All their specific complaints about Connecticut's religious establishment fell under these latter two heads.[17]

The Baptists' principal objection was that Connecticut's laws, especially the tax laws, gave the Calvinists a favored position. This advantage was fostered by an act allowing a majority of qualified voters in any locality to select ministers and to establish taxes for their support. Because the Calvinists were numerically predominant, only Calvinist ministers were settled under this act. Quite aside from this *de facto* position of power, the state's superficially neutral laws created a *de jure* presumption that everyone was a member of the Standing Order societies with officially settled ministers. Therefore all who did not file a qualifying certificate continued to be taxed for the benefit of the local Calvinist society. These taxpayers included, in addition to actual members of the established societies; 1) those who chose to attend no religious services; 2) sincere dissenters who were unable to "continue ordinarily, to attend the Worship and Ministry" in a dissenting congregation; 3) non-resident dissenting landowners; and 4) "widows, strangers, persons newly come of age, and all [others] who do not legally dissent." Baptists thought that the state's requirement that the taxes of dissenters be paid over to the support of their dissenting church was particularly officious and pernicious. Baptist "ministers [could not] consistently with such their principles receive monies for their support, which [had] been collected by force of law, and especially from persons who never agreed to pay the same."[18]

Although the Baptists failed in their initial efforts to disestablish Calvinism in Connecticut, their petitions stimulated a good deal of debate. In addition to petitioning the state legislature, the Connecticut Baptists sought assistance from President Thomas Jefferson. In reply, Jefferson offered moral support and coined his famous phrase "a wall of separation between church and state." Needless to say, the Standing Order clergy were not sympathetic. In a subsequent election sermon, Asahel Hooker talked about the "deluge of tears and blood" caused by the "modern philosophers" who disestablished religion in France. Similarly the Connecticut legislature offered no support and instead appointed a select committee chaired by Ellsworth to consider the Baptists' initial, general petition.[19]

The appointment of Ellsworth was a shrewd choice. Even among non-Calvinists, he was one of the most respected men in the state and a key member of the state's political power structure. In addition, he had a serious interest in religion and was quite orthodox in his views on the proper relationship between church and state. At the select committee's first meeting, he reaffirmed his support of Connecticut's establishment when he reportedly threw the Baptist petition under the table, put his foot on it, and declared, "This is where it belongs."[20]

A key to understanding his overdetermined reaction to the Baptist petition is found in God's promise to His people in *Isaiah* 49:23 that "kings shall be thy nursing father." This passage probably is the origin of Connecticut Calvinists' habit of using the word, king, as a generic word for ruler. Connecticut Calvinists frequently described the Righteous Ruler as a "nursing father," and the metaphor was part of Ellsworth's worldview. The upper house of the Connecticut legislature was commonly referred to as "the Fathers," and Ellsworth described his 1780 election to that chamber as giving him a "seat with the Fathers." This paternalistic view of government also is found in a section of Ellsworth's *Summary of Christian Doctrine* that treats society as a family headed by a King. This paternalism turned the Baptists' Petition into an insulting complaint by children about their fathers' stewardship of the family—a violation of the children's filial duties.[21]

Consistent with this paternal metaphor, the Righteous Rulers had obligations to their family. In particular, the Standing Order ministers preached that, "the ruler ought to be a nursing father to a religion, which is calculated to root out iniquity, and make men good citizens." The notion of a nursing father being neutral in religious matters was described as "absurd" and "the greatest quackery." To the contrary, a Righteous Ruler had a positive duty to foster the Christian religion as a counter to man's natural depravity. Although the church was a beneficiary of this duty, Connecticut's clergy also stressed the secular objects of the duty. One of Ellsworth's former ministers explained, "religion and its institutions are the best aid of government, by strengthening the ruler's hand, and making the subject faithful in his place, and obedient to the general laws." The orthodox clergy recognized the general importance of separating Church and State. In particular, they objected to European-type establishments built on "laws prescribing faith, binding the conscience, and distinguishing by civil privilege the several classes of religion, or magistrates usurping the throne of the creator, and claiming the prerogatives of the supreme head of the church." Nevertheless, they obviously were not strict separationists. As one minister frankly stated, "A sweet and harmonious union of church and state to promote the general good, must meet the full approbation of heaven."[22]

After a deliberation of less than a week, Ellsworth's committee issued a report that basically restated the orthodox position. The report, which was published in the state's leading newspaper under Ellsworth's sole signature, began with the Lockean axiom that "the primary objects of government are the peace, order and prosperity of society." Because good morals are essential to the promotion of these objects, "Institutions for the promotion of good morals, are therefore objects of legislative provision and support: and among these, in the opinion of the committee, religious institutions are eminently useful and important." Connecticut Federalists had advanced the same argument in a mid-1790's dispute over the proper use of the proceeds from the sale of the state's Western Reserve. Although this argument for the state support of religion frequently was made by New England Calvinists, the argument was not unique to Calvinists.[23]

To clarify his reference to "the promotion of good morals," Ellsworth emphasized that he was not talking about "speculative opinions in the theology and mere rites and modes of worship." Like the Standing Order ministers, he was opposed to European-type establishments. Instead he endorsed state support of religious institutions because they are "wisely calculated to direct men to the performance of all the duties arising from their connection with each other, and to prevent or repress those evils which flow from unrestrained passion."[24]

In addition to supporting the general idea of the state's providing financial support to religion, Ellsworth squarely addressed the Baptists' central objection. He stated and restated that "every member of society should, in some way, contribute to the support of religious institutions." He concluded his report with a clever lawyer's analogy comparing religious institutions to courts of justice and schools. All three institutions serve valuable secular functions. Therefore no "individual [should be] allowed to refuse his contribution, because he has no children to be instructed—no injuries to be redressed, or because he conscientiously believes those institutions useless."[25]

This secular idea of comparing religious institutions to courts and schools was not original. Noah Webster had suggested the same analogy about ten years earlier. Webster served on Ellsworth's Committee, and he probably had a hand in drafting the Committee Report that appeared under Ellsworth's sole signature. Nevertheless Webster probably was not the principal drafter. A preliminary draft by Webster reached the same conclusion as the final report but was significantly different in the presentation of supporting reasons.[26]

The General Assembly adopted Ellsworth's report by a large majority and dismissed the petition. The next year the more detailed petition was lodged and another committee was appointed. The second committee dismissed the more detailed petition on the basis of Ellsworth's original report and for many years afterwards Ellsworth's report was cited as the definitive defense of Connecticut's religious establishment.[27]

## ☙ OLIVER ELLSWORTH AND FREEDOM OF CONSCIENCE

Although Ellsworth was a staunch supporter of Connecticut's preferential support of particular protestant sects, he was equally adamant in defending freedom of conscience in matters of religion. Fifteen years before his 1802 report, and a year before he wrote the Establishment Clause, he vigorously defended the proposed federal Constitution's provision forbidding religious test oaths. In this earlier essay, he wrote forcefully against the idea of a religious test as a prerequisite to holding public office. By religious tests, he meant any "act to be done, or profession to be made, relating to religions (such as partaking of the sacrament according to certain rites and forms, and declaring one's belief of certain doctrines)." His argument was based upon a shrewd combination of historical fact, human nature, and political theory.[28]

Ellsworth's central proposition was, "In our country every man has a right to worship God in that way which is most agreeable to his conscience." He explicitly based this fundamental freedom on the cruel lessons of English history. Before the Protestant Reformation, "tyrannical kings, popes, and prelates [enforced] systems of religious error [i.e., Catholicism] by severe persecuting laws." After the Reformation, religious persecution was continued by the Church of England, then by the puritans under Cromwell, and finally once more by the Church of England upon Charles II's restoration. Ellsworth concluded his history lesson by reminding his readers, "The pretense for [the post-restoration persecution] was to exclude the baptists; but the real design was to exclude the protestant dissenters."[29]

Ellsworth's brief history lesson was more than a simple scholarly flourish to edify the reader. He was a pragmatic advocate—not a scholar. His history lesson was aimed at the heart—not the mind. He did not have to remind his readers that the "protestant dissenters" who were the real targets of the post-restoration persecution were the direct ancestors and coreligionists of Connecticut's Calvinists. Just four years earlier, Joseph Huntington, in the course of an election sermon, had reminded Connecticut that the "hateful persecution. . . . of our progenitors, many and great, for their religion and strict piety, impelled them to forsake their native land." Nor did he have to mention the Old Light outrages of the 1740's. By invoking past persecutions directed at New England-style Calvinists, he evoked in his readers a personal sense of empathy with the victims of religious persecution.[30]

Ellsworth continued on his empathic tack when he moved from history to demography. He advanced an argument similar to one later made by James Madison in Virginia: "if [a national religious oath] were in favour of either congregationalists, presbyterians, episcopalians, baptists, or quakers, it would incapacitate more than three-fourths of the American citizens for any publick office; and thus degrade them from the rank of freemen." Like the history lesson, this general analysis was a veiled invitation to consider the issue in a personal context. For example, his distinction between congregationalists and presbyterians probably is a reference to the modified presbyterianism of the Saybrook Platform. Both New Lights and Old Lights had used the Platform to mount vicious attacks on each other. This sensitive issue of church governance finally had been resolved by deleting the Platform from the 1784 revision of the state's laws, and most in Connecticut were glad to put the issue behind them. Perhaps of even greater significance, little imagination was necessary to deduce that a detailed national oath was unlikely to embody Connecticut Calvinism.[31]

Ellsworth's argument against a detailed national test oath was cogent and compelling. He then turned to what he considered "the least exceptional" type of religious oath, one "requiring all persons appointed to office to declare, at the time of their admission, their belief in the being of God, and in the divine authority of the scriptures." Here was no strawman. The state's then existing statutory crimes against religion were directed primarily at individuals who denied God and the scriptures, and there was support in Connecticut for a general, Christian test oath. Furthermore, Ellsworth explicitly recognized a self-evident policy consideration favoring a general oath: "One who believes these great truths, will not be so likely to violate his obligations to his country, as one who disbelieves them; we may have greater confidence in his integrity."[32]

Ellsworth began his attack on this "least exceptional" form of oath by presenting a pragmatic analysis resonating with Calvinism. The "declaration of such a belief is no security at all. For . . . an unprincipled man, who believes neither the word nor the being of God and [is] governed merely by *selfish motives* [easily will] dissemble." This insight was not original. Joseph Bellamy and others had previously made the same argument. The argument's real power comes from an unspoken assumption shared by Ellsworth and his Calvinist readers. There are, in fact, many unprincipled men who are ruled by selfishness. The reference to "selfish motives" is an invocation of the Calvinist doctrine that man, by his very nature, is depraved and ruled by self-love.[33]

For empirical proof of the danger posed by selfish manipulators, Ellsworth pointed to England where "the most abandoned characters partake of the sacrament, in order to qualify themselves for public employments." Indeed, he argued that the English system actually had a negative impact on religion. By mixing civil and religious matters, "the clergy are obliged . . . to . . . prostitute the most sacred office of religion, for it is a civil right . . . to receive the sacrament." In view of selfish men's propensity to dissemble, religious oaths serve only to "exclude . . . honest men, men of principle, who will rather suffer an injury, than act contrary to the dictates of their conscience."[34]

In referring to honest men of principle who might refuse to swear on oath, Ellsworth did not mean individuals who were not Christians. In the next sentence, he clarified this potentially radical idea by noting that he was referring to honest men of principle who nevertheless "are sincere friends of religion." Perhaps he had in mind Quakers. About a year later when he drafted the Judiciary Act, he included a provision allowing Quakers to affirm rather than swear an oath in judicial proceedings. Senator Maclay argued that the provision was too narrow because "all persons conscientiously scrupulous of taking an Oath, should [be permitted to] take the affirmation." Over Ellsworth's objection, the Senate agreed to expand the provision.[35]

Ellsworth's arguments about selfish men and the English system were, however, secondary to his principal objection to religious test oaths. In the penultimate paragraph of his essay, he stated "the true principle" by which this question ought to be decided:

> The business of civil government is to protect the citizen in his rights, to defend the community from hostile powers, and to promote the general welfare. Civil government has no business to meddle with the private opinions of the people.

To justify this restriction of government to secular matters, he stated what he evidently regarded as a truism: "I am accountable not to man, but to God, for the religious opinions which I embrace, and the manner in which I worship the supreme being." These arguments virtually duplicated passages from John Locke's *Letter Concerning Toleration*.[36]

Ellsworth's ideas about freedom of conscience were by no means original. The celebration of religious freedom was a common theme of Connecticut election sermons dating at least from Joseph Bellamy's of 1762. Similarly, the argument that the correction of religious errors should be left to God is derivative, either directly or indirectly, from John Locke. Ellsworth owned a copy of Locke's *Letter on Toleration* and even borrowed some of Locke's imagery. Locke frequently used the phrase "fire and sword" to describe religious persecution while Ellsworth used the phrase "her bloody axe and flaming hand." A particularly significant aspect of Ellsworth's espousal of Locke's analysis is the brevity of the presentation. Although Ellsworth urged this analysis as the central argument of the entire essay, he limited his presentation to a single brief and conclusory paragraph. A reasonable inference is that he knew that his readers already accepted this "true principle" as a matter of course.[37]

Locke's analysis would have been particularly appealing to pragmatic individuals like Ellsworth who earned their political spurs in a state where political power was divided among three competing religious corps of New Lights, Old Lights, and Episcopalians. During and after the Great Awakening, first the Old Lights and later the New Lights used the state's civil power to intervene in religious matters. Although the New Lights eventually gained control of the civil government, they never gained predominant control, which necessitated coalition building with Episcopalians. Later the Revolutionary War encouraged a stable working relationship between the Old and New Lights. Among all the rebelling colonies, Connecticut stands out as the most politically stable state during the Rebellion. Clearly the erstwhile warring religious factions were able to set aside their traditional hostility. This Calvinist coalition probably took a number of years to accomplish and was symbolized by the deletion of the Saybrook Platform from the 1784 revision of the state's acts. Given this prior history, Ellsworth could state with confidence that civil government has no business meddling in religious affairs.

Although Ellsworth was a firm advocate of freedom of conscience in religious matters, he saw no conflict between this freedom and Connecticut's limited establishment of religion. He clearly approved of the state's financial support of protestantism in general and Calvinism in particular, and throughout his political life he consistently endorsed a limited civil power to interfere in religious affairs. A hundred years before Ellsworth wrote his essay defending freedom of conscience, John Locke had argued that civil authority might properly intervene in matters where secular and religious concerns coincide. Ellsworth agreed in the final paragraph of his essay against religious test oaths. The state, he wrote, "has a right to prohibit and punish gross immoralities and impieties; because the open practice of these is of evil example and detriment." Therefore he "heartily approve[d] of our laws against drunkenness, profane swearing, blasphemy, and professed atheism." Again Ellsworth was doing little more than reciting Locke and the then current understanding of religious freedom embodied by Connecticut's laws. His subsequent defense of Connecticut's official support of Christianity was founded upon an identical analysis.[38]

## ☙ THE FIRST AMENDMENT'S RELIGION CLAUSES

Although there is no surviving record of what Ellsworth actually said during the Senate's consideration of the Bill of Rights, his understanding of the First Amendment's religion clauses is fairly easy to deduce from his writings before and after the First Amendment was drafted. The Bill of Rights originated in the House of Representatives, and the House's proposed amendments included two articles that dealt with religion:

### Article the Third

Congress shall make no laws establishing Religion, or prohibiting to free exercise thereof, nor shall the rights of conscience be infringed.

✳    ✳    ✳    ✳

Article the Fourteenth

> *No State shall* infringe the right of trial by Jury in criminal cases, nor *the rights of conscience*, nor the freedom of speech, or of the press.

After the House approved a number of amendments, including these two articles, they were submitted to the Senate.[39]

When the Senate took up the House's third article respecting congressional power over religious matters, some of the senators evidently believed that the House's prohibitions were too broad. Rather than use general terms, someone moved to replace the House's language with a simple and more specific prohibition against establishing "One Religious Sect or Society in preference to others." This motion, however, failed to pass. Next a motion was made to strike the entire third article, but it too failed. Then a substitute article was proposed that would have forbidden Congress to "make any law, infringing the rights of conscience, or establishing any Religious Sect or Society." Again the motion failed. A fourth motion was made that would have retained the House language except that the general prohibition against "establishing Religion" would have been replaced by more specific language against "establishing any particular denomination of religion in preference to another." After this motion was defeated, someone—perhaps in exasperation—called the question in the House's original proposal, but that too was rejected.[40]

Careful grammarians have teased a number of meanings out of these various motions, but the bottom line is that the Senate rejected each and every one of them. Obviously many—probably a majority—of the senators believed that the House language was too broad, but no one was able to devise an acceptable alternative approach. The senators were, however, able to reach an agreement on the House proposal that "the rights of conscience [shall not] be infringed." The Senate agreed to strike all reference to "the rights of conscience."[41]

After reaching an impasse on the House's third proposed article, the Senate considered the rest of the articles in sequence and also considered a number of matters not covered by the House proposals. During this process, the House's fourteenth article protecting rights of conscience from state action was rejected. Finally on the last day of debate, the senators returned to the House's third article and agreed to change it to read that "Congress shall make no law establishing articles of faith or a mode of worship, or prohibiting the free exercise of religion." This change was incorporated into Ellsworth's consolidated motion that passed the Senate and was sent back to the House.[42]

In sending these and other proposed changes to the House, the Senate was, in effect, formally opening negotiations between the two chambers on the final wording of the Bill of Rights. The House agreed to many of the Senate's changes but stood firm on the original wording of the third and fourteenth articles on religion. In response, the Senate voted to recede from or give up on its proposed version of the third article's establishment and free exercise clauses but to "insist on all the others." Disagreements like this are inevitable in any legislative body having two co-equal chambers. The same problem routinely arose in Great Britain when the House of Commons and the House of Lords disagreed on proposed legislation. The British solution to this kind of disagreement was to convene a Committee of Conference in which representatives or managers from each chamber would confer with each other and work out a compromise that would be recommended to their respective chamber. Not surprisingly, this same procedure was used by Congress, and a Committee of Conference was formed to resolve the differences between the House and Senate versions of the Bill of Rights. The Senate appointed three managers, with Ellsworth as chairman, to confer with three managers from the House, who were led by Madison.[43]

The differences between the House and the Senate were quickly resolved, and Ellsworth personally penned the Conference Committee report embodying the House and Senate managers' agreement. Notwithstanding the Senate's prior recession from its proposed establishment and free exercise clauses, the Committee of Conference recommended changing the establishment clause to read:

> Congress shall make no law *respecting an establishment of Religion*, or prohibiting the free exercise thereof.

The Committee also agreed to the Senate's insistence on striking the House's proposed fourteenth article forbidding infringements of rights of conscience by the states. The Senate's version of the Bill of Rights as modified by the Conference report was immediately approved by both chambers. Ten of the twelve proposals were subsequently ratified by the states, and became the first ten amendments of the Constitution.[44]

### ❦ FREE EXERCISE AND RIGHTS OF CONSCIENCE

Ellsworth's Committee of Conference Report followed the general philosophy of Church and State that he consistently advocated before and after the Bill of Rights was framed. Consistent with his firm belief in freedom of religion, his report recommended that "Congress shall make no law . . . prohibiting the free exercise [of Religion]." Although this recommendation technically deleted the House's additional language guaranteeing "rights of conscience" against congressional infringement, Ellsworth undoubtedly viewed the deletion as simply a matter of style and not substantive. In the eighteenth century, rights of conscience and freedom of religion were synonymous terms. The leading example of equating rights of conscience with freedom of religion is John Locke's influential *Letter Concerning Toleration*, which he wrote in terms of freedom of conscience.[45]

The same rights-of-conscience phraseology was commonly used in Connecticut to refer to freedom of religion. Connecticut's toleration act was called "An Act for securing the Rights of Conscience," and Connecticut writers and ministers routinely wrote and spoke in terms of rights of conscience when they meant freedom of religion.

Those who vigorously opposed the preferences that Connecticut conferred upon Calvinism used the same phraseology. Two years after the Bill of Rights was framed, John Leland, a leading Baptist theoretician and minister, strenuously attacked Connecticut's preferential laws in a pamphlet entitled *The Right of Conscience Inalienable*. Similarly both petitions in the Baptist Petition movement began their criticism of Connecticut's laws by invoking "the rights of conscience." Finally when Ellsworth, himself, wrote about religious freedom, he used the term rights of conscience. Therefore the deletion of "rights of conscience" from the Bill of Rights should not be viewed as a decision to narrow the scope of rights under the Constitution. Instead Ellsworth almost certainly viewed the deletion as a matter of style.[46]

A detailed account of what Ellsworth may have understood the free exercise of religion to mean is difficult to reconstruct. To be sure, there was a consensus among Connecticut's Standing Order that the state had no business in interfering with the personal religious beliefs of its citizens. Nevertheless in one of his *Landholder* essays, Ellsworth had written, "while I assert the rights of religious liberty, I would not deny that the civil power has a right, in some cases, to interfere in matters of religion." Ellsworth's touchstone was whether the civil power was being exercised to accomplish secular goals. Thus he had no objection to the punishment of "gross . . . impieties . . . profane swearing, blasphemy, and professed atheism" because "the open practice of these is of evil example and detriment." In his time, this position was neither anomalous nor even extreme. It was virtually a restatement of Connecticut's criminal laws related to religion. Moreover, John Locke and Connecticut religious liberals like Zephaniah Swift agreed.[47]

Ellsworth's attitudes on freedom of religion and state support for religion also provide an explanation of the Conference Committee's rejection of the House's fourteenth article forbidding the states to "infringe . . . the rights of conscience." Ellsworth certainly approved of the general principles embodied by the rights of conscience. Similarly, the House may have passed the fourteenth article as an expression of general principle without taking into account the article's potential for a national intrusion into local relations between church and state. Although there probably was general agreement within the Congress regarding the general principle, specific applications of the principle might be subject to dispute. The problem was that general phrases like establishment of religion and rights of conscience are ambiguous and subject to dramatically diverse interpretations. We are painfully aware of this problem today, and the Founding Generation was no less sophisticated. While the House of Representatives was pondering the prohibition of religious establishments and guaranty of rights of conscience, Peter Silvester of New York specifically expressed an apprehension that these concepts were "liable to a construction different from what had been made by the committee." Indeed, Silvester "feared it might be thought to have a tendency to abolish religion altogether."[48]

Silvester's concerns were essentially general and theoretical, but Connecticut's representatives fully understood how a constitutional provision for religious rights might affect their state's religious establishment. Benjamin Huntington stated Connecticut's objection in the clearest possible terms. These "words," he said, "might be taken in such latitude as to be extremely hurtful to the cause of religion." He specifically noted that the "ministers of their congregations to the Eastward [by which he meant New England is general and Connecticut in particular] were maintained by the contributions [i.e., taxes] of those who belonged to their society; the expense of building meeting houses was contributed in the same manner." He went on to raise the specific fear that the religion clauses might empower "a Federal Court" to interfere with Connecticut's approach to supporting religion.[49]

The proposed amendment prohibiting the states from interfering with individuals' rights of conscience clearly presented problems for Connecticut's establishment. When the Baptists later vigorously attacked Connecticut's system of taxation, they did so on the express basis that the system infringed their rights of conscience.[50] Calvinists like Ellsworth sincerely believed that the tax structure did not infringe rights of conscience. Nevertheless the phrase rights of conscience was ambiguous. When the Baptists subsequently petitioned the Connecticut legislature, this ambiguity was taken care of by appointing a committee of right-thinking Calvinists who put a proper spin on the issue. But Connecticut's Standing Order did not control the national government. Therefore the creation of federal rights of conscience that might be enforced against Connecticut in a national forum was quite unacceptable.

Given the firm basis for opposing the creation of ambiguous federal rights regulating state establishments, the decision of the Committee of Conference to excise this proposed right from the Bill of Rights is entirely understandable. Obviously Ellsworth, who chaired the managers from the Senate, was a firm defender of Connecticut's establishment. In addition his friend, Roger Sherman, was one of the House managers and would have been equally firm on this issue.

## ☙ AN ESTABLISHMENT OF RELIGION

Ellsworth's recommendation that "Congress shall make no law respecting an establishment of Religion" requires a more complicated explanation. There is no doubt that he believed that a government should provide direct financial assistance to protestant churches even to the extent of preferring one protestant denomination over all others. Therefore his role as the father of the Constitution's Establishment Clause seems at first glance peculiar. In fact, however, the most plausible explanation of his role in drafting the Clause is that he simply did not care whether the Bill of Rights included an establishment clause.

Ellsworth's indifference to the Establishment Clause was multilayered. In the first place, Calvinist political psychology provided little support for the adoption of a Bill of Rights. In the words of a Standing Order minister, written laws "exist only on paper and ink." What counts is the presence of righteous rulers who will provide good government. This reasoning had led Ellsworth and other Connecticut Calvinists to dismiss the need for a Bill of Rights during the ratification process.[51]

In addition to this Calvinist inclination to view declarations of rights as mere "paper and ink," some aspects of the Bill of Rights seemed doubly superfluous. After the Constitutional Convention in Philadelphia, Ellsworth and Roger Sherman had penned a joint letter explaining that the powers "vested in Congress . . . extend only to matters respecting the common interests of the Union." Among other things Sherman believed that matters of religion were basically of local interest and therefore essentially beyond the national government's powers. In the House of debates on the Establishment Clause, Sherman flatly stated that "the amendment [was] altogether unnecessary, inasmuch as congress had no authority whatever delegated to them by the constitution, to make religious establishments."[52]

Ellsworth was of much the same mind. When he thought of religious establishments, he thought of the imposition of a single type of protestantism upon an entire nation similar to the establishment of the Church of England. In view of the rampant pluralism of American protestantism, such an establishment obviously was a practical impossibility. As he had explained in one of his Landholder letters, to establish any one type of protestantism would be to the detriment of "more than three-fourths of the American citizens." Like Sherman, he believed that matters of religion were essentially of local rather than national concern. As he had noted during the Constitutional Convention, the federal government "could only embrace objects of a general nature. He turned his eyes therefore for the preservation of his rights to the State Govts." Similarly, during the ratification process, he flatly denied that Congress had "power to prohibit . . . liberty of conscience." His practical understanding that religion is primarily a local matter is evident in a letter that he and William Samuel Johnson, his fellow Connecticut senator, wrote to their governor about six months after the Bill of Rights was framed. In response to an enquiry from Governor Huntington as to whether President Washington would proclaim a "General Fast" later in the Spring, Ellsworth and Johnson stated that "except on great National Occasions the appt of both Fasts & Thanksgivings should be left to the particular states." Because Ellsworth thought that matters of religion generally should be left to the states, his approval of government support for religion was not implicated by the Establishment Clause, which applied only to the federal government.[53]

Consistent with this view, Ellsworth approved a federal entanglement with religion in a few instances involving a clear federal interest. He obviously thought that the President could declare national days of Fasts and Thanksgivings "on great National Occasions." Similarly he was the Senate chairman of a joint committee that recommended the appointment of House and Senate chaplains, and he presumably voted for the provision of chaplains to the armed forces. A 1795 Treaty providing the Oneida Indians with money to rebuild a church destroyed by the British when the Oneida were our allies during the Revolutionary War fits this same pattern. The paucity of these *ad hoc* entanglements with religion indicates that the early Congresses agreed with Ellsworth's idea that religion was generally a matter for the states rather than the national government.[54]

In addition to viewing the Establishment Clause as relatively unimportant and even superfluous, Ellsworth almost certainly would have limited the Clause's impact to forbidding federal establishments similar to Great Britain's establishment of the Church of England. This narrow view of religious establishments was the orthodox Standing Order doctrine espoused by leading Connecticut Calvinists. Ellsworth's friend, Timothy Dwight, who sometimes was called the "Pope" of Connecticut, recognized that some believed that the state had an *ecclesiastical establishment.*" He explained, however, that the critics (undoubtedly the Baptists) were in error because the "phrase . . . denoted *the establishment of a national or state church, or the establishment of exclusive privileges in the possession of one class of christians.*" Ellsworth's subsequent legislative report on the Baptist Petitions indicates that he subscribed to Dwight's particular view of religious establishments. Under this narrow view of religious establishments, the Establishment Clause in the Bill of Rights was virtually nugatory.[55]

Although Ellsworth held a narrow view of improper religious establishments, others had a far broader view. In fact, the concept of improper religious establishments was ambiguous in the late eighteenth century. In 1761, Ezra Stiles, later Ellsworth's friend and President of Yale College, had described Connecticut's relationship between church and state as one of the British colonies' "provincial establishments." In the same decade, separationists in Connecticut already were attacking the colony's system as an improper establishment. Indeed during the years before and after Ellsworth penned the Establishment Clause, there actually was a general agreement that Connecticut's laws created an establishment of religion. The dispute was over whether the establishment was proper or improper. Timothy Dwight denied that Connecticut had an establishment like the Church of England, which obviously was improper. In the same paragraph, however, Dwight conceded that Connecticut had a religious establishment, which he called *"the legal establishment of the public worship of God in this state.*"[56]

Ellsworth was a sophisticated lawyer who had drafted countless contracts, statutes, resolutions, and other documents, and his experience had made him well-versed in the problems of ambiguity. "Perhaps no two men," he once wrote, "will express the same sentiment in the same matter, and by the same words; neither do they connect precisely the same ideas with the same words. From hence arises an ambiguity in all languages, with which the most perspicuous and precise writers are in a degree chargeable."[57] When an ambiguous rights-of-conscience clause directly applicable to the states was proposed, the clause's ambiguity led him to oppose it. But he had no qualms about drafting a similarly ambiguous Establishment Clause applicable to the federal government, because he viewed the federal government's role in religious matters to be relatively unimportant.

Presumably Ellsworth intended the Establishment Clause to have a comparatively narrow meaning, but given his knowledge that the clause was ambiguous he could not safely predict such an outcome. James Madison, who chaired the Committee of Conference managers from the House, was in an ironically similar predicament. Unlike Ellsworth, Madison had an expansive understanding of improper religious establishments, but like Ellsworth, he undoubtedly was familiar with the contrary view.[58] In other words both men were capable lawyers and politicians who consciously embraced ambiguity in framing the Establishment Clause.

Ellsworth and Madison were sophisticated men who represented opposing points of view on the proper relationship between church and state, and they can be viewed as ideal-types for the clash of ideas within the First Congress—indeed within the nation—that gave birth to the Establishment Clause. When competent negotiators and drafters consciously agree to ambiguous language in an important document, the usual explanation is that in order to reach general agreement they have tacitly postponed the resolution of the issue to a later date and perhaps a different forum. Madison had specific reservations about clearly defining the scope of religious liberties in the Constitution because he feared that such a "public definition" would be unduly narrow. When the Committee of Conference agreed to an Establishment Clause that the managers knew to be ambiguous, they must have understood that the ambiguity would have to be resolved at a later date.[59]

Some have proposed a different interpretation of the drafting of the Establishment Clause. Because the final language of the Committee of Conference differs from both the House and Senate proposals, the Clause frequently has been viewed as a compromise hammered out in the Committee of Conference.[60] Under the compromise thesis, Madison's personal beliefs and position of leadership in the House suited him as the natural advocate of separationism. For the same reasons, Ellsworth would have been the natural advocate for accommodating the direct state support of religion.

Consistent with the compromise thesis, some scholars have argued that the House and Senate managers added the word "respecting" to the Establishment Clause in order to forbid the Congress to make a "law respecting [a state] establishment of religion"—in other words, to protect existing state establishments.[61] As historical analysis, this ingeniously subtle reading is implausible. One wonders who on the Committee of Conference would have pushed a state's rights position. Ellsworth and Sherman clearly were protective of state establishments, but they considered matters of religion to be of local interest and therefore beyond the power of the national government. Surely Madison did not waste any bargaining chips in order to protect existing state establishments. In addition we will see that there was a serious parliamentary impediment to a substantive compromise by the Committee of Conference on the Establishment Clause.

In addition, the states' rights interpretation ultimately yields quite ironic results. If the Committee of Conference changed the Establishment Clause to protect state establishments, the managers presumably had in mind the existing relationships between Church and State in the various states. In order to provide complete protection, the Establishment Clause would have to be given the broadest possible reading—extending to preferential and nonpreferential establishments. But the clause at the same time clearly was meant to prohibit federal establishments. Therefore the states' rights advocates logically (albeit unwittingly) must agree with commentators like Professor Leonard Levy[62] who have cogently suggested an expansive interpretation of the Establishment Clause. Of course, the incorporation of the Establishment Clause in the Fourteenth Amendment eliminates the notion of the Clause as a protection of states' rights.

If the Establishment Clause actually was the result of a compromise between the

House and Senate managers, Ellsworth was seriously disadvantaged in his negotiations with Madison. At the same time that the Senate agreed to a Committee of
Conference, the Senate formally receded from its proposed Establishment Clause and
thereby officially accepted the House version. As a matter of technical parliamentary
procedure, this Senate action deprived the Committee of Conference of authority to
change the Clause. The English parliamentary rule for conferences between the Lords
and the Commons were quite formal and drew a technical distinction between ordinary conferences and "Free" conferences. In the former the managers were limited to
a formal reading of the reasons for their chamber's disagreement, whereas in "Free"
conferences the managers were permitted to engage in a free discussion of their disagreement. Under the English practice, a Committee of Conference was not allowed
to change the provisions upon which both the Commons and the Lords had agreed.
Therefore the Senate's recession on the Establish Clause barred the Committee of
Conference from changing the meaning of the clause.[63]

Ellsworth fully understood the concept of a Committee of Conference and the
basis of the Committee in English parliamentary practice. In the bicameral Connecticut General Assembly, he had sat upon many Committees of Conference. Similarly in
presiding over the Senate, both Vice Presidents Adams and Jefferson recognized English parliamentary practice as valid precedent. Jefferson explained that the English
parliamentary practice was the preferred basis for congressional practice because it "is
the model which we have all studied, while we are little acquainted with the modifications
of it in our several States." Ellsworth, himself, was wont to rely upon arcane parliamentary rules. When the Senate in its second session was debating the status of
unfinished business from the first session, Senator Maclay noted in his diary that
Ellsworth "had much parliamentary stuff."[64]

More importantly, less than five months before the Committee of Conference on
the Bill of Rights was convened, Ellsworth had chaired the Committee that drafted
the Congress's rule on Committees of Conference. This rule from Ellsworth's committee was clearly based on the well-established parliamentary practice and demonstrated a detailed knowledge of the practice by providing that in all conferences the
managers "shall . . . confer freely." In other words the rule allowed the managers to
discuss their differences and therefore, taking into account the English parliamentary
distinction, provided for "Free" Conferences rather than conferences that were not
"Free." Under the rule, the House and Senate managers' discussions were limited to
the "amendment to a bill agreed to in one House and dissented to in the other." This
provision evidently followed the parliamentary practice that limited committees of
conference to specific matters over which the two houses actually had disagreed. The
effect of this technical limitation was to deprive the Committee of Conference of
power to change the meaning of the House's version of the Establishment clause.
Seven years later, Vice President Jefferson explained "it is unparlimentary to strike
out, at a conference, anything in a bill which hath been agreed and passed by both
Houses." Therefore a variance from the House's version would have been subject to a
point of order by any member of the House or Senate. To be sure, the Committee

changed the precise wording of the Establishment Clause, but the most plausible explanation of the change is that the Committee viewed it merely as a matter of style—and not of substance—in which the Senate managers deferred to James Madison. This explanation resolves the apparent departure from parliamentary practice and would have been a powerful rebuttal to a point of order.[65]

In addition to this arcane parliamentary complication, the Senate recession had serious practical implications for the Senate managers chaired by Ellsworth. The recession was a substantive institutional decision to accept the House's position. Furthermore, the Senate receded on only one point and disagreed with the House on sixteen other issues.[66] Therefore at the very least Ellsworth's brief instructed him to concentrate his negotiations on the latter sixteen points.

In addition to receiving no institutional support on the Establishment Clause issue, Ellsworth was personally inclined to view the matter as unimportant. In contrast, we may infer that he was quite interested in scotching the House provision guarantying rights of conscience in the states, and we know that the Senate managers were adamantly opposed to other House proposals relating to the federal judiciary.[67] The Senate managers were not appointed until the late afternoon or early evening of September 21 and they apparently concluded their deliberations two days later. Given this press of time, Ellsworth surely would have concentrated upon the issues that he believed were really important.

Although the precise language of the Establishment Clause obviously was changed, the most plausible explanation is that the change was viewed merely as a matter of style in which the Senate managers deferred to Madison. In addition to being a powerful rebuttal to a point of order, this explanation comports with the Senate's prior recession from its more narrow establishment language. The House language formally accepted by the Senate provided, "Congress shall make no law establishing religion." The Committee changed this language to read, "Congress shall make no law respecting an establishment of religion." A careful grammarian might find substantive distinctions between these two sentences,[68] but to suggest that the change was intended to record a significant substantive compromise is wildly implausible. If Ellsworth and Madison in fact worked out a substantive change to the House's proposal, it is incredible that they did not draft language that more clearly indicated the change.

When considered in the historical context of the Conference Committee's formation and deliberations, the common assumption that the language of the Establishment Clause is the result of a compromise within the Committee is implausible. There was, in fact, no disagreement between the House and the Senate because the Senate specifically agreed to the House's language. The Conference Committee technically lacked jurisdiction to alter the House's proposal, the Senate managers lacked institutional support to negotiate a compromise, and Ellsworth, their leader, not only thought the matter was unimportant but had much more important differences to discuss.

### CHAPTER SEVEN

# The Rhode Island Trade Bill

*T*HE FIRST SESSION OF THE first Congress was quite eventful. In addition to the Judiciary Act and the Bill of Rights, a series of acts was passed to create the Departments of State, War, and Treasury, and detailed revenue measures were enacted to tax vessels and imported goods. All the while, the Union still was not complete because Rhode Island and North Carolina had yet to ratify the Constitution. Therefore these two states were not represented in the first session. By and large a pragmatic attitude was initially adopted toward them. The Congress concentrated upon putting the government in motion and essentially ignored their absence. Members of Congress assumed that these two states were bound to come into the fold and waited patiently. Rhode Island and North Carolina were technically foreign countries, but the Congress temporarily exempted them from revenue measures directed at foreign countries.[1]

In the Fall of 1789, North Carolina joined the Union, but when the Congress returned for its second session in January, 1790, Rhode Island still was not in the fold. There was hope, however, because Rhode Island had scheduled a ratifying convention that was to meet on March 1. Influenced by this encouraging news, Congress agreed to continue Rhode Island's exemption from the revenue acts until April 1, but "no later." Unfortunately, however, the Ratification Convention adjourned almost immediately on March 6 without accomplishing anything of significance. The Convention did decide, however, to reconvene about three months later at the end of May.[2]

The Rhode Island Convention's adjournment was the last straw for Ellsworth. He did not like the government of Rhode Island and was outraged that Rhode Island had failed to join the Union. He remembered the occasions during and after the Revolutionary War when Rhode Island had vetoed plans to give the Continental Congress direct taxing authority, and he viewed the state's failure to ratify the Constitution as a continuing effort to prevent the national government from being placed on a sound financial footing. The little state, however, was guilty in Ellsworth's eyes of a far greater sin. During the economic depression following the Revolutionary War, hard money became scarce in the United States, and farmers were unable to pay off their debts. Rhode Island solved this problem by printing paper money and requiring merchants to accept currency—which depreciated instantly and terribly—as lawful medium for the payment of debts.[3]

Ellsworth's draft of the Rhode Island Trade Bill. Rhode Island initially refused to ratify the Constitution, bu the threat of a complete trade embargo in Ellsworth's Rhode Island Trade Bill effectively ended that small state's recalcitrance.

This shifting of the Depression's burden from the farmers to the merchants enraged mercantile interests within and without the state. Because newspapers tended to be controlled by or at least be sympathetic to mercantile interests, Rhode Island's paper money strategy was vigorously savaged in the press throughout New England. In neighboring Connecticut, a group of poets later known as the "Connecticut Wits" assailed Rhode Island in part of a satiric poem called the *Anarchiad*. Wrote the Wits:

> Hail! realm of rogues, renow'd for fraud and guile,
> All hail, ye knav'ries of your little isle.
> There prowls the rascal, cloth'd with legal pow'r,
> To snare the orphan, and the poor devour;
> The crafty knave his creditor besets,
> And advertising paper pays his debts,
>
> \* \* \* \*
>
> The wiser race, the snares of law to shun,
> Like Lot from Sodom, from Rhode Island run.[4]

The Wits were friends and acquaintances of Ellsworth, but if anything Ellsworth was even more virulently opposed to paper money.

During the Revolutionary War, Ellsworth condemned governmental abuse of paper money as "madness, atheism and suicide," and his firm opposition to paper money had not diminished. At the Constitutional Convention in Philadelphia he wanted "to shut and bar the door against paper money." With Rhode Island in mind, he argued that the "mischiefs of the various experiments which have been made, were now fresh in the public mind and had excited the disgust of all the respectable part of America." In his opening speech to the Connecticut Ratifying Convention, he warned, with obvious reference to Rhode Island:

> Is there not in one of our states injustice too barefaced for Eastern
> despotism? That state is small; it does little hurt to any but itself. But it
> has a spirit which would make a Tophet of the universe.

When he wrote an essay a few months later urging Rhode Island to ratify the Constitution, his analysis was a seamless web of rational, moral, and religious indignation. He expressly addressed his words to "the Rhode-Island Friends of PAPER-MONEY" and immediately launched into a vigorous attack. "The singular system of policy adopted by your state," he began, "no longer excites either the surprize or indignation of mankind." The Rhode Island experience was part of "the progress of human depravity" and comparable to "Milton's lapse of the angels and their expulsion from Heaven." Nevertheless, all was part of God's plan, and Ellsworth expressly modeled his essay after Bellamy's *The Wisdom of God*: "The sentiment thrown out by some of our adventurous divines [i.e., Joseph Bellamy], that *the permission of sin* is the highest display of *supreme wisdom*, and the greatest blessing to the universe, is most successfully illustrated by the effects of your general policy."[5]

Under God's plan, Rhode Island's depravity was serving a didactic purpose. The leaders of Rhode Island were "Men full of evil and desperate fortune" who implemented their scheme to preserve themselves "from deserved poverty, and from prisons appointed to be the reward of indolence and knavery." God was using these desperate and evil men to demonstrate the need for a new Constitution:

> To silence such opposition as might be made to the new constitution, it was fit that public injustice should be exhibited in its greatest degree and most extreme effects. For this end Heaven permitted your apostacy from all the principles of good and just government. By your system we see unrighteousness in the essence, in its effects, and in its native miseries.

Obviously Ellsworth believed that the advocates of paper money were beyond redemption. In the concluding portion of his essay he urged the people of Rhode Island, whom he believed "guilty of [no] crime greater than indiscretion," to throw out the existing government and ratify the Constitution. He ended his essay with an ominous threat: "If you will not hear your own groans, nor feel the pangs of your own torture it must continue until removed by a political annihilation."[6]

Two years later all the states but Rhode Island had ratified the Constitution, and Ellsworth was ready to carry through on his threat of "political annihilation." While Ellsworth was concentrating on putting the government in motion during the 1789 session of Congress, he did not forget Rhode Island. In May of 1789, Roger Sherman wrote a friend in Rhode Island urging a speedy ratification of the Constitution and tacitly threatened that Congress might have to enact legislation forbidding trade between the United States and Rhode Island. Sherman noted that "Mr. Ellsworth . . . joins in opinion with me." Almost as soon as the Rhode Island convention adjourned the next year without taking action, the Senate selected Ellsworth and four other senators to a committee to decide what to do about Rhode Island.[7]

While the committee was pondering the problem, Ellsworth's colleague from Connecticut, Benjamin Huntington, with whom Ellsworth was boarding, received a letter from William Ellery of Rhode Island. Ellery warned:

> it is my opinion still that the Convention will adjourn again unless you do something which will touch the interest of the Antis before the Convention meets; which will be the last Monday in this month.

Ellery also raised a delicate issue that he had broached in a previous letter. The seaports were considering seceding from the state and joining the Union. If this secession resulted in hostilities, "some prudent men," wrote Ellery, desired assurances that the federal government would protect the seceding towns.[8]

Huntington replied that he could not speak for Congress, but he assured Ellery that he personally believed that Congress would protect any seceding towns from violence. He was not sanguine, however, about Congress's willingness to take immediate steps to influence Rhode Island's ratification convention. "We have so many mixuped men among us who chose to wait to see the Result of the Next Session of your Convention, that I am not Certain," wrote Huntington, "they will agree to any Coercive measures with the Little Sister until they are convinced of her final Obstinacy."[9]

While Huntington was worrying whether Congress would "agree to any coercive measure," Ellsworth was drafting just such a measure. His task was complicated by the "mixuped men" who were reluctant to take decisive action, and the political stakes were raised by the possibility of a bloody secession. Ellsworth, however, approached his task with complete confidence. A month later he confessed in private to his wife that his bill "would have exposed me to some censure had it not produced the effect which I expected." He was not, however, particularly concerned with censure from others because he was inwardly driven by his confidence that he was one of God's elect. The bill that he personally penned was harsh—even ruthless. There was no compromise. Essentially, he proposed a complete economic embargo. "No goods, Wares, or Merchandize" could be brought into the United States from Rhode Island. Nor could Rhode Island ships enter United States ports, or United States ships enter Rhode Island ports. All property, ships, and carriages used in violation of the embargo would be forfeited, and individual violators were subject to a fine of five hundred dollars and six months imprisonment. In the last section of the bill, he frankly provided that the measure would be terminated upon Rhode Island's ratification of the Constitution.[10]

Ellsworth understood that his bill was "a pretty bold measure." It was the legislative foundation for the "political annihilation" that he had threatened two years earlier in his "Landholder" essay. There was no flexibility in his bill because he viewed the other side to be utterly without merit. As he had written earlier, the political leaders of Rhode Island were "full of evil and desperate fortune." Moreover he did not have to compromise in order to obtain a sufficient majority in the Senate. He undoubtedly did some head counting in the Senate and knew that he had the votes. His bill was an exercise of righteous political power. There was no mercy.[11]

When the Senate took up Ellsworth's bill, it was vehemently attacked as an unfair and misguided exercise of raw political power. Senator Maclay of Pennsylvania argued that the bill would impose "a kind of Commercial Coventry" and "plainly that this was playing the Tyrant." Pierce Butler of South Carolina called it "a declaration of war" and compared it to Britain's Boston Port Bill that closed Boston after the Boston Tea Party. In private, Senator Gunn of Georgia was speculating that "the agitating the affair of Rhode Island, is only to furnish a Pretext to raise more Troops."[12]

In addition to these visceral attacks, the "mixuped" opponents suggested that until word arrived from the Rhode Island convention "the Whole Business [was] premature." They also hinted that the Bill might drive the state into "foreign Engagements." In response, "Ellsworth spoke with great deliberation, often and long." The Senate finally passed the Bill by a vote of 13–8, but this vote did not silence the opposition. Arthur Fenner, who was president or governor of Rhode Island, wrote a letter to President Washington complaining that "a Measure of such an Hostile appearance and so degrading to this State as [Ellsworth's bill] would not be expected by us." In the House of Representatives, John Steele of North Carolina denounced the Bill to his state governor as "tyrannical and arbitrary in the highest degree and the author of it [i.e., Ellsworth] indeed the Senate by passing it, seem to have lost sight of" Rhode Island's sacrifices during the Revolution.[13]

When the Bill was sent to the House, the rhetoric of censure continued. John Page of Virginia assailed it as "improper, unjust, and highly impolite." But the House debates were essentially irrelevant. The fundamental purpose of Ellsworth's bill was to coerce Rhode Island—not to regulate its trade. Toward this end a copy of the bill had been immediately sent to Rhode Island where it was quickly published in the state's newspapers before the ratifying Convention was reconvened. To quote Tench Coxe, who was a well-informed Federalist in Philadelphia, the issue of ratification in Rhode Island was "touch and go." The Federalists in the Convention made overt use of Ellsworth's Bill, and finally the delegates voted to ratify the Constitution by a narrow margin of 34 to 32.[14]

Whether Ellsworth's bill in fact effected Rhode Island's ratification cannot be known with certainty, but the final vote was quite close. If the publication of his bill throughout the state changed even a single negative vote to a positive one, then the bill indeed played a significant role. Certainly Ellsworth believed that his bill had its intended effect. Finally the great work that had begun three years earlier in Philadelphia to create a stronger more energetic national government was complete. Ellsworth wrote to his wife with obvious satisfaction:

> The Constitution is now adopted by all the States, and I have much satisfaction, and perhaps some vanity, in seeing, at length, a great work finished, for which I have long labored incessantly.[15]

### CHAPTER EIGHT

# Ellsworth's Disillusionment with the Federal Government

RHODE ISLAND'S ENTRY into the Union was the last significant step in the creation of the federal republic and also may have marked the high tide of Ellsworth's faith in the Constitution as a positive element of God's plan for human society. The basic problem was that Calvinists like Ellsworth placed enormous emphasis on striving for a society of harmony and order, but the United States, in contrast to the individual states, has always been more pluralistic than cohesive. Therefore Ellsworth's vision of a perfect society was doomed never to come to pass.

Throughout the 1790s the Federalists, with whom Ellsworth was aligned, maintained a fairly comprehensive control of the national government. Presidents Washington and Adams were Federalists and so were all the Supreme Court justices. In Congress the Federalists never lost control of the Senate, and they frequently had at least a working control of the House. At the same time, however, a political coalition of individuals who came to call themselves Republicans and who were opposed to Federalist policies steadily gained power throughout the decade. To Ellsworth, the Republicans' political opposition was an assault on the Federalists' righteous political order, but for most of the decade he perservered in a faith that all would come right with the federal government. By the end of the decade his faith in the federal government was virtually gone. When the opposition coalition led by Thomas Jefferson completely ousted the Federalists from control of the Executive and Legislative Branches in the 1800 election, Ellsworth had had enough and resigned from national political service.

The opposition to Federalist policies was evident early in the decade in connection with issues like the creation of a national bank and the Washington administration's policy of strict neutrality in the European war arising from the French Revolution. Then in the middle of the decade, the Jay Treaty served as a national political watershed that enabled the Jeffersonian Republicans to focus upon their extensive disagreement with Federalist policies and to solidify their coalition of interests into a loose organization resembling an opposition political party. Before the Treaty, the Republicans more or less deferred to George Washington's Federalist administration. The Treaty, however, convinced the Republicans of the need for firm and open opposition.[1]

*Traité avec les Etats-Unis*, lithograph by C. Motte after a painting by V. Adam.
Ellsworth accepts the Treaty of Mortefontaine from Napoleon.
COURTESY ANNE S.K. BROWN MILITARY COLLECTION, BROWN UNIVERSITY LIBRARY.

In the early spring of 1794, an effective British maritime campaign against American commerce in the West Indies brought the two countries to the brink of war. While the Congress was enacting legislation to prepare for war, a small group of influential senators, including Ellsworth, decided that war could be best averted by simultaneously preparing for war and sending an envoy to England to adjust the two countries' differences. Ellsworth went to President Washington as the group's representative and proposed the mission. The President agreed, and in the spring of 1794 Chief Justice Jay was despatched as special envoy to Great Britain. Jay returned the next year with a treaty and almost immediately resigned his chief justiceship to become Governor of New York. President Washington then offered the position of chief justice to John Rutledge of South Carolina.[2]

Meanwhile the Jay Treaty was being considered by the Senate in closed executive session where it met severe opposition from southern senators. Nevertheless, the Federalists, led by Oliver Ellsworth, approved the Treaty by a close vote of 20-10. When the terms of the treaty were published, most of the nation was furious. Britain had prevailed on virtually every issue in controversy. From the American point of view, the best that could be said was that the Treaty avoided a war and established a diplomatic precedent that under certain circumstances Britain was willing to enter into a treaty with the United States. Many viewed the Treaty as a national humiliation. Laborers demonstrated on the Fourth of July in Philadelphia, the nation's capital. They burned

John Jay in effigy, and overpowered a force of cavalry called out to quell the "riot." Alexander Hamilton was stoned in New York. In the midst of these ignominious affronts to Federalist policy came a hubbub in Charleston, South Carolina. Mobs rioted for two days in opposition to the Treaty, and on the third day at a public meeting John Rutledge vehemently attacked the Treaty and Jay. Unfortunately for him a detailed account of his intemperate speech was published in newspapers throughout the nation, and his appointment as chief justice was doomed. Although he served briefly under a recess appointment as the second Chief Justice of the United States, the Senate rejected his nomination in December of 1795.[3]

### ☙  ELLSWORTH BECOMES CHIEF JUSTICE

Rutledge was, above all else, a gentleman whom Washington trusted. After Rutledge was rejected by the Senate, the President turned to another trusted personal acquaintance—Patrick Henry—but Henry declined. The President wrote that this inability to find a new Chief Justice was "embarrassing in the extreme," and perhaps in desperation he nominated William Cushing, the Court's senior Associate Justice. But Cushing also declined. Washington was unwilling to take any more chances, and he turned to Oliver Ellsworth. The President presumably did not nominate Ellsworth earlier because Ellsworth was the linchpin to the Federalists' control of the Senate. But Washington needed a Chief Justice with solid Federalist credentials and an equally solid reputation for sound judgment, and Ellsworth was the man.[4]

Ellsworth was nominated on March 3, 1796 and confirmed by the Senate the next day. Almost immediately he became embroiled in another facet of the general controversy over the Jay Treaty. As a practical matter, the Treaty could not be implemented without money, and the Treaty's opponents had seized upon the appropriations process in the House of Representatives as an opportunity to reconsider the Treaty's merits. Ellsworth was keenly aware of these legislative maneuvers, and just a few days before he became Chief Justice he wrote his wife, "there remains yet to be made one violent effort in the House of Representatives to destroy the Treaty." He had faith, however, "that the effort will be unsuccessful and that the Treaty will be carried into effect, which the honor and interest of this Country very much requires."[5]

On March 7, 1796, the day before Ellsworth took his oath of office as Chief Justice, the House demanded that the President turn over all documents relevant to the Treaty's negotiation. Today most Justices would remain aloof from controversies between the executive and legislative branches, but Ellsworth apparently saw no reason for restraint. On March 13, five days after becoming Chief Justice, he wrote a detailed private advisory opinion on the House's authority to demand the documents.[6]

Ellsworth's opinion took the form of a nine page letter to Connecticut Senator Jonathan Trumbull and was intended to be an advisory opinion. Senator Trumbull had discussed the Treaty a few days earlier with President Washington, and after that discussion Trumbull asked Ellsworth for a legal analysis of the issues. Ellsworth's letter contains no chit-chat and no customary closing enquiry about the well being of

Trumbull's family or mutual friends. Instead the letter is devoted exclusively to the legal questions presented by the House's demand for documents. Ellsworth predictably concluded that the House lacked authority either to reject the Treaty or to demand the documents. Although the letter was addressed to Senator Trumbull, it wound up in President Washington's files docketed under the subject "treaty making power." Whether Ellsworth knew that his opinion would be passed on to the President is not known to a certainty, but as a shrewd and knowledgeable politician he must have known or anticipated this event. In any case the letter obviously was intended by the Chief Justice as a detailed advisory opinion on a hotly debated constitutional controversy.[7]

Almost as soon as Ellsworth delivered his advisory opinion, he wrote his wife with "some pain" that he had to ride the Southern Circuit that spring and preside over the federal circuit courts in each southern state. A month later he convened the Circuit Court in Savannah, Georgia, and delivered a grand jury charge that was published in at least twelve newspapers in eight different states. Following the custom of the times, Ellsworth's charge was not so much an explanation of criminal law as it was a political essay extolling the federal government's righteous order. In particular, he explained that

> The national laws are the national ligatures and vehicles of life. Tho'
> they pervade a country, as diversified in habits, as it is vast in extent, yet
> they give to the whole, harmony of interest, and unity of design.

His emphasis upon "harmony of interest, and unity of design" is a restatement of the Calvinist vision of a perfect society, and in the next sentence he expressly affirmed that the federal government was part of God's plan. The national laws, he said, "are the means by which it pleases heaven to make of weak and discordant parts, one great people."[8]

While Ellsworth was penning his grand jury charge, he was undoubtedly concerned about the Jay Treaty's fate in the House of Representatives. In the charge he applauded the wisdom of distributing legislative power to two "maturing and balancing bodies, instead of the subjection of it to momentary impulse, and the predominance of faction." In this regard he probably considered the Senate to be "maturing and balancing" and the House to be subject to "momentary impulse, and . . . faction." Notwithstanding his concern about the Treaty's fate, his private conviction was that the Treaty would be funded, and on April 30 the House approved the required funds by a close vote of 51–48.[9]

The legislative victory in the House confirmed Ellsworth's Calvinist understanding of government under the relatively new Constitution. Soon after learning about the Jay Treaty's victory in the House, he reiterated the basic principle of *The Wisdom of God* to his son-in-law, Ezekiel Williams. "Of politicks," he wrote Williams, "I will converse with you when I come, and am satisfied in the mean time that God governs the world, & will turn all the wrath & folly of men to good account." At about the same time, he reassured President Washington that "the publick mind, as well Southward as elsewhere, is pretty tranquil, and much more so than it would have been had our Country [, through a failure to fund the Treaty,] been dishonored and exposed by a violation of her faith."[10]

After defending the wisdom of the federal government in his charge to the Georgia grand jury, Ellsworth proceeded from Savannah to South Carolina where he dealt with the important neutrality question of whether the Jay Treaty forbade the French to sell British prizes in American ports notwithstanding an ambiguous provision possibly to the contrary in the Treaty of Alliance with France. The British Consul in Charleston initially asked the local Federal District Judge to rule on this issue, but the judge, who usually ruled against the British, seized upon a technicality and refused to decide the matter. As soon as Chief Justice Ellsworth arrived in town, the Consul renewed his petition, and Ellsworth immediately heard the case and gave full effect to the Jay Treaty."[11]

Later that spring the Chief Justice held court in North Carolina and in *Hamiltons v. Eaton* addressed a conflict between British creditors' treaty rights to recover debts and a North Carolina statute designed to impede those rights. Ellsworth had not participated in the Supreme Court's earlier decision of *Ware v. Hylton* in which the Court held that national treaties override state laws, so he used the North Carolina case to pronounce his views on the subject and to reaffirm the supremacy of federal law over state law. Among other things, he brushed aside the defendant debtor's argument that the Treaty of Paris was an improper taking of the defendant's private property. Ellsworth met the argument head on and bluntly ruled, "It is justifiable and frequent, in the adjustments of national differences, to concede for the safety of the state, the rights of individuals."[12]

## ☙ CHIEF JUSTICE ELLSWORTH'S SUPREME COURT OPINIONS

Ellsworth had played a commanding role in the creation and initial operations of the Federal government, but his service as Chief Justice was somewhat anticlimactic. He took his oath of office too late to participate in the Court's decisions in *Ware v. Hylton*, holding that national treaties override state laws, and *Hylton v. United States*, giving an expansive reading to the government's constitutional power to tax. Similarly, four years later in 1800, he was in Europe on an important diplomatic mission when the Court decided *Bas. v. Tingy* and *Cooper v. Telfair*. In between these four decisions, illness caused him to miss most of the Court's February terms. So far example, he did not participate in *Calder v. Bull*.[13]

Ellsworth probably viewed *United States v. La Vengeance* as his most important Supreme Court decision. The case involved a french privateer, *La Vengeance*, that was seized by the government for exporting arms and munitions in violation of a federal embargo act. The government obtained a judgment of forfeiture from a federal district court sitting as an admiralty court without a jury, but on appeal to the circuit court, this judgment overturned. The government then took the case to the Supreme Court where Attorney General Lee argued that the whole case should be thrown out because the suit was not tried to a jury.[14]

This objection was based upon Ellsworth's Judiciary Act that required all issues of fact to be tried by jury except in Admiralty cases. Relying upon settled principles of Admiralty law, Attorney General Lee argued that Admiralty cases must arise wholly upon the sea and the exportation of munitions is done partially on land. This argument seems a bit technical, but it made a good deal of sense to eighteenth-century lawyers. Just five month's earlier, the Supreme Court followed settled English precedent in holding that admiralty jurisdiction did not extend to enforcing a contract for the construction of a ship. Moreover, Peter Du Ponceau, counsel for the privateer, was convinced that Attorney General Lee's jury-trial analysis was correct—so correct that Du Ponceau planned to "make no opposition." This planned capitulation was not based solely upon Du Ponceau's personal judgment. Before the case was argued, he wrote his co-counsel, "The general sense of the Court & Bar is in favor of the Jury trial."[15]

Du Ponceau could not have been more mistaken. Two days later, when argument in the case began, the Court peremptorily announced that the case was within the federal courts' admiralty jurisdiction. Nevertheless, the Attorney General was allowed to present a detailed argument on the issue. The case was then taken under advisement overnight, and the next morning Chief Justice Ellsworth announced that "the court did not feel any reason to change the opinion, which they had formed upon opening the case." Dallas's report of the case does not indicate that Ellsworth gave an explanation of this decision other than to assert that "exportation is entirely a water transaction."[16]

Ellsworth's seemingly summary treatment of the Attorney General's argument is puzzling in view of Du Ponceau's report that the "general sense of the Court & Bar is in favor of the Jury trial." Some twelve years later Justice Chase explained what had happened. Justice Chase recollected that the Court had not been concerned about traditional principles of Admiralty law. Instead, he explained, "The reason of the legislature for putting seizures of this kind on the admiralty side of the court was the great danger to the revenue if such cases should be left to the caprice of juries."[17]

Perhaps some members of the Court in *La Vengeance* were initially persuaded by the Attorney General's analysis, but at least two of the Justices were not. If Chase's recollection that the Court's decision was based upon a legislative intent to protect revenue collection from "the caprice of juries" is accurate, the rationale of legislative intent undoubtedly came from Chief Justice Ellsworth and Justice Paterson. As senators, they had personally drafted the Judiciary Act, and they were especially interested in establishing an adequate and dependable stream of federal revenue.

In drafting the statutory language vesting the federal district courts with an admiralty jurisdiction to enforce revenue laws, Ellsworth had expressly expanded the Court's admiralty jurisdiction well beyond the traditional common-law limits. *La Vengeance* was not a suit to enforce revenue laws, but the statutory language at issue also governed forfeitures under revenue laws. Therefore, a Supreme Court decision following the Attorney General's analysis would almost inevitably have expanded the right to a trial by jury in revenue cases. When the Judiciary Act was being debated in the Senate, Justice Paterson had successfully argued that revenue collection should not be left to state courts because "state officers will feel it their Interest to consult the Temper of the People of the State in which they live rather than of the Union." If Justice Chase's recollection was correct, Paterson and Ellsworth used a similar argument in *La Vengeance* to exclude juries—who represented the local temper of the people—from the federal courts' enforcement of revenue laws. Of course, the rationale was applicable only to revenue laws bearing upon maritime commerce, but in the 1790s such laws accounted for almost 90 percent of federal revenues.[18]

The Court's expansive approach to federal admiralty jurisdiction in *La Vengeance* is similar to an earlier decision in *Glass v. The Sloop Betsy*. In both cases the expansion of federal judicial power was at the expense of settled rules of admiralty jurisdiction. Moreover, both decisions were evidently motivated by national security concerns. In *Glass*, the Court was confronted with an ongoing crisis caused by the depredations of French privateers. In *La Vengeance*, the Court facilitated revenue collection necessary to finance the federal government, including its military establishment. In each case the Court was willing to issue a fiat overturning settled admiralty law with little or not explanation. In contrast, in cases like the ship-contract case where national security was not at issue, the Court followed settled admiralty law without a qualm.[19]

Another significant aspect of *La Vengeance* involves the manner in which the Court announced its opinion. Before Ellsworth became Chief Justice, the Court frequently had followed the English common-law practice in which, beginning with the Court's junior member, each Justice would deliver his individual opinion and justification of how the case before the Court should be decided. In *La Vengeance*, however, this tradition of delivering seriatim opinions was not followed. Nor did the Court issue a per curiam decision. Instead, Chief Justice Ellsworth delivered a consolidated majority opinion from which Justice Chase dissented.

In eschewing seriatim opinions, Ellsworth was simply following the practice to which he had become accustomed when he served upon the Connecticut Superior Court from 1784 to 1789. The year that he became a state judge, the Connecticut legislature passed a statute requiring that in cases turning upon an issue of law, "each one [of the Superior Judges must] give his opinion *seriatim* with the Reasons thereof, and the same reduce to Writing." The purpose of this statute was to facilitate appeals from the Superior Court and to lay "a foundation . . . for a more perfect and permanent System of Common Law in this State." Although the statute called for written seriatim opinions, the Superior Court adopted an almost uniform practice of writing majority and dissenting opinions. Perhaps the judges adopted this approach to save the judicial labor involved in having every judge write a formal opinion in every case.[20]

Before Ellsworth became Chief Justice, the Court had not developed a firm tradition regarding the use of either seriatim or majority opinions. In some cases it delivered seriatim opinions, and in others it might deliver a simple majority opinion coupled with a dissenting opinion. In one case the Court delivered seriatim opinions on one aspect of the case and a majority opinion on another aspect. In 1795 an attorney reported that the Court delivered seriatim opinions when "a difference in opinion exists on the Bench," but his statement cannot be taken literally. The Court subsequently used seriatim opinions to announce unanimous decisions in *Talbot v. Jansen* and *Hylton v. United States* and a majority opinion to announce a split decision in *United States v. Peters.*[21]

After Ellsworth became Chief Justice, a clear pattern emerged in which he would personally deliver short opinions of the Court, infrequently supplemented by dissenting or concurring opinions. From Dallas's Reports it appears that the Court delivered seriatim opinions only once when Ellsworth participated in the decision. When Ellsworth was not participating, the Court might deliver seriatim opinions, or the senior associate Justice might deliver a majority opinion. By 1800 the practice was so well established that Justice Chase was surprised when the Court delivered seriatim opinions in *Bas v. Tingy* while Chief Justice Ellsworth was in Europe. "The Judges agreeing unanimously in their opinion, I presumed," said Chase, "that the sense of the Court would have been delivered by the president."[22]

This custom of using majority rather than seriatim opinions became entrenched during Chief Justice Marshall's tenure and has endured to the present. Majority opinions have played a subtle but significant role in establishing the Supreme Court's hegemony over the Constitution's interpretation. A contrary tradition of seriatim opinions would have splintered many of the Court's opinions into the relatively isolated and more or less different views of the various Justices. In contrast, a single majority opinion makes it easier for the Court to speak with a single authoritative voice.

In *La Vengeance*, Ellsworth was not so much concerned with legal theory as he was with bolstering the government's effective enforcement of revenue laws. His decision supports the judgment of a fellow Connecticut lawyer who knew and respected him and who wrote that Ellsworth's services in the Senate had "accustomed [him] to view things as a politician, rather than a lawyer." This same *realpolitik* is evident in two of the Chief Justice's decisions on the important Constitutional issue of Congressional control over the federal courts' subject matter jurisdiction. In *Wiscart v. Dauchy* and *Turner v. The Bank of North America*, he supported a virtually plenary Congressional control over the courts' jurisdiction.[23]

Chief Justice Ellsworth, however, did not view judicial decisionmaking as simply the unbridled exercise of political power. His decisions in *Wiscart* and *Turner* were based upon a sophisticated and careful analysis of the words of the Constitution and the agreements reached in the Convention, which the Constitution's words were intended to embody. Today, some two hundred years later, his understanding of Congressional control over the federal courts' jurisdiction is the orthodox view of this complicated issue. In politically sensitive cases, Chief Justice Ellsworth typically was more interested in the long term consequences of his decisions than in the immediate result. In *Moodie v. The Ship Phoebe Anne*, he dealt with the sensitive issue of the extent to which America's Revolutionary War Treaty with France gave French privateers the right to refit their cruisers in America ports. The attorney for the British argued "the impolicy and inconvenience of suffering privateers to equip in our ports." Ellsworth had no desire to support the French, but he firmly rejected this analysis. "Suggestions of policy and conveniency cannot be considered," he said, "in the judicial determination of a question of right: the Treaty with France, whatever that is, must have its effect." He then ruled in favor of the French privateer. Ellsworth was more interested in the long term enforcement of United States treaties than in the immediate result of the case before him.[24]

## ☙ EVENTS LEADING TO ELLSWORTH'S RESIGNATION

Although President Washington finally decided that summer not to seek a third term of office, Ellsworth's faith in the federal government was not shaken. In the Fall of 1796, he optimistically wrote a good friend and fellow Calvinist that "we may however yet hope that the gates of Hell will not prevail." His reference to the Book of Matthew 16:18 was used by Connecticut Calvinists to assure themselves and others that God was looking after their institutions. Ellsworth continued in a Calvinist strain by "pray[ing] especially that good men everywhere may make their Election sure." Ellsworth was clearly writing about politics, but he could not have meant the word "Election" to refer specifically to the coming political elections because all "good men everywhere" were not running for election. Instead, he was referring to God's election of good men for salvation. In Ellsworth's mind, God's elect were voters who supported the federal government, and they found further evidence of their personal Election when they voted properly in the November elections. When the Fifth Congress was convened in 1797, the Federalists had a majority in both houses. Moreover, John Adams, whom Ellsworth had fully supported, continued the Federalists' control of the Presidency.[25]

Notwithstanding the Federalist electoral triumphs, 1797 was a bad year for Ellsworth. The Supreme Court was convened in early February, but Ellsworth could not attend because he was sick. He probably was suffering from gout and gravel. The latter extremely painful illness usually appears in middle age and is caused by either a hereditary metabolic disorder or excessive accumulations of lead in the body (among eighteenth-century English-speaking people typically from drinking large quantities of port wine). The illness is not degenerative, but it afflicted him with sporadic bouts of intense pain until he died in 1807. By the middle of March he reported to his son-in-law that his health was "pretty well restoring," and he was ready to ride the Eastern Circuit.[26]

While Ellsworth was recovering from his illness, he and other Federalists were deeply disturbed by a worsening of relations with France and the impact of Franco-American relations upon domestic American politics. The previous year the French had unsuccessfully attempted to bring about the election of Thomas Jefferson to the presidency. After John Adams was elected, they refused to accredit a new American minister to France and increased their maritime depredations on American commerce.

These hostile actions caused the Federalists to believe that war with France was likely. At the same time Jeffersonian Republicans seemed to support France. The Republicans' domestic support for French misconduct outraged New England Federalists. In early April, Ellsworth's friend Connecticut Senator Uriah Tracy wrote, "I presume we shall see at the coming Session of Congress the humiliating spectacle of a considerable number of the members of the Government take side with France & justify all the depredations." Tracy continued, "if we must suffer the French Nation to interfere with our politics—by reason of a Geographical division of Sentiment, perversely bent on humiliating their own government to a foreign one—why then, Sir, I hesitate not a moment in saying a separation of the Union is inevitable."[27]

On the same day that Senator Tracy was speculating about a "separation of the Union," Chief Justice Ellsworth delivered an embarrassing grand jury charge in New York. The combination of his painful kidney ailment and uncertainty about the impact of relations with France upon domestic politics caused him to rail against "the baleful influence of those elements of disorganization, & tenets of impiety." He warned the nation that there were "impassioned" and "impious" people who are "radically hostile to free government." Even worse, this "disaffection . . . opens a door to foreign [i.e., French] influence, that 'destroying angel of republics.'" All in all, the charge verged upon disjointed hysteria.[28]

A writer in the New York *Argus* disliked the religious undertone of Ellsworth's charge and wrote, "I like neither his politics nor his religion." After reading the charge, Abigail Adams was so exasperated that she wrote her husband, "did the good gentleman never write before? can it be genuine? . . . I am Sorry it was ever published." Perhaps during this time Ellsworth—like his friend Senator Tracy—began to have serious doubts about the viability of the new federal government. Within three years the Chief Justice was privately stating "that there is in a government like ours a natural antipathy to system of every kind." These were strong words indeed for a man who worshiped system and order.[29]

If Ellsworth was pessimistic as early as 1797 about the federal government's basic viability, his doubts were temporarily abated by a speech that President Adams delivered to a special session of Congress in the middle of May. To counter the French depredations, Adams chose the same strategy that Ellsworth had recommended to President Washington three years earlier during the war scare with Great Britain. Adams committed the nation to attempt an "amicable negotiation" with France and simultaneously urged Congress to enact "effectual measures of defense." This strategy received immediate widespread public approval, and by the end of May Ellsworth was feeling "triumph[ant]" that the President's speech had strengthened the Federalists' "political faith."[30]

The next winter of 1798 brought a recurrence of Ellsworth's painful illness. In January he was "considerably unwell." By February he was somewhat better but reported that his "want of health . . . requires that my movements shall be gentle & cautious." The illness continued into March, and he determined to ride a reduced circuit comprising only the states of Vermont and New Hampshire. He asked his

Calvinist friend, Justice Cushing, to take Massachusetts and Rhode Island and offered "to furnish a little money for [Cushing's] expenses." Ellsworth explained that he was offering money "as it may never be in my power to repay you in kind [i.e., by riding circuit for Cushing]." This ominous explanation indicates that as early as April, 1798, Ellsworth was contemplating vacating his position by resignation or possibly death.[31]

There is no evidence that Ellsworth's illness recurred in the winter of 1799, and that year he was able to preside over the Supreme Court's February term for the first and only time during his chief justiceship. With his health restored he bent to the wheel of government and vigorously participated in attempts to resolve domestic and foreign policy issues arising from the ongoing dispute with France. Ellsworth had been pleased with President Adams' decision in 1797 to attempt an "amicable negotiation" of the two nations' differences, but the upshot of the negotiation was disastrous. When the American diplomatic mission arrived in Europe the next year, the French demanded bribes as a condition to opening formal negotiations, and the mission fell through. The mission's failure, which became known as the XYZ Affair, exacerbated the rift in Franco-American relations. Relatively minor maritime skirmishing in the West Indies was escalated to a limited Quasi War, and on the domestic front Congress enacted the Sedition Act to discourage criticism of the government. Ellsworth began 1799 by writing private and public advisory opinions calculated to establish the Act's constitutionality. He finished the year on a diplomatic mission to Europe to negotiate an end to the war.[32]

When the Sedition Act was initially debated in Congress, the measure's opponents vehemently attacked it as unconstitutional, and the Federalists responded that the Act would be a proper use of the Constitution's "necessary and proper" clause to protect the federal government. In addition, the Federalists had a powerful argument based upon the federal courts' preexisting authority to try common-law crimes. The idea of common-law crimes was based upon a natural-law belief that certain activities were inherently criminal even in the absence of a statute formally declaring them to be criminal. These activities included conduct like counterfeiting, bribing a public officer, and seditious libel. Because the existence of the common-law doctrine of seditious libel was not seriously controverted, the only issue was whether common-law crimes against federal interests should be tried in state courts or federal courts. The Federalists believed that common-law crimes against the federal government obviously should be tried in federal court. Therefore the Sedition Act was constitutional because it was essentially a codification of a common-law authority that the federal courts already had.[33]

Because the logic of the Federalists' constitutional argument was unassailable, the opponents of the Sedition Act had to attack the argument's underlying premise. The opposition could not deny the existence of common-law crimes without appearing foolish or ignorant, so they were forced to deny that the federal courts had authority to punish them. Presumably they would have conceded that the state courts had such authority. The opposition's arguments, however, were unavailing, and Congress passed the Sedition Act in the summer of 1798.[34]

In the 1790's, Cabinet responsibility for supervising the U.S. Attorneys' criminal prosecutions in the various states was allocated to the Secretary of State rather than the Attorney General, and Secretary of State Timothy Pickering evidently had some concerns about the Sedition Act. In 1796 Secretary Pickering had noted in official correspondence that on "weighty points" of law he could consult the Attorney General and that he also could consult Supreme Court Justices, whom he called "our first law characters." Moreover, that same year Pickering actually sought Chief Justice Ellsworth's legal advice in coordinating ongoing litigation in the federal courts. Consistent with this prior practice, the Secretary evidently sought the Chief Justice's advice on the Sedition Act's constitutionality. In any event in a letter penned to Secretary Pickering in December 1798, Ellsworth opined that the Act was constitutional. Like other Federalists, the Chief Justice believed that because the Act was a codification—actually, an amelioration—of the federal courts' pre-existing authority to punish common-law seditious libel, the Act's constitutionality was not subject to serious dispute. Ellsworth evidently had no qualms about giving an advisory opinion on a statute that he might subsequently have to administer in a criminal trial.[35]

Ellsworth's remarkable advisory opinion did not end his ex-parte defense of the Sedition Act. In early 1799, the Act's opponents unveiled a new argument. The linchpin of the constitutional argument in favor of the Act's constitutionality was the federal courts' pre-existing authority over common-law crimes. During a congressional reconsideration of the Act in February of that year, Representative Wilson Cary Nicholas challenged the federal courts' pretension to common-law jurisdiction as a dangerous arrogation of federal authority. Because the common law was "a complete system" that regulated all human relations, the federal courts' jurisdiction must extend to all human conduct, and Congress's legislative authority must be equally comprehensive. In other words, Nicholas argued that the constitutional implication of the Federalists' position was to consolidate virtually all state authority into the federal government.[36]

Chief Justice Ellsworth almost immediately began writing another advisory opinion to counter this new argument, and in May he presented his comprehensive analysis of federal common-law crimes in a charge to a grand jury in South Carolina. The charge was published in at least eleven newspapers in eight different states. Ellsworth used a traditional natural-law analysis to establish the fundamental validity of the doctrine of federal common-law crimes. Like Representative Nicholas and virtually all American lawyers, Ellsworth assumed that the common law—like the law of gravity—existed in nature independent of government. Representative Nicholas had argued that to recognize a federal common-law jurisdiction would give the federal courts complete power over all human affairs, but Ellsworth emphatically rejected this idea. Given the fact that the common law of crimes already existed in nature, the federal courts seemed to be the most appropriate forum for punishing crimes against the national government. Ellsworth advised the grand jury (and the nation) that the doctrine was limited to acts "manifestly subversive of the national government" and emphasized that he said "manifestly subversive, to exclude acts of doubtful tendency, and confine criminality to clearness and certainty."[37]

In addition to explaining the substantive limits of the unwritten criminal law, Ellsworth saw the grand jury process itself as a procedural limit to common-law pros-ecutions. He cautioned the grand jurors that an indictment must not "be founded on suspicion; and much less on prepossession" and reminded the jurors that they were "a shield from oppression [and not] the *instruments* of it." He concluded by emphasizing that grand jurors should not investigate "the *opinions* of men, but their *actions*, and weigh them, not in the scales of *passion*, or of *party*, but in a *legal* balance—a balance that is undeceptive—which vibrates not with popular opinion; and which flatters not the pride of birth, or encroachments of power."[38]

At the same time that the Chief Justice was defending the Sedition Act and the doctrine of federal common-law crimes, he was participating directly in efforts to resolve the diplomatic impasse between the United States and France. The previous fall, the government of France intimated to William Vans Murray, the United States Minister Resident to The Hague, that a new diplomatic mission to France for the resolution of the nation's differences would be received favorably. President Adams kept this overture secret because his Secretaries of State, War, and Treasury were High Federalists. They deferred to Alexander Hamilton, abhorred Adams' modera-tion, and sought war with France. In February of 1799 Adams nominated Murray to be Minister Plenipotentiary to France without prior cabinet consultation, but this sur-prise nomination was dead on arrival. As one High Federalist wrote, when the pro-posal was made public, "Surprise, indignation, grief & disgust followed each other in quick succession in the breasts of the true friends of our country." A Select Commit-tee was appointed by the Senate to consider the matter, but a private meeting between the senators and the President degenerated into a shouting match.[39]

Although Chief Justice Ellsworth was quite friendly with and was respected by most of the High Federalists, he was not one himself. He had been a firm supporter of President Adams from the beginning. In addition Ellsworth was philosophically in-clined to seek political compromises. He was in the capital when Murray's name was submitted to the Senate and undoubtedly was appalled by the explosive shouting match between the President and the Select Committee. After this disaster, he reportedly took it upon himself to speak privately with the President and managed to convince Adams to appoint three ministers instead of one. The basic idea was that the three would represent different interests and guarantee that any peace would be negotiated on acceptable terms.[40]

The President decided to name Ellsworth and Patrick Henry as the two additional nominees, and Ellsworth was in no position to refuse. Patrick Henry, however, did refuse, and the President subsequently had a number of conversations with Ellsworth in which either Ellsworth or Adams mentioned Governor William Davie of North Carolina as a possible replacement. When Ellsworth rode the Southern Circuit that spring, he consulted with Davie and recommended his appointment. Following this recommendation, the President then formally nominated Davie.[41]

Ellsworth did not really want to go to France and feared that the voyage would bring him illness. Nevertheless, he told the President to "disregard any supposed pains or perils that might attend me from a voige at one season more than another." Finally he and Davie set sail in early November and after a rough passage of twenty-four days made a landfall in Portugal. Unfortunately, however, his journey to Paris was not even half way through. From Portugal they set sail for France, "but were 10 days in getting out of the harbour owing to contrary winds, and were afterward 25 days at sea in a succession of storms one of which lasted 8 days, and were after all obliged to put into . . . a port in Spain about . . . 900 [miles] from Paris." Then they traveled overland in the dead of winter. After a journey of nine weeks in which their carriages broke down and they wound up on horseback, they arrived in Paris in early March.[42]

During his arduous trip by sea and land, Ellsworth's painful kidney ailment recurred and continued throughout the negotiations with the French government. This personal catastrophe, however, did not keep him from playing a leading role in the negotiations, and after six months, a compromise was reached. The naval war in the West Indies was terminated, and the two countries formally agreed to suspend embarrassing Franco-American treaties dating from the Revolutionary War and the period of the Confederacy. These aspects of the compromise were all well and good, but Ellsworth and his fellow commissioners had been instructed to insist that the French government compensate the United States for almost $20 million in spoliations against American commerce. As his opinion in *Hamiltons v. Eaton* indicates, Ellsworth was perfectly willing to override individual property rights to secure safety for the nation. To obtain peace, he agreed to drop this important claim.[43]

Ellsworth knew that the abandonment of the spoliation claims would outrage his High Federalist friends who were opposed even to the idea of negotiating with France, but he did not care. He had been a politician for nearly his entire adult life and was satisfied that "more could not be done without too great a sacrifice, and . . . it was better to sign a convention than to do nothing." Moreover, his righteous self-confidence gave him the inner strength to accept the High Federalists' inevitable snide attacks with equanimity. "If," he wrote, "there must be any burning on the occasion, let them take me, who am so near dead already with the gravel & gout in my kidnies, that roasting would do me but little damage."[44]

## ☙ ELLSWORTH'S RESIGNATION AND FINAL YEARS

In addition to accepting full political responsibility for the treaty, Ellsworth did something quite uncharacteristic. He resigned his chief justiceship. Although Ellsworth's illness clearly played a role in his resignation from the Supreme Court, his health was not the primary reason for the resignation. Instead, his ill health probably made him unusually susceptible to a growing suspicion that the federal government was no longer a milestone on the direct path to a graceful national order. In 1796, he had confidently pronounced that the federal government would give "harmony of interest, and unity of design" to the country. But by 1800 he was thinking "that there is in a government like ours a natural antipathy to system of every kind." If the federal government was

Oliver Ellsworth (1800) by William Vans Murray. In 1800 William Vans Murray portrayed Ellsworth as thinner and more haggard than the Sharples pastel on the cover of this book. The Sharples picture was done three years earlier.
COURTESY LIBRARY OF CONGRESS.

not to play a direct positive role in God's plan, Ellsworth, who knew himself to be one of God's elect, would have found continued federal service to be galling and surely would have preferred devoting himself to his orderly and righteous state of Connecticut. At the same time, however, there was something inherently dishonorable about quitting. In early middle age, Ellsworth had described himself as a soldier in public service and affirmed that "when a soldier goes forth in publick service he must stay until he is discharged, and though the weather be stormy and his allowance small yet he must stand to his post."[45] His unbending noblesse oblige may have caused him to place inordinate emphasis upon his illness as the reason for not standing to his post. Certainly a good soldier in public service could not be criticized if a serious illness beyond his control forced his discharge.

Shortly after Ellsworth resigned, John Adams' loss in the 1800 presidential election confirmed Ellsworth's Calvinist pessimism about the national government. On hearing of Jefferson's victory, Ellsworth compared the task of governing under the Constitution to the legend of Sisyphus. "So," he wrote, "the Antifeds are now to support their own administration and take a turn at rolling stones up hill." This legend would have been particularly appealing to a Calvinist like Ellsworth who believed generally in predestination and specifically that governments were part of God's plan. Sisyphus was a clever ruler who tricked and betrayed the gods and who, as an exemplary punishment, was doomed by the gods to his eternal task. Like Sisyphus, Jefferson was a clever ruler, and many New England Calvinists believed that he had betrayed God. By suggesting that Jefferson was as certainly doomed as Sisyphus, Ellsworth was reaffirming that the federal government with Jefferson at the helm was part of God's plan.[46]

Notwithstanding Ellsworth's pessimism, the essential optimism of *The Wisdom of God* prevailed as he regained his health. Shortly after writing about "rolling stones up hill," he commented that

> Jefferson ... dare not run the ship aground, nor essentially deviate from that course which has hitherto rendered her voyage so prosperous. His

> party also must support the Government while he administers it, and if others are consistent & do the same, the Government may even be consolidated & acquire new confidence.

Later he confided to his son-in-law that "Mr. Jefferson's Presidency may be turned to good account if people will let their reason & not their passions tell them how to manage."[47]

The traditional explanation for Ellsworth's resignation is that "the ministerial journey to the continent broke his health," and undoubtedly his recurring sickness played a role in motivating his resignation. But the myth of broken health should not be taken at face value. In 1778 he partially justified his resignation from Connecticut's Committee of the Pay Table on the ground that "his health [had been] sensibly impaired," and in 1784 he again used "my health" as a ground for refusing an appointment by the Continental Congress to the newly created Board of Treasury. His health did not prevent him from leading an active life after 1778 and again after 1784, and it did not slow him down after 1800. He continued to be mentally and physically active. For example, upon returning to Connecticut he insisted on walking a little over a mile to church each week rather than riding a carriage. The winter after his return from Europe he invited five young men to study with him as law clerks, and in 1804 he began a regular series of essays and notes on agricultural topics in the Connecticut Courant.[48]

More significantly, his 1800 resignation was by no means a retirement from public life. He retired from the national political arena but continued to play an active role in Connecticut public life until a few months before he died. In 1802 he was elected to the upper house of the state legislature and was reelected each year for the rest of his life. As the leading member of that body, he chaired and played an active role in the 1802 attempt to resolve the Baptist Petition movement. In 1805 he led the upper house's consideration of and personally drafted the resolutions rejecting two proposed amendments to the United States Constitution. That same year he served on the three-person committee charged with remodeling the state's judiciary system.[49]

In addition to his legislative services, Ellsworth's position in the legislature automatically made him an appellate judge because in Connecticut the upper house also was the Supreme Court of Errors. Ellsworth was a dominant member of the court and personally wrote many of its opinions. Although Day's Reports does not tell who wrote the opinions, surviving dockets assigning opinion-writing responsibility for the court's June terms of 1803 and 1804 indicate that only one member of the court wrote more opinions than Ellsworth.[50]

Although Ellsworth continued to play an active part in Connecticut society and politics, his illness remained. While in Europe he had taken the waters at Bath, and back in Connecticut he frequented a mineral spring in Suffield. These treatments lessened his problems, but the illness always returned. In 1807 he accepted the newly created office of Chief Justice of Connecticut, but he declined the post that summer for reasons of health. In the fall, his illness increased to the point that he suffered excruciating pain and at times lost his reason. On November 28, 1807, he died in his home.[51]

### CHAPTER NINE

# An Assessment

OR THOSE WHO LIVE in the late twentieth century, the most fascinating aspect of Ellsworth's genius for pragmatic politics is the extent to which he so thoroughly integrated his religion into his political life. He would have been astounded by the notion that a politician's private faith might be separated from his public life. If Ellsworth lost sight of his religion in following a particular course of political action, he would have lost sight of his love of God. No matter how beneficial the action might be, it would have been done without a love of God in his heart and therefore would have been sinful. Cyprian Strong who served with Ellsworth on the committee that drafted the *Summary of Christian Doctrine* was quite clear on the impossibility of a government official being neutral on religious matters. Quoting Matthew 12:30, Strong reasoned:

> "He that is not with me is against me: and he that gathereth not with me scattereth abroad." There is according to these words of Christ, no such thing as neutrality. And this is as true, respecting civil government, as respecting an individual.[1]

In truth under Ellsworth's firm Calvinist believe in predestination, all human action— whether it be private or public—was part of the seamless web that was God's plan, and any failure by a human being to keep sight of love for God was sinful.

Ellsworth's New Divinity Calvinism provided him with a wonderfully cohesive model of human society that was impervious to critique. At the core of this model was an all-powerful, all-wise God, who had perfectly predestined all human conduct and who had selected a comparatively few human beings for salvation. This fundamental core belief generated a coherent explanation of the entire human experience and was unshakeable. The core did not give way to the jarring reality of evilness in the world. Instead evilness was made part of God's plan. Nor did the core give way to the problem of holding individuals morally accountable for actions that were utterly beyond their control because those actions were predestined by God. Instead human accountability was shifted from the theater of action to a metaphysical realm where internal disposition ruled.

Ellsworth's New Divinity faith was subject to powerful rational objections, but the objections were essentially incoherent to him. His understanding of the entire human experience was like a solar system in which God's predestined plan was the sun and complicating ideas like the existence of evil and the problem of free will were planets whose orbits were controlled by the sun. Within his mind, the doctrine of predestination achieved its absolutely privileged position on the basis of faith alone, and only a loss of faith could budge it from that position. In Ellsworth's case, a loss of faith was unthinkable because he had personally experienced his election by God. He knew that he was saved and any loss of faith in God's absolute governance would have removed the basis for his salvation.

In the realm of politics, Ellsworth's faith reinforced his steadfast inclination to hard work and made him the epitome of Max Weber's protestant work ethic. No task was too small; no task was too difficult. As a young man he embraced the tedious work of Connecticut's Committee of the Paytable. Later he relished service on legislative committees and was always ready willing and able to assume the thankless task of actually drafting complex legislation. This willingness to work hard coupled with an intelligent—though perhaps not brilliant—mind made him a good worker bee.

But Ellsworth was far more than a diligent functionary. He was a political operative of unsurpassed skills, and his effectiveness was fully supported by his faith in the New Divinity's absolute predestination. The faith gave him immense confidence in and optimism about the progress of human affairs. All obstacles and travails were temporary. He knew that all would come right because all was part of God's plan. He also knew that he had been elected by God for salvation and that one of his roles in God's plan was to be a Righteous Ruler. When he told the Senate in 1789 "that Kings were of divine appointment [and were] the head & shoulders taller than the rest of the people,"[2] he had in mind Righteous Rulers like himself. Therefore he approached all tasks with an immense confidence that he was an agent of God doing God's work.

At the same time that Ellsworth's confidence made him dauntless and indefatigable, it made him ruthless. He had no qualms whatsoever about advancing quite harsh measures because he knew that even the harshest of measures were part of God's plan. In the case of coercing Rhode Island into joining the Union, some politicians remembered that state's service during the Revolutionary War and were willing to indulge Rhode Island's recalcitrance. But not Ellsworth. There was no forgiveness in the Rhode Island Trade Bill that he drafted. Either the state would join the Union, or criminal law would be used to impose an economic annihilation.

The Rhode Island Trade Bill illustrates another aspect of Ellsworth's confidence. In dealing with difficult political issues, he was comparatively unconcerned with how people might judge him. As he told his wife, the Bill "would have exposed me to some censure had it not produced the effect which I expected it would." Nevertheless he was undeterred. Similarly when he negotiated the Treaty of Mortfontaine, he knew that the compromises in the Treaty would be exceedingly unpopular with many of his fellow Federalists, but he didn't care. If, he said, "there must be any burning on the occasion, let them take me." Like a religious martyr, he was unconcerned with what fellow human beings might do to him because he knew that he was an agent of God.[3]

Ellsworth's faith that God had a plan and that he, Ellsworth, was a part of it imparted great sincerity to his conduct. Because all of Ellsworth's actions were predestined by God, Ellsworth knew that he always acted from a principled position. In addition, he knew that his conduct was righteous because he acted with a love of God in his heart. His knowledge that he was a sincere person added to his formidableness as a political operative and negotiator because his allies and opponents inevitably perceived his unfeigned sincerity.

Without more, a politician who is a sincere, self-confident, intelligent, hardworking, and ruthless optimist is more likely to be a loose cannon than a political genius. Part of the additional ingredients to Ellsworth's genius was the fact that he sincerely embraced compromise as a valuable and legitimate political tool. His faith in predestination as elaborated in *The Wisdom of God* conclusively established the righteousness of any compromise that he fashioned with the love of God in his heart. He had no compunction about aligning himself with the Deep South slaveholders at the Constitutional Convention or about agreeing to a treaty with France that he knew would anger many of his fellow Federalists. He knew that his compromises were principled and right because they were part of God's plan.

In addition to justifying compromises, Ellsworth's Calvinism provided a psychological motivation to seek compromises. Max Weber believed that the doctrine of predestination caused the ideal Calvinist to seek evidence of his salvation in his life and that the best evidence was a consistent life of righteous rectitude. Therefore Weber concluded that the search for evidence would act as an unconscious form of behavior modification. A Calvinist like Ellsworth, who happened to be a Righteous Ruler rather than a participant in private commerce, would be subject to the same unconscious behavior modification. The notion of one of God's elect being an ineffective ruler is implausible. Righteous Rulers, to use Ellsworth's phrase, are "head and shoulders taller than the rest of the people."[4] Therefore they surely must be effective rulers. Conversely ineffectiveness on a ruler's part would be evidence that he might not be one of God's elect. Continuing this Weberian analysis, Ellsworth would have sought to be an effective ruler in order to find evidence confirming his election by God for salvation. Because compromise is the very essence of effective rule in a pluralistic society, Ellsworth must have been motivated to seek compromises.

In addition to being willing to compromise, Ellsworth was inclined to be tolerant of others' faults. In his church and community back in Windsor, he routinely dealt with people whom God had not elected for salvation, and the New Divinity pronounced that these unelected individuals were depraved sinners. Ellsworth, however, was quite willing to tolerate their "depravity." When Ellsworth stepped onto the stage of national politics, he constantly dealt with individuals from other states who did not share his religion and who opposed his views of proper public policy. His national opponents, however, were fundamentally no different from his unregenerate friends and neighbors back in Windsor. Their actions were not as important as was the fact that they had not been elected by God. If he could accept the unelected in Windsor, he could accept the unelected at the Constitutional Convention and in the nation's capital.

The Constitution of the United States is a grand scheme. Ninety years after its ratification, British Prime Minister William Gladstone proclaimed that the United States Constitution is "the most wonderful work ever struck off at a given time by the brain and purpose of man."[5] The process of creating a system of government, however, is far more complicated than putting grand ideas to paper. Even in 1787, America was a pluralistic society, and in a pluralistic society a general idea of governance has no political value unless it is generally acceptable to the elements of society that wield significant political power. Oliver Ellsworth's genius was in the details of effectively wielding political power to achieve grand purposes. In a political setting he had an unsurpassed ability to gauge who had significant power and who did not, and then to fashion compromises that at the same time assuaged the relevant power groups and advanced general interests that he believed were proper. When he confronted a legislative problem, he rolled up his sleeves and plunged into the arduous and sometimes mindnumbing task of developing a fully elaborated solution that would work.

Nowhere was the need for pragmatic political genius more evident than at the Constitutional Convention in Philadelphia. Virtually all the delegates believed that a stronger national government under a new constitution was needed. At the same time, however, the individual delegations from each state were leary of creating a stronger government that would have power over their particular states but that would not be controlled by their states. In a word, the delegates were distrustful of a more powerful government, and they focused their distrustfulness on the big state/small state controversy. Notwithstanding the common desire of the delegates to create a new government, the entire project might have foundered but for the Connecticut Compromise. If the Convention had collapsed, a new and stronger form of government probably would have been created within a few years, but it would not necessarily have been similar to the one that has lasted over two hundred years. In the late eighteenth century, the most significant source of pluralism among America's enfranchised populations was geography rather than the relative size of the particular states. Ellsworth believed that the fundamental source of political diversity was the difference between the northern states and the southern states. He feared that if the Connecticut Compromise were not accepted, America would be divided into two separate nations—one north; the other south—separated by the Delaware River.[6] Certainly the nation's subsequent history in the nineteenth century marks his fear with prescience.

The important point is that the Connecticut Compromise was not inevitable. The Compromise was born in the subtle brain of Roger Sherman, but when he initially proposed it at the Convention, it was rejected. The leaders of the Big States knew that an absolute rule of representation in proportion to population was right, and they had the bit between their teeth. They would not budge, and some of the small state leaders were equally adamant in insisting upon a continuation of an absolute rule of one state/one vote. In the face of this polarization, Sherman and Ellsworth cleaved to the fairness of their Compromise.

More than persistence was required to bring the Convention around to accepting the Connecticut Compromise. Ellsworth and his Connecticut colleagues ceaselessly reminded the other delegates that intransigence on the issue of representation would destroy the Convention, but they did not base their position entirely upon raw political blackmail. Ellsworth's comprehensive June 29 argument emphasized his belief that the Compromise was intrinsically fair to all parties. Moreover the general tone of his argument was one of respect for his fellow delegates. When he addressed James Wilson's intransigence, he prefaced his speech by reassuring the assembly that he had "the greatest respect" for Wilson.[7]

When the First Congress was convened, Ellsworth again displayed his political brilliance when he pieced together the intricate compromise that became the Judiciary Act of 1789. He had a clear understanding of what was and what was not necessary for an effective system of federal courts. He insisted upon a plenary judicial power to deal with maritime matters, to enforce federal revenue laws, and to prosecute federal crimes. He also wanted to provide for the federal enforcement of British creditors' rights under the Treaty of Paris, but he had the pragmatic wisdom to see that it was not to be, and the confidence to act on that judgment. When he fought for the Connecticut Compromise in Philadelphia and negotiated the Treaty of Mortfontaine in Paris, he "preferred doing half the good we could, rather than do nothing at all."[8] This same pragmatic wisdom served him well in drafting the Judiciary Act.

The Judiciary Act is the most prominent example of his effective service in the Senate. Over the next six years until he became Chief Justice, he continued to fashion effective compromises where appropriate, but where compromise was inappropriate—like the Rhode Island Trade Bill—he was equally willing to ride roughshod over the opposition. At the same time, he managed to gain and retain the respect of opponents like James Madison, Aaron Burr, and others.[9]

As a group, the men who created the Federal Republic were the most gifted collection of politicians in the nation's history. In the subsequent 200 years, only Abraham Lincoln and Franklin Roosevelt approach being in the same class with George Washington as a national leader. At the cabinet level of the Executive Branch, no secretary of any department has ever performed better than Alexander Hamilton did as the first Secretary of the Treasury. Similarly in the realm of political theory and polemics, no politician has ever exceeded the standards set by Hamilton and James Madison. This confluence of political genius is particularly astonishing in view of the nation's small population. In 1790 there were 3.9 million human beings in the United States, but less than forty percent—probably less than a third—were citizens with a full right to participate in the political process. African Americans, Indians, and white women were not allowed to vote or run for public office. Only white males need apply, and property qualifications disenfranchised many of them. In 1790 there were only 1.6 million white males, which is about the total population two hundred years later of the state of Nebraska or the city of Houston, Texas. The quantity and quality of political genius in the Founding Generation is simply astonishing.[10]

The list of political greatness does not stop with Washington, Hamilton, and Madison. The Founding Generation also included Thomas Jefferson and an aging Benjamin Franklin, and below this first tier we encounter the likes of John Adams, John Jay, Patrick Henry, John Marshall, James Wilson, and George Mason. Similarly the Generation included a number of gifted jurists. For example, among the early Supreme Court Justices, James Iredell and William Paterson could easily have held their own on any of the Courts in the succeeding two centuries.[11]

Among this rich collection of political talent, Oliver Ellsworth is entitled to a seat at the first table of absolute political genius. He did not have Washington's genius for national leadership, but who else in the history of the nation could be seriously described as first in war, first in peace, and first in the hearts of his countrymen. As a political theorist, Ellsworth's ideas were entirely derivative and lacking in originality. He was a gifted and effective political polemicist, and some quite capable contemporaries viewed his "Landholder" essays as more valuable than Madison's and Hamilton's contributions to the *Federalist Papers*. The passage of time, however, has made it clear that Ellsworth's polemics spoke essentially to his times, but *Publius* spoke to the ages. Political genius, however, takes many forms. Both George Washington and Alexander Hamilton were geniuses, but their abilities were incommensurable. Hamilton could never have led the nation, and Washington could never have co-authored the *Federalist Papers*. Oliver Ellsworth is entitled to a seat at the first table of genius, not because he had George Washington's abilities as a leader or Alexander Hamilton's abilities as a theorist and polemicist—but because Oliver Ellsworth was the Founding Generation's most gifted practical politician.

# Notes

### CHAPTER 1

1. The only full-scale biography is almost a hundred years old. *Brown's Ellsworth*, 225 (quoting Burr's joke). *Lettieri's Ellsworth* is a slim master's thesis that provides a valuable picture of Ellsworth's early career. James Madison to Joseph Wood, Feb. 27, 1836, *Letters and other Writings of James Madison* (Philadelphia: Lippincott, 1867), 4: 427–28.

2. Verplanck's "Sketch."

3. John Murrin, "Religion and Politics in America from the First Settlements to the Civil War," in *Religion and American Politics*, Mark A. Noll, ed. (New York: Oxford University Press, 1990), 29 & 31.


### CHAPTER 2

1. Oliver Ellsworth, Jr., Mss (1803), *quoted in Stiles' Ancient Windsor*, 2:212; G.A. Rawlyk, *Yankees at Louisbourg* (Orono, Maine: University of Maine Press, 1967); Douglas Edward Leach, *Arms for Empire* (New York: MacMillan, 1973), 224–43.

2. Oliver Ellsworth, Jr. Mss. (1803), *quoted in Stiles' Ancient Windsor*, 2:212.

3. *First Congregational Church of Windsor Records 1636–1932*, 1:201 & 214, Ct-Ar.

4. For the schism, see *Stiles' Ancient Windsor*, 1:278. J.H. Hayden, "Address," in *A Record of the Services held at the Congregational Church of Windsor, Conn.* (Windsor, Conn.: Congregational Church of Windsor, Conn., 1880), 68–70. For Jemima's status in the North Society, see Church Book of the North Windsor Congressional Church 1761–94, Ct-Ar.

5. Michael J. Crawford, "The Spiritual Travels of Nathan Cole," *William & Mary Quarterly* 3rd ser., 33 (1976), 79–126 (reprinting Cole's narrative).

6. *Id.* at 93–94; David Harlan, *The Clergy and the Great Awakening in New England* (Ann Arbor, Mich.: UMI Research Press, 1980), 50–52. Cole went on to relate a multiyear conversion process in which he came to know that he had been elected by God.

7. George Whitefield, *A Continuation of Reverend Mr. Whitefield's Journal from Savannah June 25, 1740 to his arrival at Rhode Island, his Travels in other parts of New England to his Departure from Stanford to New York* (Philadelphia: B. Franklin, 1741), 111 (Evans No. 4846).

8. For the Great Awakening in Connecticut, see *Bushman's Puritan to Yankee*, ch. XII–XIV; Maria Louise Greene, *The Development of Religious Liberty in Connecticut* (New York: 1905, Da Capo Press reprint, 1970), ch. IX–X.

9. George Whitefield, *Journal* 22, 110–11.

10. *McLaughlin's New England Dissent*, 1: ch. 18–20; *Bushman's Puritan to Yankee*, ch. XII–XIV.

11. "An Act for regulating and correcting Disorders in Ecclesiastical Affairs," in *Connecticut Colonial Records*, 8:454, analyzed in Elisha Williams, *The Essential Rights and Liberties of Protestants* (Boston:Kneeland & Green, 1744), 50–66 (Evans no. 5520); *Bushman's Puritan to Yankee*, 186–87.

12. Louis Leonard Tucker, *Puritan Protagonist: President Thomas Clap of Yale College* (Chapel Hill, N.C.: University of North Carolina Press, 1962), 132–36; *Goen's Revivalism*, 63; An Act relating to, and for the better regulating Schools of Learning, *Connecticut Colonial Records*, 8:500–02.

13. Act of May, 1743, *Connecticut Colonial Records*, 8:522; *McLaughlin's New England Dissent*, 1:366.

14. Isaac Stiles, *A Prospect of the City of Jerusalem, in its Spiritual Building, Beauty and Glory* (New London, Conn.: T. Green, 1742) (Evans No.5066), quoted and discussed in *Goen's Revivalism*, 62; *Bushman's Puritan to Yankee*, 237–38.

15. Jonathan Edwards, *A Faithful Narrative of the Surprising Work of God in the Conversion of Many Souls* (1738), in *The Works of Jonathan Edwards*, C.C. Goen ed., (New Haven, Conn.: Yale University Press, 1972), 4:154; Jonathan Edwards to Benjamin Coleman, May 30, 1735, in *id*. 102; George Whitefield, *Journal*, 111.

16. For Ellsworth's early life, see Oliver Ellsworth, Jr., Mss (1803), discussed in William Brown, *Oliver Ellsworth*, 12 n.1.

17. See *Valeri's Bellamy*; Joseph A. Conforti, *Samuel Hopkins and the New Divinity Movement* (Grand Rapids, Mich.: Christian University Press, 1981).

18. *Stiles' Ancient Windsor*, 2:213. For Bellamy's character as a teacher, see *Valeri's Bellamy*, 56–57; Tryon Edwards, "A Memoir of his Life and Times," *Bellamy's Works*, 1:vii–ix.

19. See generally Williston Walker, *The Creeds and Platforms of Congregationalism* (New York: Scribner, 1893), ch. XIII; Westminster Confession of Faith (1748), in Williston Walker, *Creeds and Platforms*, 367–402. An Act for Educating, and Governing of Children, in *Acts and Laws of his Majesty's English Colony of Connecticut in New England in America* (New London, Conn.: Timothy Green, 1750), 20–21 (Evans No. 6479). For Yale and Ellsworth's Windsor church, see Louis Leonard Tucker, *Puritan Protagonist: President Thomas Clap of Yale College* (Chapel Hill, N.C.: University of North Carolina Press, 1962), 79; *First Congregational Church of Windsor Records*, 3:37, Ct-Ar.

20. *Christian Doctrine* (Ellsworth's authorship explained in William R. Casto, "Oliver Ellsworth's Calvinism," *Journal of Church and State*, 36 (1994), 511 n.23); *Bellamy's Works*.

21. *Westminster Confession*, ch. II, VI, VII, IX, & XVI; Joseph Bellamy, *True Religion*, in *Bellamy's Works*, 25–26, 137–51, 168–73, 222–40, & 273–77; *Christian Doctrine*, ch. V, VII, VIII, & XVI.

22. *Christian Doctrine*, ch. VI, IX, & XIV.

23. Max Weber, *The Protestant Ethic and the Spirit of Capitalism*, 98–128; Joseph Bellamy, *True Religion*, in *Bellamy's Works*, 1:193–201; *Christian Doctrine*, ch. XV.

24. Joseph Bellamy, *Theron, Paulinus, and Aspasio: or Letters and Dialogues upon the Nature of Love to God, Faith in Christ, Assurance of a Title to Eternal Life* (1758–59), in *Bellamy's Works*, 2:242; *Bloomfield Congregational Church Records*, Ct-Ar.

25. *Christian Doctrine*, ch. XIV & XV ("*general walk*" emphasis original; emphasis added in last sentence); Max Weber, *Protestant Ethic*, 117.

26. Joseph Bellamy, *The Wisdom of God in the Permission of Sin* (1758), in *Bellamy's Works*, 2:1–96. See also Joseph Bellamy, *The Wisdom of God in the Permission Vindicated; in Answer to a Pamphlet entitled "An Attempt," &c* (1760), in *Bellamy's Works*, 2:97–155. *Christian Doctrine*, ch. XVII, ¶ 5. This theodicy is ably analyzed in Alan Heimert, *Religion and the American Mind* (Cambridge, Mass.: Harvard University Press, 1966), 342–43; Frank Foster, *A Genetic History of the New England Theology* (Chicago: University of Chicago Press, 1907), 118–20; and *Valeri's Bellamy*, ch.4.

27. Joseph Bellamy, *The Wisdom of God*, in *Bellamy's Works*, 2:5. See *Valeri's Bellamy* ch.4.

28. Norman Fiering, *Jonathan Edward's Moral Thought and Its British Context* (Chapel Hill, N.C.: University of North Carolina Press, 1981), ch.6; Paul Ramsey, "Editor's Introduction," in *Jonathan Edwards Freedom of the Will*, Paul Ramsey, ed. (New Haven, Conn.: Yale University Press, 1957) 1:81–89.

29. William Breitenbach, "Unregenerate Doings: Selflessness and Selfishness in New Divinity Theology," *American Quarterly* (1982), 34: 479–502; Joseph Haroutunian, *Piety Versus Moralism: The Passing of the New England Theology* (New York: H. Holt, 1932), 62–65 (Smalley); David S. Rowland & Theodore Hinsdale, *Heresy, Detected and Exposed* (Hartford, Conn.: Hudson & Goodwin, 1781), 35–40 (Evans no. 17357); *Christian Doctrine*, ch. VIII, ¶¶ 1 & 3; "Notebook of Theodore Hinsdale," n.d., Theodore Hinsdale Papers, MPBA ("Whitby on 5 Points to Oliv. Ellsworth"); Inventory of Oliver Ellsworth's Estate, 4, Ct-Ar.

30. *Bushman's Puritan to Yankee*, 209–20 & 235–66; *McLaughlin's New England Dissent*, 1:345; William Samuel Johnson to J. Beach, Jan. 4, 1763, *Samuel Johnson, President of King's College: His Career and Writings*, Herbert & Carol Schneider eds., (New York: Columbia University Press, 1929), 3:266.

31. Joseph Bellamy, "An Election Sermon," in *Bellamy's Works*, 1:588; Oscar Zeichner, *Connecticut's Years of Controversy, 1750–1776* (Chapel Hill, N.C.: University of North Carolina Press, 1949), ch. 3; Edmund Morgan & Helen Morgan, *The Stamp Act Crisis: Prologue to Revolution* (Chapel Hill, N.C.: University of North Carolina Press, 1953), ch. 13; Bruce Steiner,

"Anglican Office Holding in Pre-Revolutionary Connecticut: The Parameters of New England Community," *William & Mary Quarterly* (3rd ser.) (1974), 31:381.

32. *See* Louis Leonard Tucker, *Puritan Protagonist: President Thomas Clap of Yale College* (Chapel Hill, N.C.: University of North Carolina Press, 1962), 222–54; Jonathan Ware, "Students vs. the Puritan College," *The Connecticut Historical Society Bulletin*, 40 (1975), 50–51.

33. *Brown's Ellsworth*, 14–16, *quoting* Yale records; Jonathan Ware, "Students vs. the Puritan College," *The Connecticut Historical Society, Bulletin*, 40 (1975), 51; Yale University, *Yale College Records*, 1701–04, 1716–1857, typescript, 1:156, Yale University, New Haven, Conn.; Alexander Cowie, *Educational Problems at Yale College in the Eighteenth Century*, (New Haven, Conn.: Yale University Press, 1936), 19–20.

34. *Valeri's Bellamy*, 19 & 117; *Goen's Revivalism*, 61–62.

35. Franklin B. Dexter, *Biographical Sketches of Graduates of Yale College* (New York, N.Y.: H. Holt & Co., 1896), 2:783; James McLachlan, *Princetonians 1748–1768: A Biographical Dictionary* (Princeton, N.J.: Princeton University Press, 1976), xx.

36. *An Account of the College of New Jersey* (Woodbridge N.J.: James Parker, 1764), 15–16 (Evans No. 9752). *Accord, Charter of the College of New Jersey* (1748), in Thomas Jefferson Wertenbaker, *Princeton, 1746–1896*, (Princeton, N.J.: Princeton University Press, 1946), 402. For the *Account's* provenance, see John MacLean, *History of the College of New Jersey* (Philadelphia Lippincott, 1877), 260–61.

37. Thomas Jefferson Wertenbaker, *Princeton, 1746–1896* (Princeton, N.J.: Princeton University Press, 1946), 104; *An Account of the College of New Jersey*, 20. See also Samuel Finley to Eleazer Wheelock, nd, *quoted in* Howard Miller, *The Revolutionary College: American Presbyterian Higher Education 1701–1837* (New York: New York University Press, 1976), 98.

38. *Brown's Ellsworth*, 19.

39. Verplanck's "Sketch." For the Cliosophic Society, see generally Charles Richard Williams, *The Cliosophic Society*, (Princeton, N.J.: Princeton University Press, 1916). The clearest primary evidence of Ellsworth's participation in founding the Well Meaning Club is William Paterson, *Biography of William Paterson*, NjHi(Mss. written by William Paterson's grandson and quoting Luther Martin), 11: 89–90. *Accord*, John E. O'Connor, *William Paterson: Lawyer and Statesman 1745–1806* (New Brunswick, N.J.: Rutgers University Press, 1979), 27–29.

40. William Chauncy Fowler, "The Ministries of Connecticut in the Revolution," in *Centennial Papers Published by Order of the General Conference of the Congregational Churches of Connecticut* (Hartford, Conn.: Case, Lockwood & Brainard Co., 1877), 107–08. For New Divinity metaphysics in general and John Smalley in particular, see Stephen E. Berk, *Calvinism Versus Democracy: Timothy Dwight and the Origins of American Evangelical Orthodoxy* (Hamden, Conn.: Archon Books, 1974), ch. IV; Sidney Ahlstrom, *A Religious History of the American People* (New Haven, Conn.: Yale University Press, 1972), 404–05. For Ellsworth's regeneration, see *Church Book of the North Windsor Congregational Church, 1761–1794*, 31, 31fn., and 44–45, Conn.-Ar; Henry Augustus Rowland, *A Sermon Occasioned by the Death and Delivered at*

the Funeral of the Honorable Oliver Ellsworth (Hartford, Conn.: William Sawyer & Co., 1808), 12 (Shaw-Shoemaker no. 16108).

## ☙ CHAPTER 3

1. *Lettieri's Ellsworth*, 13–15; *The Diary of Elihu Hubbard Smith*, James E. Cronin, ed. (Philadelphia: American Philosophical Society, 1973), 467.

2. *Lettier's Ellsworth*, at 15–20.

3. *Id.* at 19–24. Oliver Ellsworth to the General Assembly, May 1780, Connecticut Archives, Revolutionary War (1st ser.), 10:236, Ct-Ar; Paytable Memorandum, June 28, 1776, Connecticut Archives, Revolutionary War (1st ser.), 32:306a, Ct-Ar; Receipt, Sept. 14, 1776, Connecticut Archives, Revolutionary War (1st Ser), 11:52a–b, Ct-Ar; Paytable Memorandum, June 23, 1777, Connecticut Archives, Revolutionary War (1st ser.), 33:326, Ct-Ar.

4. For an excellent treatment of Ellsworth's rise to political power during the Revolution, see *Lettieri's Ellsworth*. *See also* Verplanck's "Sketch" ("very considerable emolument").

5. *Id.* ch. 3.

6. Timothy Dwight, *Travels in New England and New York*, ed. Barbara Solomon (Cambridge, Mass.: Belknap Press, 1969), 1:221; Nathanael Emmons, "Sermon on American Independence" (1802), in Nathanael Emmons, *The Works of Nathanael Emmons*, ed. Jacob Ide (Boston: Crocker & Brewster, 1842), 2:228; Henry Augustus Rowland, *A Sermon Occasioned by the Death and Delivered at the Funeral of the Honorable Oliver Ellsworth* (Hartford, Conn.: Hudson & Goodwin, 1808), 12 (Shaw-Shoemaker no. 16108); Verplanck's "Sketch," 401; *Brown's Ellsworth*, 328.

7. Harry S. Stout, *The New England Soul* (New York: Oxford University Press, 1986), 3–10; *Stiles's Ancient Windsor*, 2:210–13; Oliver Ellsworth to Abigail Ellsworth, Feb. 3, 1779, *Delegates Letters*, 12:13–14.

8. Oliver Ellsworth to his wife Abigail Ellsworth, July 17, 1781, CtHi; Oliver Ellsworth to his daughter Abigail Ellsworth, Dec. 16, 1791, Williams Family Papers, CtHT; Oliver Ellsworth to this wife Abigail Ellsworth, Feb. 3, 1779, in *Delegates Letters*, 12: 13–14; Oliver Ellsworth to this wife Abigail Ellsworth, July 1, 1787, CtHi.

9. Max Weber, *The Protestant Ethic*, 110–17 & 232 n.66.

10. *Christian Doctrine* ch. VI, ¶2; *First Congregational Church of Windsor 1632–1932*, 3:37, Ct-Ar.

11. Max Weber, *The Protestant Ethic*, 117.

12. Joseph Bellamy, "An Election Sermon," (1762), *Bellamy's Works*, 1:583–85. *Accord*, Josiah Whitney, *The Essential Requisites to Form the Good Ruler's Character, Illustrated and Urged* (Hartford, Conn.: Elisha Babock, 1788), 37–38 (Evans No. 21601); A. Whitney Griswold, "Three Puritans on Prosperity," *New England Quarterly*, 7 (1934), 475–93.

13. Oliver Ellsworth, *Landholder XIII*, DHRC, 16:473.

14. William Vans Murray to John Quincy Adams, Nov. 7, 1800, in "Letters of William Vans Murray," (1912) W. Ford ed., *Annual Report of the American Historical Association for the Year 1912* (1914), 358 (discussing the negotiation in 1800 of the Treaty of Mortfontaine). *Accord*, A. Du Casse, *Histoire des Negociations Diplomatiques Relatives Aux Traits de Mortfontaine, de Lineville et D'Amiens* (Paris: E. Denton, 1855), 1:184 (Ellsworth devoted "great constancy, a slow and calculated perseverance, to the negotiations."). For Ellsworth's frugality, see Verplank's Sketch, 400; *Brown's Ellsworth*, 338; Statement of Stone Mills Account, 1799, Oliver Ellsworth Papers, Bibliotheck der Universiteit van Amsterdam.

15. Joseph Bellamy, "The Millennium," *Bellamy's Works*, 1:459.

16. Joseph Bellamy, "An Election Sermon," *Bellamy's Works*, 1:582 & 587–96; Samuel Finley, *The Curse of Meroz; or, The Danger of Neutrality, in the Cause of God, and Our Country* (Philadelphia: James Chattin, 1757), 10–13 (Evans no. 7893).

17. For the persistence of millennarianism, see Ruth Block, *Visionary Republic* (New York: Cambridge University Press, 1785) 17; Nathan Hatch, *The Sacred Cause of Liberty* (New Haven, Conn.: Yale University Press, 1799).

18. Joseph Bellamy, "An Election Sermon," *Bellamy's Works*, 1:578–79, 584, & 586. See also Joseph Bellamy, *True Religion Delineated, Bellamy's Works*, 1:13–14.

19. *Christian Doctrine*, ch. XIX & XX.

20. Judah Champion, *Christian and Civil Liberty and Freedom Considered and Recommended* (Hartford, Conn.: E. Watson, 1776), 12 (Evans no. 14675); Harry Stout, *The New England Soul*, 364 n.64; William R. Casto, "Oliver Ellsworth's Calvinism," 511–12 (citing and discussing 14 election sermons).

21. William R. Casto, "Oliver Ellsworth's Calvinism," 512 (citing and discussing 11 election sermons).

22. Joseph Perry, *A Sermon Preached before the General Assembly* (Hartford, Conn.: Eben Watson, 1775), 14–15. *Accord*, William R. Casto, "Oliver Ellsworth's Calvinism," 513 (citing 8 additional election sermons); Nathan Hatch, *The Saved Cause of Liberty*, 105–09. *See also* Oliver Ellsworth to Joseph Perry, April 14, 1783, Oliver Ellsworth Papers, CtHi.

23. *Christian Doctrine*, 54; Westminster Assembly of Divines, *The Shorter Catechism*, LXIV & LXXXI (1648), adopted, *First Congregational Church of Windsor Records 1636–1932*, 15:37, CtHi.

24. Joseph Bellamy, *An Election Sermon*, 583–86.

25. Nathan Strong, *A Sermon Delivered in the Presence of his Excellency Samuel Huntington* (Hartford, Conn.: Hudson & Goodwin, 1790), 14 (Evans no. 22913); Oliver Ellsworth Papers, Bancroft Transcript, 63, NN; Joseph Bellamy, *True Religion Delineated*, in *Bellamy's Works*, 1:150–51. *See also Christian Doctrine*, ch. XV, ¶ 1; Joseph Conforti, *Samuel Hopkins and the New Divinity Movement* (Grand Rapids, Mich.: Christian University Press, 1981), ch. 7.

26. See William R. Casto, "Oliver Ellsworth's Calvinism," 513–14, n.40 (citing seven sermons).

27. *Maclay's Diary*, 27 (emphasis original to indicate quote from New Testament, 1 Peter 2:17).

28. Elisha Williams, *The Essential Rights and Liberties of Protestants* (Boston: S. Kneeland & T. Green, 1749), 40 (Evans. no. 5520); Joseph Bellamy, *The Millennium*, in *Bellamy's Works*, 1:451; Joseph Bellamy, *True Religion, id.* 324.

29. William C. Stinchcombe, *The American Revolution and the French Alliance* (Syracuse, N.Y.: Syracuse University Press, 1969), ch. VII; Oliver Ellsworth to Theodore Hinsdale, Jan. 26, 1779, *Delegates Letters*, 11:518–19.

30. Benjamin Trumbull, *The Dignity of Man, Especially as Displayed in Civil Government* (Hartford, Conn.: 1801), 22 ("Newgates" was a reference to Connecticut's state prison) (Shaw-Shoemaker no. 1440).

31. Oliver Ellsworth to Theodore Hinsdale, Jan. 26, 1779, reprinted in *Delegates Letters*, 11: 518–19.

32. Oliver Ellsworth to William Williams, July 29, 1777, Oliver Ellsworth Papers, CtHi; The *Oxford English Dictionary*, 11:185 & 186 ("tenner" and "tenor").

33. Oliver Ellsworth to David Ellsworth, Oct. 25, 1778, CtWOe; Roger Sherman & Oliver Ellsworth to Governor Jonathan Trumbull, Sr., Nov. 10, 1778, *Delegates Letters*, 11: 194–95; Oliver Ellsworth to Samuel Lyman, Dec. 1, 1778, *Delegates Letters*, 11:270–71.

34. Oliver Ellsworth, "Thoughts on the Paper Currency," Jan. 20, 1779, *Delegates Letters*, 11:487–90.

35. Oliver Ellsworth to Abigail Ellsworth, Jan. 14, 1780, *excerpted in Delegates Letters*, 14:344 n.2; Oliver Ellsworth to Governor Jonathan Trumbull, Sr., Jan. 14, 1780, *Delegates Letters*, 14:343–44.

36. *Journals of the Continental Congress 1774–1789*, Worthington C. Ford, ed. (Washington, D.C.: Government Printing Office, 1937), 16:216–17, 263–67;

37. Oliver Ellsworth & Roger Sherman to Governor Jonathan Trumbull, Sr., March 20, 1780, *Delegates Letters*, 14: 519–21; Oliver Ellsworth to Governor Jonathan Trumbull, Sr., March 23, 1780, *Delegates Letters*, 14:537–38.

38. Oliver Ellsworth to Governor Jonathan Trumbull, Sr., March 28, 1780, *Delegates Letters*, 14:548–49.

39. Oliver Ellsworth & Roger Sherman to Governor Jonathan Trumbull, Sr., July 12, 1781.

40. *See Polishook's Rhode Island* ch. 3–4.

41. *Journals of the Continental Congress* 24:261; Oliver Ellsworth to Governor Jonathan Trumbull,

July 10, 1783, *Delegates Letters*, 20: 413–15; Oliver Ellsworth to Samuel Holton, Oct. 28, 1783, Emmet Collection, NN.

42. An Act to enable the United States in Congress assembled to levy certain duties and taxes, Connecticut Archives, Revolutionary War (1st ser.), 26: 317, Ct-Ar.

43. See *Lettier's Ellsworth*,57–59; *Collier's Sherman*, 217–18.

44. An Act Establishing the Wages of the Judges of the Superior Court, *Connecticut State Records*, 5:324–25. For Kirby and Ellsworth's relationship with him and his Reports, see Oliver Ellsworth to Ephriam Kirby, April 16, 1787, MH-H. The cases reported by Kirby are ably surveyed in Wesley W. Horton, "Day, Root and Kirby," *Connecticut Bar Journal* (1997).

45. Oliver Ellsworth, "Charge to the Grand Jury of the Circuit Court for the District of South Carolina," May 7, 1799, DHSC, 3:358; Mack v. Parsons, 1 Kirby 155, 156 (1786) (By the Court; Mss. by Ellsworth); Adams v. Kellogg, 1 Kirby 195, 186 (1786) (By the whole Court; Mss. by Ellsworth); Clark v. Bray, 1 Kirby 237, 239–40 (1787) (By the Court; Mss. by Ellsworth); Harris v. Thomas, 1 Kirby 267, 268 (1787) (By the whole Court; Mss. by Ellsworth); Gustin v. Brattle, 1 Kirby 299, 300–04 (1787) (By the Court; Mss. by Ellsworth); Bacon v. Taylor, 1 Kirby 368, 370–71 (1788) (Sherman & Ellsworth, dissenting; Mss. by Ellsworth); Fitch v. Loveland, 1 Kirby 380, 386 (1788) (Ellsworth, dissenting); Apthorp v. Backus, 1 Kirby 407, 409–14 (1788) (Opinion by Law & Ellsworth; Mss. by Ellsworth).

46. Horsford v. Wright, 1 Kirby 3 (1786) (Opinion by Law). For Ellsworth, see Adams v. Kellogg, 1 Kirby 438, 442 (1788) (separate opinion by Ellsworth).

47. Wilford v. Grant, 1 Kirby 114 (1786) (By the whole Court; Mss. by Ellsworth).

48. *Id.* at 116–17.

49. Adams v. Kellogg, 1 Kirby 195 (1786), (By the whole Court; Mss. by Ellsworth) *discussed in,* Mary Moers Wenig, "The Marital Property Law of Connecticut: Past, Present and Future," *Wisconsin Law Review*, 1990 (1990), 839–41. *See also* Fitch v. Brainerd, 2 Day 163, 176 & 186 (Conn. 1805).

50. Oliver Ellsworth to Ephriam Kirby, Dec. 23, 1788, Ephraim Kirby Papers, NcD; Judge Ellsworth's Notes, 1 Kirby 438 (1788); Giles Jacob, *A New Law Dictionary*, 6th ed. (London: Henry Lintot, 1750) (Doctrine of Relation).

51. Kirby at 438–39; William Blackstone, *Commentaries on the Laws of England* (Oxford: Clarendon Press, 1765), 1:42–43 & 54–55.

52. Kirby at 439–41.

53. *Id.* at 441.

54. *Id.* at 441–42.

55. *Id.* at 442; *Christian Doctrine*, ch. 20, ¶ 9.

56. Kirby at 443; *Christian Doctrine*, ch. 20, ⁋ 4.

57. Kirby at 443; *Connecticut State Records*, 7:103 & 245; Fitch v. Brainerd, 2 Day 163 (Conn. 1805).

## ☙ CHAPTER 4

1. *See generally* Collier's "Sovereignty;" DHRC, 3:315–32.

2. *Connecticut Courant*, Nov. 20, 1786.

3. *Collier's Sherman*; John Adams to John Sanderson, Nov. 19, 1822, *quoted in id,* at 283; *Brown's Ellsworth,* 151.

4. *See, e.g.,* Forest McDonald, *The Formation of the American Republic, 1776–1790* (Baltimore: Penguin Books, 1965), 178; Collier's "Sovereignty." For disagreements between Ellsworth and Sherman see *Lettieri's Ellsworth,* 97 n. 18; *Huntington v. Chaplin,* 1 Kirby 166 (Conn. Sup. Ct. 1786), *discussed in text accompanying note 12 in chapter 5; Farrand's Records,* 1:54 & 67.

5. *Collier's Sherman,* ch. 15.

6. *Farrand's Records,* 1:21.

7. *Id.* at 21–22.

8. James Madison to George Washington (April 16, 1787), *Madison Papers,* 9:382–87; James Madison to Edmund Randolph (April 8, 1787), *id.* 368–71.

9. *Farrand's Records,* 1:38–40.

10. *Id.* at 179 & 180.

11. *Id.* at 196 & 201–02; *Rakove's Original Meanings,* 66–68. For Sherman's proposal in the Continental Congress, see *Collier's Sherman,* 157.

12. *Farrand's Records,* 1:201.

13. *Id.* at 240.

14. *Id.* at 242–45.

15. *Id.* at 312–33, 242 n *, & 322.

16. William Paterson to Oliver Ellsworth, Aug. 23, 1787, *Farrand's Records,* 4:73.

17. *Id.,* 1:461–62 & 471.

18. *Id.,* at 468–510.

19. *Id.,* at 468.

20. *Id.,* at 474 & 468.

21. *Id.*, at 469, 475, & 478.

22. *Id.*, at 469 & 475.

23.¯ *Id.*, at 469 & 478.

24. *Id.*, at 469 & 475.

25. *Id.*, at 469.

26. Clinton Rossiter, *1787 The Grand Convention* (New York: MacMillam, 1966), 250.

27. *Valeri's Bellamy*, 11–12; Robert G. Pope, *The Half-way Covenant: Church Membership in Puritan New England* (Princeton, N.J.: Princeton University Press, 1969); *Stiles' Ancient Windsor*, 1:903.

29. *See* note 40 in chapter 2.

29. *Farrand's Record*, 1:469 & 475.

30. *Id.*, at 495–96.

31. *Id.*, at 492.

32. *Colliers' Decision*, 125–28; Luther Martin, "Genuine Information III," DHRC, 15:252 & 255–56.

33. *Colliers' Decision*, 168–69, 211–15, & 125–28.

34. Abraham Baldwin to Joel Barlow, June 14, 1789, *quoted in* DHSC, 4:23 n.8; *The United States Congressional Directories 1789–1840*, eds. Perry Goldman & James Young (New York: Columbia University Press, 1973), 14–15; Henry Clay White, *Abraham Baldwin, One of the Founders of the Republic, and Father of the University of Georgia, the First of American State Universities* (Athens, Ga.: McGregor Co., 1926).; *The United States Congressional Directories 1789–1840*, Perry Goldman & James Young, eds (New York: Columbia University Press, 1973), 14 & 15.

35. Luther Martin, "Genuine Information III," DHRC, 15:252–53.

36. George Washington to Samuel Powell, Jan. 18, 1788, DHRC, 15:398–99; Oliver Ellsworth, "Landholder X," DHRC, 16:305.

37. *Colliers' Decision*, 129; *Farrand's Records*, 1:526; Oliver Ellsworth, Expense Account, April 29, 1788, Connecticut Archives: Revolutionary War, 1st series, 35:354–55, Ct-Ar.

38. *Colliers' Decision*, 128–33; *Farrand's Records*, 4:88–89.

39. *Colliers' Decision*, 166–70.

40. George Mason's Account of Certain Proceedings in Convention, Sept. 30, 1792, *Farrand's Records*, 3:367–68.

41. *Farrand's Records*, 370 & 364.

42. Levi Hart, *The Description of Good Character Attempted and Applied to the Subject of Jurisprudence and*

*Civil Government* (Hartford, Conn.: Hudson and Goodwin, 1786), 26 (Evans No. 19699). *See also* Jonathan Edwards, *The Necessity of the Belief of Christianity by the Citizens of the State, in Order to Our Political Prosperity* (Hartford, Conn.: Hudson and Goodwin, 1794), 27 (Evans. No. 26934)("the shame of humanity and the scandal of christianity"); Oliver Ellsworth, "Landholder VI," DHRC, 3:490.

43. Oliver Ellsworth to Mrs. Abigail Ellsworth, March 7, 1790, Oliver Ellsworth Papers, CtHi; *Swift's System*, 2:349; Census of the United States, Connecticut, Hartford County, Windsor Township, 1790.

44. *Farrand's Records*, 2:370–71.

45. *Id.* at 276.

46. *Id.* at 372 & 374.

47. Oliver Ellsworth, "Charge to the Ground Jury of the Circuit Court for the District of Georgia," April 25, 1796, DHSC, 3:119; *Farrand's Records*, 2:371 & 369–70.

48. "An Act concerning Indian, Molatto, and Negro Servants and Slaves," *Connecticut Acts*, 235; Levi Hart, *Description of Good Character*, 26; Oliver Ellsworth, "Landholder VI," DHRC 3:490. *See generally* John Saillant, "Slavery and Divine Providence in New England Calvinism: The New Divinity and a Black Protest, 1775–1805," *New England Quarterly*, 68 (1995), 584; James Essig, "Connecticut Ministers and Slavery, 1790–1795," *Journal of American Studies*,15 (1981), 27–44.

49. Bernard C. Steiner, *History of Slavery in Connecticut* (Baltimore: Johns Hopkins Press, 1893), 84.

50. See text accompanying notes 28 & 29 in chapter 2.

51. *Farrand's Records*, 2:288.

52. See *Collier's Decision*, 169–79.

53. Oliver Ellsworth and Roger Sherman to Samuel Huntington, Sept. 26, 1787, DHRC, 13:470–72.

54. *Id.*

55. Oliver Ellsworth, "Landholder I," DHRC, 13:561–64; Oliver Ellsworth, "Landholder XIII," DHRC, 16:472–74.

56. Oliver Ellsworth, "Landholder XIII," DHRC, 16:473; Oliver Ellsworth, "Landholder II," DHRC, 14:93. For "righteousness," see Oliver Ellsworth, "Landholder V," DHRC, 14:338; Oliver Ellsworth, "Landholder XII, DHRC, 16:406.

57. Oliver Ellsworth, "Landholder IV," DHRC, 14:231 (Gerry); Oliver Ellsworth, "Landholder V," DHRC, 14:335 (Gerry); Oliver Ellsworth, "Landholder VI," DHRC, 14:399–403 (Gerry, Lee, and Mason); Oliver Ellsworth, "Landholder VIII," DHRC, 15:75–80 (Gerry, Mason, and five New Yorkers).

58. Oliver Ellsworth, "Landholder VIII," DHRC, 15:78. For the great mass, see Oliver Ellsworth, "Landholder X," DHRC, 16:306; Oliver Ellsworth, "Landholder VII," DHRC, 16:405–08.

59. Rufus King to Jeremiah Wadsworth, Dec. 23, 1787, *excerpted in* DHRC, 15:71. On some of the factual background to Ellsworth's *ad hominem* attacks, see DHRC, 14:403 nn. 2 & 9; *id.*, 15:79 n.3 & 80 n.4.

60. Enoch Perkins to Simeon Baldwin, Jan. 15, 1788, DHRC, 3:584; *Brown's Ellsworth*, 175 (quoting Edwards).

61. Oliver Ellsworth, "Speech of Jan. 4, 1788," DHRC, 3:541–543.

62. James Wadsworth, "Speech of Jan. 7, 1788," DHRC, 3:547; Oliver Ellsworth, "Speech of Jan. 7, 1788," DHRC, 3:548–54; Enoch Perkins to Simeon Baldwin, Jan. 15, 1788, DHRC, 3:584.

## ⛝ CHAPTER 5

1. *Senate Legislative Journal*, DHFFC, 1: 3 & 7; Oliver Ellsworth to Abigail Ellsworth, March 8, 1789, Oliver Ellsworth Papers, CtHi.

2. *Senate Legislative Journal*, DHFFC, 1:11–12; Roy Swanstrom, *The United States Senate 1787–1801* (Washington, D.C.: Government Printing Office, 1985), 268–69.

3. *See Brown's Ellsworth*, ch. 2–3; *N.Y. Journal*, April 16, 1789, DHSC, 1:611–12.

4. Paine Wingate to Timothy Pickering, April 29, 1789, *excerpted in* DHSC, 4:381–82.

5. *See Casto's Supreme Court*, 10–15.

6. George Mason, *Objections to the Constitution* (1787), DHRC 13:40–46; "Richard Henry Lee's Proposed Amendments," *reprinted and discussed in* DHRC 8:59–67.

7. Holt's "Judiciary Act," 1440–58; Dunlop v. Ball, 6 U.S. (2 Cranch) 180, 182–83 (1804).

8. *See generally*, Holt's "Judiciary Act."

9. *Id.* at 1445–49; George Mason to Patrick Henry, May 6, 1783, Robert A. Rutland, ed., *The Papers of George Mason, 1725–1792* (Chapel Hill, N.C.: University of North Carolina Press, 1970), 2:769.

10. "Amendments Proposed by the Virginia Convention (1788), DHFFC, 4:15–19; Oliver Wolcott, *British Influence on the Affairs of the United States, Proved and Explained* (Boston: Young and Minns, 1804), 10 (emphasis original) (Shaw Shoemaker No. 7793).

11. Oliver Ellsworth, "Landholder V," DHRC, 14:338.

12. 1 Kirby 166 (1786) (by the Court). The manuscript in the Connecticut State Archives is in Ellsworth's hand.

13. William Blackstone, *Commentaries on the Laws of England* (Oxford: Clarendon Press, 1765), 64. *See also id.* at 45, 67, 73.

14. *Id.* at 69 & 70 (emphasis original). *See also id.* at 63–64. Fitch v. Brainerd, 2 Day 163, 194 (Conn. 1805), *discussed in Brown's Ellsworth*, 332.

15. Osborn v. Bank of the United States, 22 U.S. (9 Wheat.) 738 (1824).

16. Senate Judiciary Bill § 24, DHSC, 4:86.

17. *Id.* § 21, DHSC, 4:80–81.

18. *Id., as amended; Bakove's Original Meanings*, 320–22; *Casto's Supreme Court*, 37; *Swift's System*, 2:275.

19. *See* William R. Casto, "The Origins of Federal Admiralty Jurisdiction in an Age of Privateers, Smugglers, and Pirates," *American Journal of Legal History*, 37 (1993), 117–57.

20. Davis Rich Dewey, *Financial History of the United States* 12th ed (New York: Longmans, Green and Co., 1934), 110; Otho Williams to David Humphries, May 12, 1789, *quoted in* DHSC, 4:377n.

21. John McCusker & Russell Menard, *The Economy of British America, 1606–1789* (Chapel Hill, N.C.: University of North Carolina Press, 1985), 362–63; Edgar Maclay, A *History of America Privateers* (New York: D. Appleton, 1899), vii–ix.

22. The Flad Oyen, 165 Eng. Rep. 124 (Adm. 1799) (condemnation facilitates sales); J. Franklin Jameson, ed., *Essays on the Constitutional History of the United States in the Formative Era, 1775–1789* (Freeport, N.Y.: Books for Libraries Press, 1970, orig. ed., 1889), 25–26 (quoting the petition).

23. Jacob E. Cooke, ed., *The Federalist* (Middletown, Conn.: Wesleyan University Press, 1961), No. 80: 538.

24. Osborn v. Bank of the United States, 22 U.S. (9 Wheat.) 738 (1824).

25. Edmund Randolph to James Madison, June 30, 1789, *excerpted in* DHSC, 4:432–33. *But see* Edmund Randolph, *Report on the Judiciary* (1791), DHSC, 4:162 (conceding the propriety of an amount in controversy limitation).

26. Judiciary Act § 9. *See Casto's Supreme Court*, 7–8 & 43.

27. Judiciary Act §§ 8 & 11.

28. *See* William R. Casto, "The Federal Courts' Protective Jurisdiction over Torts Committed in Violation of the Law of Nations," *Connecticut Law Review* (1986), 18:506; Charles S. Hyneman, *The First American Neutrality* (Urbana, Ill.: University of Illinois Press, 1934), 133–42.

29. Judiciary Act § 9.

30. Dwight F. Henderson, *Courts for a New Nation* (Washington, D.C.: Public Affairs Press,

1971), 62 & 156 n.36. *See also* Richard Peters to Timothy Pickering, Dec. 8, 1806 (explaining a glitch in the statutory language), Pickering Papers, MHi.

31. William Paterson, "Notes for Remarks on Judiciary Bill," June 23, 1789, DHSC, 4:416.

32. William Loughton Smith to Edward Rutledge, August 9–10, 1789 (quoting Ellsworth), *excerpted in* DHSC, 4:496–99.

33. James Madison, "Notes of Debates in the Continental Congress," Jan. 16, 1783, *Madison Papers*, 6:46–47; DHRC, 3:544.

34. William Paterson, "Notes on Judiciary Bill Debate," June 24–27, 1789, DHSC, 4:421–23; William R. Casto, "The First Congress's Understanding of its Authority over the Federal Courts' Jurisdiction," *Boston College Law Review* (1985), 26:1113–14 n. 93.

35. *Casto's Supreme Court*, 47 n. 39.

36. Wiscart v. Dauchy, 3 U.S. (3 Dall.) 321, 329 (1796).

37. DHSC, 4: 409, 410 & 471–73.

38. *Id.* at 408.

39. Oliver Ellsworth, "Speech of Jan. 4, 1788," DHRC, 3:542. *See also* Oliver Ellsworth, "Landholder V," *id.* 3: 480–84.

40. Oliver Ellsworth, "Speech of Jan. 4, 1788," DHRC, 3:553.

41. William Paterson, "Notes for Remarks on Judiciary Bill," June 23, 1789, DHSC, 4:415–16; Oliver Ellsworth, "Landholder V," DHRC, 14:348.

42. Oliver Ellsworth to Richard Law, April 30, 1789, *excerpted in* DHSC, 4:392; *Casto's Supreme Court*, 50 n. 46.

43. *Senate Legislative Journal*, DHFFC, 1:85.

44. Jeremiah Wadsworth to Pierpont Edwards, July 27, 1789, *quoted in* DHSC, 4:483 n. 3; James Madison to Samuel Johnston, July 31, 1789, *excerpted in* DHSC, 4:491–92; DHFFC, 5:1171 n.29.

45. See *Casto's Supreme Court*, 51.


# ☙  CHAPTER 6

1. Leonard W. Levy, *Original Intent and the Framers' Constitution* (New York: Macmillan, 1988), ch.8; *see also* Rakove's *Original Meanings*, 318–38.

2. Oliver Ellsworth, "Landholder IX," DHRC, 15:192; Samuel Huntington to Samuel Johnston, Sept. 23, 1788, DHRC, 3:362–63 (microfiche supp.). *See also* Rufus King to Jeremiah Wadsworth, Dec. 13, 1787, *excerpted in Supplement to Max Farrand's The Records of the Federal*

*Convention of 1787*, James Hutson, ed. (New Haven, Conn.: Yale University Press, 1987), 290.

3. Timothy Stone, *A Sermon, Preached before His Excellency Samuel Huntington* (Hartford, Conn.: Hudson & Goodwin, 1792), 13 (Evans no. 24820). *Accord,* Moses Mather, *Sermon, Preached in the Audience of the General Assembly* (New London, Conn.: Timothy Green, 1781), 9–10 (Evans no. 17236); Ezra Stiles, *The United States elevated to Glory and Honor* (New Haven, Conn.: Thomas & Samuel, 1783), 25; Andrew Lee, *The Origins and Ends of Civil Government* (Hartford, Conn.: Hudson & Goodwin, 1795), 18–20 (Evans no. 28957). "An Act containing an abstract and Declaration of Rights and Privileges of the People of this State, and securing the same," *Connecticut Acts,* 1–2. *See also* Christopher Collier, "The Connecticut Declaration of Rights before the Constitution of 1818: A Victim of Revolutionary Redefinition," *Connecticut Law Review,* 15 (1982) 87–98.

4. Roger Sherman, "Countryman II," DHRC, 14:173. *See also* Roger Sherman, "Countryman III," DHRC, 14:296–97; Roger Sherman, "Countryman IV," DHRC, 14:356–58; Roger Sherman, "Draft Letter," Dec. 8, 1787, DHRC, 14:386–89. Speech of Oliver Wolcott, Sr., DHRC, 3:558. Oliver Ellsworth, "Landholder XIII," DHRC, 16:473.

5. Oliver Ellsworth, "Landholder VI," DHRC, 14:400.

6. DHFFC, 4:43–45.

7. DHFFC, 4:47–48.

8. See *James Madison on Religious Liberty,* Robert Alley, ed. (Buffalo, N.Y.: Prometheus Books, 1985).

9. *McLaughlin's New England Dissent,* 1:264; *Connecticut Colonial Records,* 5:87. *See generally* Williston Walker, *The Creeds and Platforms of Congregationalism,* (New York: Scribner, 1893); Paul R. Lucas, *Valley of Discord: Church and Society along the Connecticut River, 1636–1725* (Hanover, N.H.: University Press of New England, 1976).

10. See *McLaughlin's New England Dissent,* 1:ch. 15 & 2: ch. 47–50.

11. "An Act in Addition to a Law of this Colony entitled an Act for the due Observation and Keeping the Sabbath or Lord's Day, and for preventing and punishing disorders and Prophaneness on the Same," *Connecticut Colonial Records,* 13:360. For the elimination of the Saybrook Platform, *see* Bushman's *Puritan to Yankee,* 219; *McLaughlin's New England Dissent,* 2:923–24.

12. *Swift's System,* 1:42.

13. *Swift's System,* 2:321, 325, & 347; An Act for the Punishment of divers capital and other Felonies, in *Connecticut Acts,* 67; An Act for the due Observation of the Sabbath or Lord's-Day, in *id.,* 213, *discussed in* Jesse Root, "Introduction," 1 Root xxii (Conn. 1793) and *Swift's System,* 325.

14. An Act for the Punishment of divers capital and other Felonies, *Connecticut Acts,* 67; Abel

Flint, Secretary of the Connecticut Missionary Society, to the London Missionary Society, May 14, 1804, CtHUCC; *Swift's System*, 2:322–23.

15. "An Act to Enforce the Observances of Days of Public Fasting and Thanksgiving," *Connecticut State Records*, 7:313; Richard Purcell, *Connecticut in Transition*, 55–56 & 90; Maria Greene, *The Development of Religious Liberty in Connecticut*, 378.

16. *See McLaughlin's New England Dissent*, 2: ch. 50.

17. "The Baptists' Petition," *Connecticut State Records*, 11: Appendix D, at 369–71; "The 1803 Petition," *id.* at 374–80.

18. *See McLaughlin's New England Dissent*, 2: ch. 50; "The Baptist Petition" and "The 1803 Petition."

19. Asahel Hooker, *The Moral Tendency of Man's Accountableness to God* (Hartford, Conn.: Hudson & Goodwin, 1805), 33–35 (Shaw-Shoemaker no. 8635); Danbury Baptists Association to Thomas Jefferson, Oct. 1801, *quoted and discussed in*, *McLaughlin's New England Dissent*, 2:1004–05; Thomas Jefferson to Nehemiah Dodge, Jan. 1, 1802, Thomas Jefferson, *Writings* (Library of America, 1984), 510.

20. Ellen D. Larned, *History of Windham County, Connecticut* (Worcester, Mass.: Ellen D. Larned, 1880), 296.

21. *See e.g.*, Joseph Bellamy, *An Election Sermon*, quoted in text accompanying note 18 in chapter 3; Charles Backus, *A Sermon preached before his Excellency Samuel Huntington* (Hartford, Conn.: Hudson & Goodwin, 1793), 22 (Evans. no. 25130). For the upper house, *see* Oliver Ellsworth to Abigail Ellsworth, May 30, 1780, *quoted in* Delegates' Letters, 15:216 n.2. *Accord*, Josiah Whitney, *The Essential Requisites to Form the Good Rulers' Character* (Hartford, Conn.: Elisha Babcock, 1788), 29 & 30 (Evans. no., 2160); Ammi R. Robbins, *The Empires and Dominions of this World* (Hartford, Conn.: Hudson & Goodwin, 1789), 26, 30, & 32–33. *Christian Doctrine*, ch. xx ¶ 9. For the son's filial duties, *see id.* ¶¶ 5 & 7.

22. Charles Backus, *A Sermon, Preached before his Excellency Samuel Huntington* (Hartford, Conn.: Hudson & Goodwin, 1793), 22 (Evans no. 25130); Timothy Stone, *A Sermon Preached before his Excellency Samuel Huntington* (Hartford, Conn.: Hudson & Goodwin, 1792), 23 (Evans no. 24820); Benjamin Trumbull, *The Dignity of Man, Especially as Displayed in Civil Government* (Hartford, Conn.: Hudson & Goodwin, 1801), 23 (Shaw-Shoemaker no. 1440); Cyprian Strong, *The Kingdom is the Lord's* (Hartford, Conn.: Hudson & Goodwin, 1799), 17–18 & 40 (Evans. no.36380); Timothy Dwight, *Virtuous Rulers a National Blessing* (Hartford, Conn.: Hudson & Goodwin, 1795), 18 (Evans no. 23341); Zebulon Ely, *The Wisdom and Duty of Magistrates* (Hartford, Conn.: Hudson & Goodwin, 1804), 34 (Shaw-Shoemaker no. 6243). *See also* Asahel Hooker, *The Moral Tendency of Man's Accountableness to God* (Hartford, Conn.: Hudson & Goodwin, 1805), 24 (defending "a union of religion with civil government, as has always existed in this State") (Shaw-Shoemaker no. 8635).

23. "Report of the Committee to whom was referred the Petition of Simeon Brown and others, complaining of certain existing laws respecting the support of the Gospel," 1802,

*reprinted in Connecticut State Records*, 11:371–74. James Beaseley, "Emerging Republicanism and the Standing Order: The Appropriation Act Controversy in Connecticut, 1793 to 1795, *"William & Mary Quarterly* (3d ser.) 29 (1972), 595 & 609; Linda Kerber, *Federalists in Dissent* (Ithaca, N.Y.: Cornell University Press, 1970), 208–12 (using many Calvinist examples and a few non-Calvinist ones). *See generally McLaughlin's New England Dissent*, 2:ch. 50.

24. "Ellsworth's Report," *Connecticut State Records*, 11:373.

25. "Ellsworth's Report," *Connecticut State Records*, 11:371, 373, & 374.

26. Noah Webster, *A Collection of Essays and Fugitiv[sic] Writings* (Worcester, Mass.: Thomas & Andrews, 1791), 345. (Evans no.23053). *Accord*, John Devotion, *The Duty and Interest of a People to Sanctify the Lord of Hosts* (Hartford, Conn.: Eben Watson, 1777), 31 (Evans no. 15285). Noah Webster, "Draft Report," 1802, Noah Webster Papers, NN.

27. *McLaughlin's New England Dissent*, 2:989–94.

28. United States Constitution, Art. VI; Oliver Ellsworth, "Landholder VII," DHRC, 14:448–52.

29. *Id.*

30. Joseph Huntington, *God Ruling the Nations for the Most Glorious End* (Hartford, Conn.: Hudson & Goodwin, 1784), 13 (Evans no. 18530); Benjamin Trumbull, *A Complete History of Connecticut Civil and Ecclesiastical* (Hartford, Conn.: Hudson & Goodwin, 1797), 128 (discussing Old Light "outrages").

31. Oliver Ellsworth, "Landholder VII," DHRC, 14:450; Jonathan Elliot, ed., *The Debates in the Several State Conventions, on the Adoption of the Federal Constitution, as Recommended by the General Convention at Philadelphia in 1787*, 2d ed. (Philadelphia: J.B. Lippincott, 1876), 3:330 (James Madison), *Bushman's Puritan to Yankee*, 211–12 & 215–19.

32. For the "strawman," compare William Williams to the Printer, Feb. 2, 1788, DHRC, 3:588–90; with Oliver Ellsworth, "Landholder VII," DHRC, 14:450. For Connecticut support for a general, Christian test oath, see William Williams to the Printer, Feb. 2, 1788, DHRC, 3:588–90; Samuel Parsons to William Cushing, Jan. 11, 1788, DHRC, 3:573; "A New Test," New Haven Gazette, Jan. 31, 1788, DHRC, 3:588; "Elihu," American Mercury, Feb. 18, 1788, DHRC, 3:590–92.

33. Oliver Ellsworth, "Landholder VII," DHRC, 14:451; Joseph Bellamy to a friend, circa 1766, *Bellamy's Works*, 1:xxxi–xxxiii, William Paley, *The Principles of Moral and Political Philosophy* (1785), *The Works of and Life of William Paley*, Alexander Chalmers, ed. (London: F.C. and J. Rivington, 1819), 2:36. Inventory of Oliver Ellsworth's Estate, 7 ("Payley's Moral Philosophy"), Ct-Ar.

34. Oliver Ellsworth, "Landholder VII," DHRC, 14:451. *See generally* Norman Sykes, *Church and State in England in the XVIIth Century* (Hamden, Conn.: Archon Books, 1962).

35. Oliver Ellsworth, "Landholder VII," DHRC, 14:451; "A Bill to Establish the Judicial Courts of the United States," § 9, DHFFC, 5:1176; *Maclay's Diary*, 88–89

36. Oliver Ellsworth, "Landholder VII," DHRC, 14:451; John Locke, *Letter Concerning Toleration* (W. Papple transl. 1789), John Locke, *The Second Treatise of Civil Government and a Letter Concerning Toleration*, J.W. Gough ed. (Oxford: B. Blackwell, 1946), 122, 134, 152–54.

37. Compare Oliver Ellsworth, "Landholder VII," DHRC, 14:451, with John Locke, *Letter Concerning Toleration*, 124, 125, 134, 146, & 147. See "Inventory of Ellsworth's Estate," 6.

38. John Locke, *Letter Concerning Toleration*, 150–59; Oliver Ellsworth, "Landholder VII," DHRC, 14:451. On punishing atheism, *see id.*; John Locke, *Letter Concerning Toleration*, 156; John Locke, *A Vindication of the Reasonableness of Christianity* (1696), in John Locke, *The Works of John Locke* (London: Thomas Tegg, 1823), 7:161; Nathan Strong, *A Sermon Delivered in the Presence of his Excellency Samuel Huntington* (Hartford, Conn.: Hudson & Goodwin, 1790), 21–20 (Evans no. 22913).

39. DHFFC, 4:36 & 39 (emphasis added).

40. *Id.*, 1:151.

41. *Levy's Establishment Clause*, 81–82; Rodney K. Smith, *Public Prayer and the Constitution* (Wilmington, Del.: Scholarly Resources, 1987), 87–89; *Senate Legislative Journal*, DHFFC, 1:182.

42. DHFFC, 1:158, 166 & 4:43–45.

43. *Id.*, 1:181–82.

44. *Id.*, 4:47–48.

45. *See, e.g.*, John Locke, *Letter Concerning Toleration*, 141 & 153.

46. *Connecticut Acts*, 21–22; Elisha Williams, *The Essential Rights of Protestants*, 7–8 & 42–45; Joseph Huntington, *God ruling the Nations for the most glorious end*, (Hartford, Conn.: Hudson & Goodwin, 1784), 13 (Evans no. 18530); Levi Hart, *The Description of a Good character attempted and applied to the subject of jurisprudence and civil government* (Hartford, Conn.: Hudson & Goodwin, 1786), 23 (Evans no. 19699); John Leland, *The Right of Conscience Inalienable, and Therefore Religious Opinions not Cognizable by Law; or, The high-flying church-man Stripped of his Legal Rule, Appears a Yaho, 1791*, L.F. Greene, *The Writings of the Late Elder John Leland* (New York: G.W. Wood, 1845), 177–92; *Connecticut State Records*, 11:369–374.

47. Oliver Ellsworth, "Landholder VII," DHRC, 14:451; Oliver Ellsworth, "Landholder VI," DHRC, 14:401; notes 14 & 38 in this chapter and accompanying text.

48. *Curry's First Freedoms*, 204–06. DHFFC, 11:1260. *See also id.* 1257.

49. DHFFC, 11: 1261–61.

50. John Leland, *The Right of Conscience Inalienable*; John Leland, *A Stroke at the Branch, Containing Remarks on Times and Things* (Hartford, Conn.: Elisha Babcock, 1801), 23–24 (Shaw-Shoemaker no. 813); "The Baptist Petitions," *Connecticut State Records*, 10:369 & 374.

51. Moses Mather, *Sermon, Preached in the Audience of the General Assembly* (New London, Conn.: Timothy Green, 1781), 9. *See* text accompanying notes 3 & 4 in this chapter.

52. Oliver Ellsworth and Roger Sherman to Samuel Huntington, Sept. 26, 1787, DHRC 3:351–53; DHFFC, 11:1261.

53. Oliver Ellsworth, "Landholder VII," DHRC, 14:450; Oliver Ellsworth, "Landholder VI," DHRC, 14:401; William Samuel Johnson and Oliver Ellsworth to Samuel Huntington, March 18, 1790, William Samuel Johnson Papers, CtHi. *See* text accompanying note 29 in chapter 4.

54. *Senate Legislative Journal*, DHFFC 1:12 & 16; Act of March 3, 1791, ch. 28 § 6, 1 Stat. 222, 223; Act of March 5, 1792, ch. 9, § 7, 1 Stat. 241, 242; Act of March 27, 1794, ch. 12, § 2, 1 Stat. 350; A Treaty between the United States and the Oneida, Tuscarora, and Stockbridge Indians, dwelling in the Country of the Oneidas, Art. IV, 7 Stat. 47, 48 (1795).

55. Timothy Dwight, *Travels in New-England and New York*, Barbara Miller Soloman, ed. (Cambridge, Mass.: Harvard University Press, 1969, original ed. 1822), 4:283. *See also* Isaac Lewis, *The Political Advantage of Godliness* (Hartford, Conn.: Hudson & Goodwin, 1797), 27 (Evans no. 32377). Dwight's *Travels* was published posthumously based upon essays and notes written between 1798 and 1814.

56. *Curry's First Freedoms*, 178–84 & 209–17; Ezra Stiles, *A Discourse on the Christian Union* (Boston: Edes and Gill, 1761), 80–83 (Evans no. 9018); Ebenezer Frothringham, *A Key to Unlock the Door* (1767) *discussed in McLaughlin's New England Dissent*, 1:ch.22; Timothy Dwight, *Travels*, 4:283.

57. Oliver Ellsworth, "Landholder V," DHRC, 14:335.

58. *See* William McLaughlin, "The Role of Religion in the Revolution," in *Essays on the American Revolution*, Stephen G. Kurtz & James H. Hutson, ed. (New York: W.W. Norton, 1973), 219–22.

59. James Madison to Thomas Jefferson, Oct. 17, 1788, *Madison Papers*, 11:297. For somewhat different analyses reaching similar conclusions, *see* Cushing Strout, *The New Heavens on Earth: Political Religion in America* (New York: Harper & Row, 1974), 93–98.

60. *See, e.g.*, Chester James Antieau, Arthur T. Downey, & Edward C. Roberts, *Freedom from Federal Establishment* (Milwaukee, Wisc.: Bruce Publishing Co., 1964), 130–31 & 140–42; Michael J. Malbin, *Religion and Politics: The Intentions of the Authors of the First Amendment* (Washington, D.C.: American Enterprise Institute, 1978), 13–15; Robert L. Cord, *Separation of Church and State: Historical Fact and Current Fiction* (Grand Rapids, Mich.: Baker Book House, 1982), 8–9; *Levy's Establishment Clause*, 83; Rodney K. Smith, *Public Prayer and the Constitution* (Wilmington, Del.: Scholarly Research, 1987), 90–96. *See also* Philip Kurland, "The Origins of the Religion Clauses of the Constitution," *William & Mary Law Review*, 27 (1986), 855–56; Douglas Laycock, "'Nonpreferential' Aide to Religion: A False Claim about Original Intent," *William & Mary Law Review*, 27 (1986), 879–81 & 904.

61. Chester Antieau, *Freedom from Federal Establishment*, 140–42; Michael Malbin, *Religion and Politics*, 15–16; Robert Cord, *Separation of Church and State*, 15.

62. *Levy's Establishment Clause*, 95.

63. John Hatsell, *Precedents of Proceedings in the House of Commons*, 2d ed. (South Hackensack, N.J.: Rothman, 1971, orig. ed. 1818), 4:48–55; *id.* 4:35 (discussing sixteenth century precedent).

64. Thomas Jefferson, *Manual of Parliamentary Practice* (1796), H.R. Doc. No. 277, 98th Cong., 2d less., at 113 n.a. (1985); *Maclay's Diary*, 189.

65. *Senate Legislative Journal*, DHFFC, 1:12 & 16 Thomas Jefferson, *Manual of Parliamentary Practice*, § XLV. *Accord*, John Hatsell, *Precedents of Proceedings*, 4:35.

66. *Senate Legislative Journal*, DHFFC, 1:16, 181, & 182.

67. James Madison to Edmund Pendleton, Sept. 23, 1789, *Madison Papers*, 12:418–20.

68. On Ellsworth's use of the article "an" and the participle "respecting," compare *Levy's Establishment Clause*, 94–96, with Rodney Smith, *Public Prayer and the Constitution*, 92–93.

## ☙ CHAPTER 7

1. Act of Sept. 16, 1789, 1st Congress, 1st sess., ch. 15, 1 Stat. 69–70.

2. *Polishook's Rhode Island*, ch.9; Act of Feb. 8, 1790, 1st Congress, 2d sess., ch. 1, § 7, 1 Stat. 100–101.

3. *Polishook's Rhode Island*, ch.6.

4. *Id.*, 168.

5. *Farrand's Records*, 2: 309–10; Oliver Ellsworth, "Speech of Jan. 4, 1788," DHRC, 3:542; Oliver Ellsworth, "Landholder XII," March 17, 1788, DHRC, 16: 405–08 (emphasis added to Ellsworth's paraphrasing of Bellamy's *The Wisdom of God*).

6. *Id. Accord*, Oliver Ellsworth, "Landholder V," DHRC, 14:338.

7. Roger Sherman to David Howel, May 6, 1789, RPB-JH; Senate "Legislative Journal," DHFFC, 1:294–95.

8. William Ellery to Benjamin Huntington, May 3, 1790, William Ellery Letters, R-Ar.

9. Benjamin Huntington to William Ellery, May 8, 1790, William Ellery Letters, R-Ar.

10. Oliver Ellsworth to Abigail Ellsworth, June 7, 1790, Oliver Ellsworth Papers, CtHi, *excerpted in Brown's Ellsworth*, 200–01; Rhode Island Trade Bill, DHFFC, 6:1812–14.

11. Oliver Ellsworth to Abigail Ellsworth, June 7, 1790, Oliver Ellsworth Papers, CtHi, *excerpted in Brown's Ellsworth*, 200–01.

12. *Maclay's Diary*, 255, 260, 264, & 458.

13. *Maclay's Diary*, 260 & 263; Arthur Fenner to George Washington, May 20, 1790, DNA RG59;

John Steele to Governor Alexander Martin, May 17, 1790, Governor's Letterbook, 10:51–52, NC-Ar.

14. DHFFC, 13:1356–57 n.40, 1446–47, 1458–59; Tenche Coxe to Francis Tenche, May 31, 1790, Tenche Coxe Papers, PHi; *Polishook's Rhode Island*, 226–30.

15. Oliver Ellsworth to Abigail Ellsworth, June 7, 1790, Oliver Ellsworth Papers, CtHi, *excerpted in Brown's Ellsworth*, 200–01.

## ☙ CHAPTER 8

1. See generally *Combs' Jay Treaty*.

2. *Casto's Supreme Court*, 87–90.

3. *Combs' Jay Treaty*, 159–62; *Annals of Congress*, 4:862–63; *Casto's Supreme Court*, 90–94; Ronald Schultz, *The Republic of Labor: Philadelphia Artisans and the Politics of Class, 1720–1830* (New York: Oxford University Press, 1993), 137–39.

4. *Casto's Supreme Court*, 95; George Washington to Henry Lee, Jan. 11, 1796, DHSC 1:829.

5. *Combs' Jay Treaty*, 171–87; Oliver Ellsworth to Abigail Ellsworth, Feb. 26, 1796, CtWOe.

6. *Combs' Jay Treaty*, 175–77; Oliver Ellsworth to Jonathan Trumbull, March 13, 1796, George Washington Papers, DLC.

7. DHSC, 3:88 n.7; Oliver Ellsworth to Jonathan Trumbull, March 13, 1796, George Washington Papers, DLC.

8. Oliver Ellsworth to Abigail Ellsworth, March 20, 1796, DHSC 3:99–100; Oliver Ellsworth, "Charge to the Grand Jury of the Circuit Court for the District of South Carolina," April 25, 1796, in *ibid.*, 3:119–20.

9. *Ibid.*; Oliver Ellsworth to Abigail Ellsworth, Feb. 26, 1796, CtWOe; *Annals of Cong.* 5:1291.

10. Oliver Ellsworth to Ezekiel Williams, Jr., May 29, 1796, Williams Family Papers, CtHT; Oliver Ellsworth to George Washington, June 19, 1796, George Washington Papers, DLC.

11. See *Casto's Supreme Court*, 115–17; Alexander DeConde, *Entangling Alliance: Politics & Diplomacy under George Washington* (Durham, N.C.: Duke University Press, 1958), 437–38.

12. Hamiltons v. Eaton, 11 F. Cas. 336 (C.C.D.N.C. 1796) (No. 5980).

13. *Ware v. Hylton*, 3 U.S. (3 Dall.) 199 (1796); Hylton v. United States, 3 U.S. (3 Dall.) 171 (1796); Bas v. Tingy, 4 U.S. (4 Dall.) 37 (1800); Cooper v. Telfair, 4 U.S. (4 Dall.) 14 (1800); Calder v. Bull, 3 U.S. (3 Dall.) 386 (1798). These cases are discussed respectively in *Casto's Supreme Court*, 98–101, 101–05, 225–27, & 227–30.

14. *United States v. La Vengeance*, 3 U.S. (3 Dall.) 297 (1796), *discussed in Casto's Supreme Court*, 105–09.

15. *Id.* at 299–301; United States v. Judge of the District Court of the United States for the District Court of Virginia, unreported (U.S. 1796), *discussed in* William R. Casto, "The Origins of Federal Admiralty Jurisdiction in an Age of Privateers, Smugglers, and Pirates," *American Journal of Legal History* 37 (1993): 154–55 n. 91; Peter Du Ponceau to Brockholst Livingston, Aug. 8, 1796, Edward Livingston Papers, NjP.

16. 3 U.S. (3 Dall.) at 301.

17. United States v. The Schooner Betsy, 8 U.S. (4 Cranch) 443, 446 n. (1808).

18. See text accompanying notes 20 & 41 in Chapter 5.

19. Glass v. The Sloop Betsy, 3 U.S. (3 Dall.) 6 (1794), *discussed in Casto's Supreme Court*, 83–87.

20. An Act Establishing the Wages of the Judges of the Superior Court (1784), *Connecticut State Records*, 5:324–25; Preface, 1 Kirby iii–iv.

21. *See Casto's Supreme Court*, 110–11.

22. *See id.* at 111.

23. Letter to David Daggett, April 20, 1798, CtY; Wiscart v. Dauchy, 3 U.S. (3 Dall.) 321 (1796); Turner v. The Bank of North America, 4 U.S. (4 Dall.) 8 (1799); *Casto's Supreme Court*, 241–45.

24. Moodie v. The Ship Phoebe Anne, 3 U.S. ( Dall.) 319 (1796), *discussed in Casto's Supreme Court*, 114.

25. Oliver Ellsworth to Caleb Strong, Oct. 25, 1796, Caleb Strong Papers, MNF. The phrase "gates of Hell" is explained in Casto, "Oliver Ellsworth's Calvinism," 520 n.74. For Ellsworth's support of John Adams, see Oliver Wolcott, Sr., to Oliver Wolcott, Jr., Dec. 12, 1796, Wolcott Papers, CtHi.

26. Oliver Ellsworth to Ezekiel Williams, March 16, 1797, Conarroe Collection, PHi.

27. See DeConde, *Entangling Alliance*, ch.xiv; *DeConde's Quasi-War* ch.I; Uriah Tracy to Samuel Dana, April 1, 1797, PHi.

28. Oliver Ellsworth, "Charge to the Grand Jury of the Circuit Court for the District of New York," April 1, 1797, DHSC 3:158–60.

29. *Argus*, April 11, 1797; Abigail Adams to John Adams, April 17, 1797, in DHSC 3:161–62; Alexander Hamilton to James McHenry, Feb. 19, 1800 (quoting Ellsworth), in *The Papers of Alexander Hamilton*, ed. Harold Syrett (New York: Columbia University Press, 1976), 24:237–38.

30. James D. Richardson, ed., *Messages and Papers of the Presidents* (Washington, D.C., 1896),

1:233–39; George Cabot to Oliver Wolcott, Jr., May 31, 1797, in Cabot Letters, 139–140; Oliver Ellsworth to Oliver Wolcott, Jr., May 29, 1797, in DHSC 3:182.

31.  Frederick Wolcott to Oliver Wolcott, Jr., Jan. 23, 1798, in *Ibid.*, 1:857; Oliver Ellsworth to William Cushing, Feb. 4, 1798, in *Ibid.*, 1:857; Abigail Adams to Hannah Cushing, March 9, 1798, in *Ibid.*, 1:859; Oliver Ellsworth to William Cushing, April 15, 1798, in *Ibid.*, 3:251.

32.  *DeConde's Quasi-War*, ch. II–III.

33.  See James Morton Smith, *Freedom's Fetters: The Alien and Sedition Laws and American Civil Liberties* (Ithaca, N.Y.: Cornell University Press, 1956), ch. VII–VIII.

34.  See *Casto's Supreme Court*, 148–50 & 155–62.

35.  *Ibid.*, 116–17, 149; Timothy Pickering to Ambassador Rufus King, July 27, 1796, King Papers, CSmH; Oliver Ellsworth to Timothy Pickering, Dec. 12, 1798, Pickering Papers, MHi, *excerpted in* Henry Flanders, *The Lives and Times of the Chief Justices of the Supreme Court of the United States* (New York: James Cockcroft, 1875), 2:193–94.

36.  *Casto's Supreme Court* 149–50.

37.  Oliver Ellsworth, "Charge to the Grand Jury of the Circuit Court for the District of South Carolina," May 7, 1799, DHSC, 3:357–59 (emphasis in original); *Casto's Supreme Court*, 149–52.

38.  Oliver Ellsworth, "Charge to the Grand Jury of the Circuit Court for the District of South Carolina," May 7, 1799, DHSC, 3:357–59 (emphasis in original).

39.  *DeConde's Quasi-War*, ch. V–VI; George Cabot to Rufus King, March 10, 1799, in *The Life and Correspondence of Rufus King*, ed. Charles R. King (New York: G.P. Putnam's Sons, Da Capo Press ed. 1971), 2:551–52.

40.  *DeConde's Quasi-War*, 185.

41.  *DeConde's Quasi-War* 185–87; Oliver Ellsworth to Timothy Pickering, March 21, 1799, William R. Davie Papers, NC-Ar; Raleigh, North Carolina; John Adams to Timothy Pickering, May 8, 1799, in *The Works of John Adams*, ed. Charles F. Adams (Boston: Little Brown, 1856), 8:641.

42.  Oliver Ellsworth to John Adams, Sept. 26, 1799, Adams Manuscript Trust, MHi; Oliver Ellsworth to Abigail Ellsworth, Feb. 10, 1800, Oliver Ellsworth Papers, CtHi.

43.  See Peter P. Hill, *William Vans Murray Federalist Diplomat: The Shaping of Peace with France 1797–1801*, (Syracuse, N.Y.: Syracuse University Press, 1971), ch.XIV–XV. For the *Hamilton* Case, see footnote 36 and accompanying text.

44.  Oliver Ellsworth to Oliver Wolcott, Jr., Oct. 16, 1800, in George Gibbs, *Memoirs of the Administrations of Washington and John Adams* (New York: W. Van Norden, 1846), 2:434; Oliver Ellsworth to Elias Perkins, Oct. 10, 1800, CtNlHi.

45. Oliver Ellsworth to David Ellsworth, March 24, 1780, CtWOe, *quoted in Brown's Ellsworth*, 74.

46. Oliver Ellsworth to Rufus King, Jan. 21, 1801, Rufus King Papers, CSmH; Casto, "Oliver Ellsworth's Calvinism," 509, 520–21.

47. Oliver Ellsworth to Rufus King, Jan. 24, 1801, Rufus King Papers, CSmH; Oliver Ellsworth to Ezekiel Williams, March 20, 1801, CtHi.

48. DHSC, 1:118; Michael Kraus, "Oliver Ellsworth," in *The Justices of the United States Supreme Court, 1789–1969: Their Lives and Major Opinions*, ed. Leon Friedman and Fred L. Israel (New York: Bowker, 1969) 1:234; *Lettieri's Ellsworth* 88; *Connecticut Courant*, Dec. 9, 1807, 3; Oliver Ellsworth to The Honorable General Assembly, May ?, 1778, Connecticut Archives: Revolutionary War, 1st series, 10:236, Ct-Ar; Oliver Ellsworth to Charles Thompson, Oct. 20, 1784, Continental Congress Papers, DNA.

49. 1 Day 1, 91, 189 (Conn. 1802–04); 2 Day 1, 227, 399 (Conn. 1805–07). For the Baptist Petition, see *McLaughlin's New England Dissent* 2: ch. XLVII–L; Casto, "Oliver Ellsworth's Calvinism," 521–25. For the Constitutional amendments, see *Connecticut Public Records*, 12:221–22; Connecticut Archives: Civil Offices, 2d ser., pp. 24–26 (manuscript resolutions in Ellsworth's hand and marginalia noting his leadership in the upper house) Ct-Ar. For the state judicial system, see *Connecticut Public Records*, 12:xl–xli.

50. *Brown's Ellsworth* 331–33. Accord Anonymous Bench Notes, 1802–03, RG3, box 5, Ct-Ar. Supreme Court of Errors Docket, 1803 & 1804, Oliver Wolcott Jr. Papers, CtHi.

51. Oliver Ellsworth to the Public, Jan. 16, 1806, in *Connecticut Courant*, July 6, 1806; Brown's Ellsworth, 334 & 343; Oliver Ellsworth to Jonathan Trumbull, June 5, 1807, Oliver Ellsworth Papers, CtHi.


## ❦ CHAPTER 9

1. Cyprian Strong, *The Kingdom is the Lord's* (Hartford, Conn.: Hudson & Goodwin, 1799), 16 (Evans no. 36380).

2. See text accompanying note 27 in chapter 3.

3. See text accompanying notes 10 & 33 in chapters 7 & 8.

4. See text accompanying note 27 in chapter 3.

5. William Gladstone, "Kin Beyond Sea," *The North American Review* (1878), 127:185.

6. See text accompanying note 19 in chapter 4.

7. See text accompanying notes 17–28 in chapter 4.

8. See text accompanying notes 23 & 33 in chapters 4 and 8.

9. See text accompanying note 1 in chapter 1.

10. United States Department of Commerce, *Historical Statistics of the United States: Colonial Times to 1970* (Washington, D.C.: Government Printing Office, 1975), 1:8 & 14.

11. *Casto's Supreme Court*, 250.